Australia's Greatest
ESCAPES

Also by Colin Burgess:

Aircraft
Pioneers of Flight
Prisoners of War (with Hugh Clarke and Russell Braddon)
Laughter in the Air: Tales from the Qantas Era (with Max Harris)
More Laughter in the Air: Tales from the Qantas Era
Barbed Wire and Bamboo: Australian POW Stories
(with Hugh Clarke)
Freedom or Death: Australia's Greatest Escape Stories from
Two World Wars
Destination: Buchenwald
Australia's Dambusters: The Men and Missions of 617 Squadron
Bush Parker: An Australian Battle of Britain Pilot in Colditz
Space, the New Frontier
Oceans to Orbit: The Story of Australia's First Man in Space,
Paul Scully-Power
Australia's Astronauts: Three Men and a Spaceflight Dream
Teacher in Space: Christa McAuliffe and the Challenger Legacy
Fallen Astronauts: Heroes Who Died Reaching for the Moon
(with Kate Doolan)
NASA's Scientist-Astronauts (with David Shayler)
Animals in Space: From Research Rockets to the Space Shuttle
(with Chris Dubbs)
Into That Silent Sea: Trailblazers of the Space Era, 1961–1965
(with Francis French)
In the Shadow of the Moon: A Challenging Journey to Tranquility,
1965–1969 (with Francis French)
The First Soviet Cosmonaut Team: Their Lives and Legacies
(with Rex Hall)
Australia's Astronauts: Countdown to a Spaceflight Dream
Selecting the Mercury Seven: The Search for America's First Astronauts
Moon Bound: Choosing and Training the Lunar Astronauts
Freedom 7: The Historic Flight of Alan B Shepard Jr
Liberty Bell 7: The Suborbital Mercury Flight of Virgil I Grissom
Friendship 7: The Epic Orbital Flight of John H Glenn Jr
Aurora 7: The Mercury Space Flight of M Scott Carpenter
Interkosmos: The Eastern Bloc's Early Space Program
Sigma 7: The Six Mercury Orbits of Walter M Schirra, Jr
Faith 7: L Gordon Cooper, Jr and the Final Mercury Mission
The Last of NASA's Original Pilot Astronauts: Expanding the Space
Frontier in the Late Sixties (with David J. Shayler)
Shattered Dreams: The Lost or Canceled Space Missions

Australia's Greatest ESCAPES

GRIPPING TALES OF WARTIME BRAVERY

COLIN BURGESS

SIMON &
SCHUSTER

London · New York · Sydney · Toronto · New Delhi

A CBS COMPANY

AUSTRALIA'S GREATEST ESCAPES: GRIPPING TALES OF WARTIME BRAVERY
First published in Australia in 1994 as FREEDOM OR DEATH: AUSTRALIA'S
GREATEST ESCAPE STORIES FROM TWO WORLD WARS
This revised edition published in 2020 by Simon & Schuster (Australia) Pty Limited
Suite 19A, Level 1, Building C, 450 Miller Street, Cammeray, NSW 2062

10 9 8 7 6 5 4 3 2 1

A CBS Company
Sydney New York London Toronto New Delhi
Visit our website at www.simonandschuster.com.au

NATIONAL
LIBRARY
OF AUSTRALIA

A catalogue record for this
book is available from the
National Library of Australia

Cover design: Luke Causby
Cover image: POWs at Stalag 11B at Fallingbostel welcome their liberators, 16 April
1945, used by permission of the Imperial War Museum, London (front); Panther Media
GmbH/Alamy Stock Photo (back)
Map design: Xou
Index: Puddingburn Publishing Services
Typeset by Midland Typesetters, Australia
Printed and bound in Australia by Griffin Press

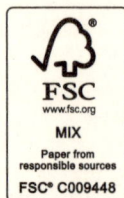

FSC
www.fsc.org
MIX
Paper from
responsible sources
FSC® C009448

The paper this book is printed on is certified
against the Forest Stewardship Council®
Standards. Griffin Press holds FSC chain
of custody certification SGS-COC-005088.
FSC promotes environmentally responsible,
socially beneficial and economically viable
management of the world's forests.

CONTENTS

The Escaper's Prayer

Endeavour more with death before,
Whene'er once captive soul,
May spur the will to freedom's hill,
And soon a steadfast goal.

Behold a gleam of homeland dream,
Soon drink of freedom's wine.
May boldness be a friend to me,
Endurance pray be mine.

– C.E.B.

officer's duty to try to do so, and to make life as difficult as possible for the enemy whilst they were held captive.

My admiration for these amazing Australian warriors increased as my research continued. How could one not be thrilled at their courage, ingenuity and audacity, or be moved by meeting such awe-inspiring people as a bold and successful escaper from a German prison camp during the Great War of 1914–1918; or someone who took part in a mass tunnel escape from a notorious Italian POW camp; or an airman who fled German captivity and after many hazardous exploits – including an attempt to steal a Messerschmitt fighter and fly it back to England – finally crossed the Pyrenees to Spain under brutally freezing conditions in which other escapers and guides perished from the extreme cold.

When first published, these stories appeared under the title of *Freedom or Death*, a reflection of what the end result of such an escape might be. Not only might escaping POWs die while trying to reach home, there were also reprisals for those caught in escape attempts and their severity differed according to the theatre of war and even the year. In the early years of the war in Europe, punishment for recaptured POWs might consist of several days in solitary confinement, although towards the end of the war many paid the ultimate price for their audacity, including the 50 airmen shot in cold blood after the so-called Great Escape from Stalag Luft III in March 1944.

The outcome was even harsher for recaptured prisoners of the Japanese, who faced being tortured to death or a barbarous beheading. There was another confronting predicament: savage reprisals – even killings – could be inflicted on mates they had left behind. It was a daunting proposition.

For those captured or forced to surrender to Japanese forces, such as the 50 000 Allied soldiers ordered to meekly lay down their arms by their superiors after the devastating loss in Singapore, the future was now in the callous hands of a barbarous regime. Their ultimate survival was never guaranteed in this inhumane new world of humiliation, malnutrition, tropical diseases, punishing workloads and brutal bashings. Rebellion of any kind could result in serious injury or death, with little or no accountability exercised on the part of their captors. Many former prisoners told me of the horrors of the notorious Burma–Siam railway and the appalling mass slaughters at Sandakan and Ambon, but they also spoke of the unselfish courage of many fellow prisoners such as medical officers Edward ('Weary') Dunlop and Kevin Fagan.

And then there was a series of revealing meetings with Sydney-sider Nelson Short, one of only six servicemen who managed to escape from the abject horrors of the Sandakan–Ranau death marches in wartime Borneo. Out of sheer desperation, they escaped their Japanese captors while another 2434 Australian and British servicemen, their starved, beaten and abused bodies covered in suppurating sores and pitted with deep ulcerated cavities, were either shot or bayoneted to death, or died of extreme starvation. In early 1945, hundreds of critically ill or diseased men too feeble to take part in these death marches were callously executed and buried in mass dirt graves at the Sandakan base camp. Those weary souls still remaining were forced to carry heavy sacks of rice and other supplies along mountainous jungle tracks thick with glutinous mud. Many eventually gave up, knowing they would die, but exhausted beyond comprehension. Unable to go another step further on the endless back-to-back treks between Sandakan and Ranau, they bade farewell

1

ESCAPE FEVER

AUSTRALIANS HAVE OFTEN BEEN RECOGNISED for their audacity, sardonic humour and improvisation in the face of adversity. Their brief history is festooned with romantic, craggy heroes such as Clancy of the Overflow, whose silhouette against the cloudless blue skies of the outback is as Australian as the frontiersman Daniel Boone to America. So too our fighting men bring to mind an indelible image of valorous audacity.

Allied officers were continually frustrated by their perception of the Australian units under their command as indisputably courageous and determined, but undisciplined when it came to taking orders. They could not easily understand that these men saw beyond the braid on a man's sleeve – it was leadership by example and plain guts that they respected. The Australian soldier did not, and does not, suffer fools gladly.

At Anzac Cove the tenacity and daring of the Australian soldier gave this country its national identity and brought about a whole new treasury of folklore and tradition. The gallantry of our fighting men stamped our country and Australians with pride, touching and moulding future generations through the spirit of our countrymen at war. This same essence of boldness, resourcefulness and grim determination was the key to survival when Australians found themselves prisoners of their enemies during the dark years of two world wars.

In the First World War, the Geneva Convention of 1906 and the Hague Convention of 1907 bound all major European countries to comprehensive rules regarding prisoners of war. Humane treatment of prisoners was the principal consideration of these agreements. Limited punishment only could be administered to prisoners for 'acts of insubordination', including an officer's sworn duty – to escape.

Unforeseen complications resulted in several bilateral agreements being reached during the course of the war, specifically on the use of other-rank (OR) prisoners as labourers. Both the Allied and Central Power armies were so huge and demanding on manpower that home labour forces were greatly depleted. By mutual agreement, these ORs could only be used in agriculture, specified industries, transport and public utilities. As well, the repatriation of sick or wounded prisoners was written into the bilateral undertakings, while a limited exchange of prisoners by internment in neutral countries was permitted.

Despite strict guidelines, the treatment of captives and prisoners depended to a great degree on the humanity of the captors or the camp commandants. Delegations of neutral observers visited camps of the major belligerents periodically to check on conditions demanded by the Hague Convention. However, breaches of the Convention rules soon occurred. The Germans, supremely confident of ultimate and rapid victory, largely ignored all such agreements, although attitudes began to change when an Allied victory became a real possibility.

As related by a repatriated prisoner of war, front-line soldiers sometimes lost all sense of humanity and regulation. On 5 April 1918, Corporal C.H. Campbell was part of an Allied force holding a railway embankment between Albert and Dernancourt. The Germans launched an attack, overrunning and capturing the embankment. 'After we had given ourselves up, and just as we climbed out of the trench, a German officer came up and asked who we were. A private answered him and told him we were Australians. This officer drew his revolver and deliberately shot the Australian private through the stomach.'

'We were called the "Somme murderers",' reported Private J.D. Andrews, another Australian held in a POW camp at Dülmen, 'because the Germans insisted we had killed all the prisoners we captured on the Somme'. Many POWs were used as reluctant front-line labourers. 'I was captured at Hangard Wood, near Villers-Bretoneux on the 7th or 8th of April [1918],' related Corporal D.L. Patterson, who was forced to carry and stack heavy calibre shells. 'We were kept on this job for about two weeks. During this period we were well within our own artillery fire zone, close up to the German batteries.'

In some instances, medical treatment was given with reluctance and even open hostility. One infantry diarist, whose name is not recorded but who was later repatriated from Germany, was captured at Fleurbaix on 19 July 1916 after being badly wounded in the left calf by shrapnel

The hospital at Valenciennes was a venereal hospital, and we had to bathe at the same time as venereal patients. On Sunday, the 23rd, they amputated my left leg. There was no comfort in the hospital.

The orderlies did not try to make the bed comfortable or air it, and the food was bad. The meat served to us was blue and was, I believe, horse flesh.

The orderlies would not bring me water to wash. The only way I was able to wash was by getting comrades who could move about to bring some water. We had only one towel to ten men. A corporal was dressing my wound, and I called out in pain. On this a doctor came and hit me hard on the ribs . . .

At Valenciennes the doctor expressed the view that Australians ought not to have fought against the Germans, with whom (as he said) they had no quarrel. I attribute the rough treatment of the Australians to the unpopularity of the Australians on this account.

The inadequacy of enemy rations caused near-starvation, and it was only the vital lifeline of food parcels from home that saved many lives. Officer prisoners were able to rely on a relatively constant supply of these parcels, almost to the exclusion of the low-nutrition, unpalatable German rations. The ORs, who suffered a more irregular supply of these parcels, were able to supplement the German starvation ration from time to time. Lieutenant I.N. Archer gave this contemporary account of a life of hunger in one German prisoner-of-war camp:

On about 17th June, I was sent from the Strohen Camp Hospital into the camp itself. This was what is known as a 'strafe' [punishment] camp, and the conditions are very bad indeed. The camp itself is situated on a miserable moor, with nothing else in view and in a very bleak sort of place. We had iron-framed beds and mattresses stuffed with straw. The sanitary arrangements were anything but nice or adequate. The water for washing and drinking was taken from wells in the yard, right against which were cesspools, and about a month ago – August – there was an outbreak of dysentery. The barracks were divided by passageways, on one side of which were rooms to accommodate two senior officers and on the other rooms to hold about eight junior officers. We had to cook our own meals, as the British orderlies had too much to do.

After we had been at Ströhen a short while, our parcels started to come through. They arrived regularly, and in good condition . . . but I know of one case where a package, coming through the American Express Company, was filled with bricks instead of food.

The rations issued to us by the Germans here were very bad. They consisted of: breakfast – a cup of cocoa substitute without milk or sugar; midday – soup made from a kind of cockle and water, or potatoes and fish (which smelt very much and was very hard), or meat occasionally – evidently horses which had been badly blown about at the front. In the afternoon, tea made from leaves and grass; in the evening, some kind of thin soup and perhaps a cup of coffee substitute (burnt barley). The food was totally inadequate, and if it had not been for the parcels we received from home, we should undoubtedly have starved.

In addition to those held captive by the Germans, a further 255 Australians were held captive by the Turks – 33 officers and 222 other ranks.

Though it may have been an officer's duty to attempt to escape from the enemy, one obstacle – the resentment of fellow prisoners – was the hardest to overcome. In his First World War autobiography, *The Escaping Club* (Jonathan Cape, 1921), RAF Major A.J. Evans recorded the difficulty he and other newly taken prisoners of war had in comprehending the attitude of those in a Turkish POW camp who had already suffered under more protracted captivity:

> When I first came to the camp, escaping was looked upon almost as a crime against your fellow prisoners. One officer stated openly that he would go to considerable lengths to prevent an escape, and there were many who held he was right. There is much to be said on the side of those who took this view. Though it was childishly simple to escape from the camp, to get out of the country was considered next to impossible. An attempt to escape brought great hardships and even dangers to the rest of the camp, for the Turks had made a habit of strafing with horrible severity the officers of the camp from which the prisoner had escaped.

Breaching the barbed wire from a newly formed German POW camp was also relatively easy for determined escapers. Escape techniques and knowledge accumulated with each attempt, so much so that escaping from prison camps increased quite dramatically.

In the later war years, when communication was established with relatives and friends at home, the possibilities of escape multiplied. One of the great difficulties experienced by early escapers was that of clothing. The Germans issued a dark uniform to some, with bright yellow banding around the sleeves and down the trouser legs. The ribbon was easy to remove, and with a little needlework the uniforms were converted into passable civilian attire. An escape for those in khaki uniforms demanded that special precautions be taken. But once those at home realised what was wanted, a quantity of civilian clothing disguised as uniform parts was sent to the various camps.

The Germans, noting the gold braid and metal buttons, would allow the parcel to go to the prisoner who quickly tore off the finery and replaced the buttons with those of a civilian type.

Another problem to be overcome before escaping was that of false papers. Every man in Germany – other than a soldier in uniform – was required to be in possession of a pass on which was stated his name, address, business and so on. As in the Second World War, the Germans seemed to love rubber stamps and never lost an opportunity of adding one to any document which came their way. Thus the average document was covered in a mass of violet Prussian eagles in varying sizes, shapes and attitudes. The result was imposing and, as was probably intended, increased the difficulties of forgery. However, skilled forgeries were soon being produced, and the more stamps the better.

Thus escaping from prison camps in the later war years had become an organised and scientific operation. Once out of the German camps prisoners generally headed for neutral Holland, Switzerland or Denmark, or in some cases travelled by boat to Sweden. A few even made their way across the battle front into Allied territory, but crossing into northern Holland bypassed the more formidable water crossing over the Rhine or Maas rivers.

One of the classic examples of wartime escapes was provided by a group of British officers who, in 1918, tunnelled their way out of the German prison camp at Holzminden, a small town on the Weser near Hanover, about 160 kilometres east of Holland. The camp was commanded by Hauptmann Karl Niemeyer, a veteran of the Prussian wars who had lived in the United States for seventeen years before World War I. Despite this, he had a heinous reputation as a bully and for his harsh mistreatment of the British and

British Empire prisoners held at the camp. One British officer later described Niemeyer as, 'A thickset man with a big stomach, who spent his time either posing straddle-legged with a stick in his hand or walking about bullying and threatening to shoot us; he did everything possible to make life unbearable.'

Transformed in September 1917 from a former cavalry training facility, the fortress camp at Holzminden was surrounded by a stone wall two metres high, on top of which was another high barbed-wire fence. The inside of the wall was regularly patrolled by sentries, while outside there were more sentries, as well as a number of savage dogs. Around 550 officer prisoners and 100 orderlies were sent to occupy the camp, managing to register seventeen unsuccessful escape attempts in the first month alone.

Work on the tunnel began in November 1917. Three of those who assisted through to its completion were Australians: Lieutenant Peter W. Lyon from the sixth reinforcement of the 11th Battalion, AIF; Captain Lionel C. Lee, 19 Squadron, RFC; and Captain George G. Gardiner of the 13th Battalion, AIF.

Lieutenant Lyon, from Perth, was captured during a counter-attack at Bullecourt on 17 April 1917. He had been transferred to Holzminden from the camp at Ströhen after an unsuccessful attempt in which he and some other prisoners tried to escape by the crude method of cutting the barbed wire during a thunderstorm and making a mad dash away from the camp. The sentries opened fire and Lyon was captured after falling down in a field near the camp. Having spent six weeks in solitary confinement at Holzminden he became one of the principals behind the plan to tunnel out of the camp from beneath a four-storey stone barracks. 'The escape was the result of months of preparation,' Lyon told a *Western Mail* reporter in 1938. 'There were about twelve of us in the party at the start and we used to take it in turns to tunnel under the outer wall of the prison. We started under a wooden floor and tunnelled below some stone steps, digging out a little earth whenever the opportunity occurred. The big problem was to dispose of the dirt, but we overcame that by flushing it away in the latrines.'

While the tunnel was being dug, Lyon's friends in England were doing all they could to assist the prisoners in their escape attempt. 'I had received many useful and unauthorised presents including a compass, which arrived in the heel of a second-hand boot; a road map of Germany, which came in a big hunk of bacon; 10,000 marks in the handle of a tennis racquet, and a pair of wire cutters.'

As Captain Gardiner described in the H.G. Durnford book, *The Tunnellers of Holzminden*, the tubular tunnel was '70 yards long, 24 inches wide, and 18 inches high. Every inch of it was hacked out using a broken table knife.' It would take nearly nine months to complete. The man at the face of the tunnel would crawl there with the knife and a wash basin dragging behind him on a rope. He would then light a small candle so he could see what he was doing. A rope was tied to the other side of the basin, held by another man occupying a small station cut out at the foot of the entrance slope. He also had to pump a set of bellows, made from an old football, providing the man up front with air issuing through a pipe made from a series of tin cans. When the basin was full the second man would haul it back, while still keeping up work on the bellows, and empty the spoil into a sack, which he would pass back to a third man for disposal out in the camp. This procedure was repeated endlessly, with shifts of three hours at a time. After his time at the face, the exhausted tunneller, dripping with perspiration, would drag himself backwards.

Night after night the digging continued, with each of the twelve diggers taking their turn in rotation at the face. Another eight prisoners would later become part of the tunnelling team. Meanwhile the Germans never suspected what was going on beneath them. Even Hauptmann Niemeyer felt there was no way anyone could escape from his prisoner fortress, boastfully telling some: 'Gentlemen, if you want to escape you must give me two days' notice first'.

One night prior to the planned escape a group of officers gathered at a fourth floor window, anxiously surveying a row of beans in a field beyond the wall. Suddenly a piece of paper on the end of a stick nosed up through the ground, remaining in sight for a few seconds before being withdrawn. They determined that the tunnel was too short, and so digging resumed for another week, and this time all was in readiness.

On the night of the escape, 23–24 July 1918, the twenty tunnellers drew lots to determine the order in which they would escape. They had already nominated ten friends each to follow them down the tunnel. Beyond that, anyone else who wanted to join in could go, so long as there was still time before dawn.

Starting at around midnight, the first men began to crawl through the tunnel in twos and threes. All went well for a while, although some nearly fainted with suffocation in the confines of the tunnel, most taking nearly an hour to reach the exit hole. Eventually, however, twenty-eight men managed to crawl out of the far end of the tunnel and flee on foot. Then word was passed down the tunnel that part of the roof had collapsed and it would need to be cleared. The twenty-ninth escaper had been covered in collapsing dirt, but he managed to make it to the exit hole and pull himself through; however the tunnel was blocked behind him.

'The man in front of me stopped moving,' George Gardiner recalled, 'and he guardedly called back that there was a blockage somewhere. I was black and blue about both legs, the result of the pinches the man behind me gave me as he whispered for me to move along. By this time the atmosphere in the tunnel was so stifling that it was difficult to breathe. There was only one thing to do. The luminous dial of my watch showed 6 a.m., broad daylight, so back we crawled, this time feet first.' Some of the men, half-unconscious with the lack of oxygen, had to be dragged back by their heels.

'Back in the camp, Niemeyer nearly went mad. We chipped him, and in a fit of rage he marched into the yard about sixty soldiers, and lined them up with fixed bayonets in front of us. Then he gave the order to advance, but he then thought better of it, and ordered us back to our quarters.'

Of the twenty-nine men who safely made it through the tunnel, ten managed to cross the Dutch border. The other nineteen were eventually recaptured, either singly or in pairs, and returned to Holzminden. The most senior British officer held in the camp, Lieutenant Colonel Charles E.H. Rathbone, was one of those who made it through the tunnel and managed to avoid capture, reaching neutral Holland and freedom just twenty-four hours later. He was more fortunate than most in having a forged passport, knowing the German language, and being able to jump onto a train soon after making his escape.

Peter Lyon was one of those who made good his escape from the fortress, travelling by night with companions towards the Dutch border. 'Each day we had to hide, and when night came and things were quiet, we would set out again. We had two rivers to cross and at one of them I stole a boat, which capsized in the middle of the stream. We had to swim for our lives. For thirteen days we travelled in this manner, covering 185 miles. Then I was captured trying to crawl over the Dutch frontier near Groenlo. One has to have been a prisoner of war and suffered solitary confinement to realise just what this frustration meant to me.'

The recaptured prisoners were sent back to Holzminden, where they faced a court martial for escaping and were each awarded nine months' solitary confinement. As Lyon later reflected, 'What this meant will be realised when I tell you that when I was taken prisoner I weighed 15 stone, 10 pounds [100 kg]. When I came out of Germany I weighed 9 stone, 2 pounds [60 kg].'

Captain Lionel Lee was another of those unlucky enough to be stuck in the tunnel and reluctantly forced to withdraw. Prewar, he had been a friend of famed aviator Charles Kingsford Smith, and postwar would help him get his first job in Sydney with the Diggers Aviation Company. 'Although I was one of the unfortunates who did not get right through the tunnel, I shall never forget our anxiety for those who did,' he mused. 'We wondered how far they would get to the Dutch border.'

Among the twenty-nine men who escaped that night and successfully made it into neutral Holland was Scottish engineer Captain Stanley Purves from 19 Squadron, RFC (the same squadron as Lionel Lee). He escaped using a hand-drawn map and a small improvised compass made from a pair of needles concealed in a paper wrapper for a Gillette safety razor blade. After the war he emigrated to Australia with his wife Sybil and found work at the engineering company that constructed the Sydney Harbour Bridge. He later became the general manager of the Goliath Cement Works in Tasmania.

*

The first Australian serviceman to escape from the clutches of the Kaiser and make it to freedom was Victorian-born Captain John Eldred (Jack) Mott from the 48th Battalion, AIF, who was serving with the British Expeditionary Force in France. While trying to reorganise a company at Bullecourt on 11 April 1917, he sustained five successive wounds in the hand, arm, ear, chest and neck, the last touching the spine and knocking him from a parapet to the bottom of a trench, rendering him unconscious. After dressing his wounds as best they could, the rapidly retreating troops left him in a German dugout, where he remained undiscovered for three days. Despite the freezing cold he managed to cling to life until he was found and sent to Germany as a prisoner of war. Following further treatment, he was transported to Karlsruhe POW camp in south-west Germany, and later to the punishment camp at Ströhen Moor, in the Hanoverian marshlands.

On the evening of 26 September 1917, together with Sydney-born Lieutenant Henry Fitzgerald of the 19th Battalion, AIF, they managed to creep from their barracks to the main gate, which they unlocked using a key Mott had manufactured from a piece of steel plating.

Mott later related to the *Bendigonian* newspaper:

We reached a potato field, every moment expecting bullets from the guards. A quarter of a mile further on we got into a scrubby moor. There was no sign of pursuit. We hurried forward, floundering and falling in the black bog. Avoiding roads and farms, we covered miles and miles past sleeping villages. At daybreak we lay down in a wood exhausted, regardless of the rain. We travelled only at night, and one was always awake on guard.

The men soon found their planned route involved crossing a number of broad watercourses and drains which were either too wide or too deep to tackle, necessitating constant changes of direction while trudging through boggy fields and damp forests. Twice they came close to being recaptured, but Mott had been born in the country in Victoria and spent several years on the goldfields of Western Australia, so his experience of the bush proved invaluable. Using this knowledge, the men carried out several ruses designed to shake off any possible pursuers, at times walking backwards and retracing their steps to deceive enemy trackers and their dogs. Continuing his story, Mott said:

> On the sixth night we crossed a river by a bridge adjacent to a tavern. We saw a sergeant and two privates drinking and neglecting to guard the bridge. At a second river I drew my spare socks over my boots and crossed alone. The sentry challenged, so I rushed back and rejoined Fitzgerald. The sentry did not fire. We made a detour around another sentry and reached a bank. Packing our wet clothes, boots and food on our backs in the darkness, we jumped into the icy water. Halfway across we heard the cry 'Halt!' but did not heed it. We reached the bank, staggered forward, and fell into a muddy ditch. We heard the sentries shouting as we rushed into the forest. I lost my dear old pal. I waited a long time for him, and I suppose he was recaptured.

Once he had wrung out his clothes, a cold and despondent Mott set off alone, stumbling through the forest until he came across a wide expanse of water. Still weak from his wounds and unable to raise his right arm above the shoulder, he knew he could not hope to swim the 200 metres to the other side. Moving along the bank he finally found a much narrower stretch he felt he could handle. After tying his boots and food pack around his neck he took a deep breath and dived in. When he finally reached the far side, Mott realised he was on an island, but was excited to come across a small boat – only to discover that it was chained and padlocked to a sturdy tree. He also found that his precious food supply had gone missing during the crossing.

The next day, after swimming across the brackish water from the far side of the island, and now only five kilometres from the frontier, Mott rested up, hungry but exhilarated before facing his final hurdle to freedom. When nightfall came he was ready and set off, but as he got closer to the border area he became increasingly cautious:

I took off my boots and crept the last two miles, stopping and watching for sentries, thinking that every bush was an enemy. My nerves conjured up soldiers everywhere. I came to a road I had expected, crossed it, and knew that I was safely in Holland.

Following his escape, Mott elected to return to the front and was soon back in action, ending the war with a Military Cross and bar for his escape and bravery in battle.

Just as Jack Mott presumed, Fitzgerald had been recaptured and spent two weeks in solitary confinement at Ströhen before being sent off to Holzminden, where he continued in his relentless attempts to escape. Following one such attempt, the Germans found he was carrying several prohibited articles: money, passports, compass and a map. He and his escape companion were also wearing camp-made imitations of German uniforms. He was charged, tried, and remanded. Eventually he was court martialled and found guilty, being ordered to pay a 250-mark fine or face fifty days' imprisonment. He was reluctant to give the Germans the money, but as he was now involved in helping dig another tunnel he paid the fine.

Henry Fitzgerald never did manage to flee his captors, but on his return to Australia was awarded the Military Cross for his numerous escape attempts.

Many books were published dealing with escapes from European camps during the Great War, and they were appealing bestsellers. As A.J. Evans remarks in his book, *Escape and Liberation: 1940–1945*, this popularity had an undesired effect on those who became POWs in the Second World War.

> In this war, both the prisoners and their guards had far greater knowledge than in World War I, and much of the knowledge was gained from the numerous escaping books which were published between the two wars. Some of these books were translated into German and Italian and even became compulsory reading for the camp commandants and prison guards in those countries. Little was left untold so that the prison guards were, from the start, fully aware of nearly every trick that had been used in former days. The prisoners also read the books, for frequently copies of some of these old escaping stories found their way under various guises into the camps.
>
> It is probably true, however, that the guards gained more from these books than the prisoners, for the possible tricks which the prisoner can play, the disguises he can adopt and the bluffs which can be attempted, are strictly limited by the conditions in which he lives; these conditions are controlled to a large extent by his guards.

Of nearly 170 000 British and Commonwealth servicemen held captive by the Axis forces during the Second World War, just over 6000 managed to escape and return to England – with Australians to the fore. This figure was even more remarkable considering that not one Axis POW ever escaped from Britain.

The revised Geneva Convention of 1929 stated that no prisoner could be punished by more than 30 days' solitary confinement for a single escape. To longer term prisoners, this period was even considered a blessing in disguise after an unsuccessful escape attempt as it provided a chance to be away from fellow POWs and overcrowded quarters for a while.

Participation in an escape attempt was both a means of defiance and of occupying the long, tedious days behind brick walls and barbed wire. Men worked diligently and laboriously on shafts and tunnels, more often than not in the full knowledge that the scheme had little, if any, chance of success. But they were gainfully employed. Shift-digging in a tunnel, tailoring escape clothing, compiling maps or forging documents, the men felt useful once more, and part of a team effort to confound and harass the enemy.

Occasionally, with persistence and a sizeable dose of good fortune, many POWs found themselves scrambling away from their place of captivity. But this was only the first stage of the operation, for now they faced a more formidable foe – their own spirit of endurance. Ahead of them lay the likelihood of weeks, possibly months, crossing enemy territory with little prospect of adequate food or shelter. These creature comforts could only be gained by stealth. The escaper virtually lived as a tramp but he could never allow himself the luxuries of indolence or incaution; capture could be lurking around the next bend in the road, and it was essential he remain alert and wary. He was a fugitive in a belligerent country, a fox on the run.

To further daunt him was the knowledge that, even at journey's end, he had to confront yet another perilous barrier – that of crossing a guarded frontier safely. Little wonder that desperation weighed heavily on even the staunchest heart, and it is a sad but understandable truth that many recaptured prisoners even expressed relief at being caught. Some – in despair, cold and hungry – even turned themselves in.

Despite heavy Allied bombing and strafing of railway utilities and rail lines, train travel was still the preferred method of the escaper in Germany. It was convenient and, despite wartime conditions, fairly reliable. A single train journey could eliminate the need to spend many days and nights slogging across enemy territory by foot, with the inherent lack of food, sleep and shelter, and the imminent chance of capture.

The disadvantage in using the rail system was a reliance on forged travel papers, which would be scrutinised several times by officials on the lookout for just such forgeries.

The lack of German vernacular was not a serious problem. The massive movement of seven million legitimate foreign workers throughout Germany meant a plethora of tongues were spoken, and a good excuse for travel corroborated by official-looking forged documents gave the escaping prisoner a reasonable chance of bluffing his way through.

Several escapers came unstuck through the unintentional use of everyday mannerisms or habitual exclamations, including profanities. The study of body language is almost a science these days, but

Having usurped administrative control over the prisoners, the Germans moved equally swiftly in evacuating Allied POWs north-wards into Germany. They were especially keen to transfer and contain air force personnel in their Luftwaffe-controlled camps. Logistically, it was a time of considerable chaos, and many POWs took advantage of the situation to make good their belated escapes.

Lieutenant Athol Hunter (2/6th Battalion, AIF) and Flight Lieu-tenant Geoff Chinchen (No. 3 Squadron, RAF) were among those herded out of PG 19* at Bologna in north-east Italy and placed in cattle trucks for transhipment to Germany. En route, while they were held at Fort Bismarck in Strasbourg, the two Australians made arrangements to be bricked up by some friends inside a small damaged section of a disused passageway. The transfer occurred on 9 October 1943 and Hunter and Chinchen moved into the small niche and were soon concealed behind a freshly-reconstructed section of the wall. When all sounds of activity had passed they broke free of their small enclosure and made their way out of the fort. Three days later they reached French soil, from where they were guided into Switzer-land and eventual freedom.

Prisoners in work camps around Vercelli, to which several hundred Australians had been transferred from PG57, Gruppignano, were fortunate that the German presence was almost negligible. As a result, 400 Australians safely reached neutral Swiss territory, some in epics of endurance. South Australian George Mason Clark (2/43rd Battalion) escaped with three fellow Australians from a working party and set off to cross the Alps into Switzerland. As he recalls, it was a journey none of them could ever forget.

---

* Campo PG is short for Campo concentramento di prigioneri di guerra – permanent POW camp.

We fought on, inching up to the towering peaks, every step an agony and an effort of will, every foot of the way negotiated with the chance of falling or being blown to our deaths in the tugging winds. It would have been a relief to slump, curl up and rest.

When my aching body demanded this rest I reached back into my mind to windswept bleak afternoons walking a bare prison compound, staring at the barbed wire, sentries and gun towers; back to the memory of long, cold, hungry, despairing, lonely nights, listening to the howling of the wind, thinking of home and the lovely girl waiting there, wondering if I would see her again. It was then I found the strength to take another step forward and upwards, strike another blow, roll with another punch and tell that old mountain he would never beat us. We were survivors and we'd come too far and taken too much to lie down.

The men's spirit carried them through, and they finally knew the exultation of having beaten the odds.

We stood on a mountain on the border of Italy and Switzerland, the four of us, and we laughed, shook hands and pummelled backs. Years of planning, scheming, surviving, brushing with death, suffering frustration, hunger and reversals, waiting, escaping, climbing the mountains. We'd made the dream come true!

Many of those who had not been rounded up by the Germans made for the Allied lines in southern Italy or for the rumoured invasion bridgeheads near Venice and Genoa. Most, however, remained in the vicinity of their former prison camp or took to the hills. When it became apparent that the Allied advance in the south had ground to a temporary halt, and with the risk of capture by the

Germans or Fascists growing daily, these fugitives formulated plans to get out of Italy.

The majority followed three major routes. Those in the north and north-west generally opted for crossing the frontier into neutral Switzerland; others in the north-east looked to the Yugoslav border; while most of those hiding out in central Italy made their way south through the German defensive lines.

For those who experienced it, life as a prisoner of war in Europe was a drab routine in which frustration and uncertainty grew as the war continued without them. The battle to maintain their health, sanity and dignity in an existence fraught with inadequate rations and demeaning captors was unceasing. The vision of escape and the dream of freedom caused them to secretly and actively engage in schemes both practical and fanciful, fruitful and futile.

Escape literature is replete with many fine examples of brilliant individual efforts. The appeal of these stories is undeniable; a lone escaper fleeing over open countryside, scavenging or stealing food, sleeping in lice-infested haystacks and finally crossing a frontier to safety under the very noses of the border guards. One of the most incredible true stories of this genre is that of Lieutenant David James, RNVR, who managed to escape from a bathhouse at Marlag und Milag Nord naval camp and, brazenly dressed in full Royal Navy uniform, made his way quite openly by day to Bremen and then the Baltic Sea port of Lübeck. From here, he was hidden aboard a Swedish ship which carried him to Stockholm and freedom. Boldness saw James reach freedom but there was also a great deal of prisoner's whimsy involved in his escape. He had told a fellow prisoner that his intention was to 'bugger off' from Germany and this is precisely what he did – among the forged documents he carried were a letter and a pass to the Baltic area declaring him to be a Bulgarian seaman by the name of I. Bagerov!

In June 1943 the prisoners at Oflag VIIB, Eichstätt, in northern Bavaria set about constructing a tunnel that inched out from beneath a hut and forged upwards inside a rocky hill which formed the northern boundary of the camp. Tonnes of spoil from the tunnel was shifted without arousing the suspicions of the German guards, who later admitted they would never have thought to look for a tunnel going uphill! On the evening of 3–4 June, 65 prisoners went through the vast tunnel. Although most were recaptured, they had created an unprecedented diversion of tens of thousands of troops and civilians to seek them out. All of the recaptured prisoners, including seven AIF officers, were bundled straight off to Oflag IVC, Colditz, north-east of Leipzig. Lieutenant Jack Champ (2/6th Battalion) told the author their efforts were considered worthwhile.

> It may seem to some that we wasted our time digging this tunnel which hardly seemed to reach a successful conclusion, but the escape caused a tremendous nuisance to the Germans. We shifted over 40 tonnes of earth and rocks without their knowledge, and we occupied 60 000 enemy personnel for over a week. We caused the camp Kommandant and his security officer to be sent to the dreaded Russian Front, and at the same time gave our own morale an enormous boost, believing that in some small way we had contributed to the Allied war effort as a whole, and the eventual victory.

Perhaps the most audacious escape story of the Second World War took place in October 1943 from the East Compound of Stalag Luft III, set amid the tranquil, scented fir trees around Sagan. In staging this escape, the prisoners constructed a large, sturdy vaulting horse. Each day four men would carry the equipment to the same place in the compound, near the perimeter wire and right under the noses of the bemused sentries. What the Germans did not realise was that one or two men were concealed inside the vaulting horse. Their job was to open up the concealed entrance to a tunnel, and while other prisoners bounded over the equipment, making noise that covered the activities within, the tunnellers were digging away and placing the soil removed into bags. Once the 'exercise period' was over, the tunnellers would disguise the entrance once again, and the vaulting horse was carried back into the hut where it was housed. The dirt was then covertly dispersed into the roof of the hut, vegetable gardens and elsewhere. When the tunnel was 30.5 metres long, three airmen – flight lieutenants Eric Williams and Oliver Philpot, and Lieutenant Michael Codner – were carried out, made their way through the tunnel, and eventually reached freedom through the port of Stettin. Eric Williams' later book, *The Wooden Horse*, is witness to the triumph of ingenuity.

Tragically, another escape was mounted from Stalag Luft III on 24–25 March 1944. The sad aftermath of the mass escape bid that became known as 'The Great Escape' was the deliberate, cold-blooded shooting of 50 of the 76 escapers by the Gestapo, acting on the direct orders of Hitler. Among those murdered after recapture were five Australians – Squadron Leaders J.E.A. Williams and J. Catanach, Flight Lieutenants R.V. Keirath and T.B. Leigh, and Warrant Officer A.H. Hake – who with others were taken out into the countryside and gunned down singly or in small groups on deserted highways.

In *The Great Escape* (Faber and Faber Ltd, 1951), Australian Flight Lieutenant Paul Brickhill recalls the shock he and the other prisoners felt after being told the appalling news. Worse was still to come, for at the time the Senior British Officer, Group Captain Herbert Massey, had only been told of the deaths of 41 officers.

Still in a stunned silence we filed out of the theatre and within two minutes the news had spread to everyone in the compound. Horror lay over the camp. Mass murder was something new in the quiet backwater of prison camp, however unpleasant the life was. A lot of us wouldn't believe it. 'I know the Huns are murderous bastards,' said a man in my room, 'but they've never been game so far to murder British or American people openly in mass and I can't see their point in starting that sort of thing on relatively harmless prisoners'.

It about summed up the feeling. I suppose if the truth be known we wouldn't believe it because we didn't want to believe it. The mind builds up its own defences. Most of us thought the whole thing was a bluff; that the forty-one had been moved to another camp, and that we, believing they were dead, would be intimidated into stopping all escape activity. But there was no getting away from the fact that it had been officially announced. We held a memorial service and every man in the compound sewed a little black diamond on his sleeve.

Now there was blood on the barbed wire. This savage barbarity had an instant and sobering effect on prisoners and their guards alike, but there was now a war within a war, and prisoners faced further uncertainties regarding their fate behind the wire.

Back in 1899 a young British war correspondent covering the Boer War for the *Morning Post* was captured and placed in a prison camp.

extended to them by their superiors, they felt an inculpable justification when inflicting the death penalty on recaptured POWs.

Even with these consequences in mind, the Japanese-held prisoner of European descent faced many obstacles in any bid for freedom. The most obvious was his appearance. Another was the vastness of the Asian theatre, with any escape necessitating travel through pestilential jungle in extreme and generally unpredictable tropical weather conditions, and sometimes crossing vast tracts of water. In many areas some of the local population were on the lookout for runaways, knowing the Japanese offered substantial rewards to those assisting in their recapture. Added to these difficulties were a generally weakened condition caused by starvation diets and medical neglect, hunger, a lack of proper escape aids and information on Allied positions, insidious tropical diseases and little more than a vague idea as to their destination.

For many there was also the omnipresent thought that their escape could incur severe reprisals on the mates they had left behind. Little wonder that these escapers were desperate men, driving themselves on with an almost fanatical single-mindedness, and with only a faint spark of eventual freedom as their spur.

At a ceremony of remembrance in 1986, Canon E.H.V. Pitcher addressed the Newcastle Branch of the New South Wales Ex-POW Association on what he called 'the sombre events that together make up one of the darkest and most tragic chapters in our nation's history'. Some excerpts from his stirring eulogy are well worth recording:

> In the grim and unaccountable chances of battle there are always
> the possibilities of death, of wounding, of survival, or finally

of capture and imprisonment. That fate might be thought by members of a soldier's family to be the most fortunate outcome of all, because to them it would seem the war was now over for their loved ones. But of course they would be mistaken as the war never ends; for the prisoner the conflict becomes more intense. Some soldiers never give up trying to escape so that they could take their full part in the struggle again. But for all of them who are captured a prolonged battle begins; a long, agonising battle of the spirit, a struggle to endure the privations of inactivity, and that oppression of the soul that comes from doubts about the welfare of those left at home.

The full extent of their terrible sufferings, and the measure of the harsh brutalities perpetrated upon them, has only in recent years begun to emerge. With tragic hindsight we can see that they entered the battles poorly equipped, with insufficient strategic awareness of the strength of their enemy's forces, and with inadequate knowledge of his equipment and resources. Most all of we now know that they were the tragic victims of a barbarous medieval code which assumed that capture in battle incurred a disgrace which could only be wiped out by death. A prisoner of war was therefore a symbol of shame to be accorded no mercy and no humane considerations whatever.

The consequences are well documented now, but they still have the power to touch our hearts and to stir deep anger. Citizens can be notoriously forgetful; memories are so tragically short. But we are sure that this nation would be the poorer without the knowledge of these events. The glib reiteration of fashionable shibboleths about 'standards of living' would assume new meaning if we could retain the memory of sacrifices and suffering endured, and the sum total of what it has cost to preserve our way of life.

The barbaric ill-treatment of prisoners of war by the Japanese was a natural consequence of what was recognised by them as the code of bushido; in this the soldier realised his greatest honour in life was the opportunity to give his life for his Emperor. Conversely, his greatest disgrace would be to surrender to the enemy. This solemn code was inculcated into the Japanese soldier during his basic training. Grim witness to this was the suicidal mass break-out of Japanese prisoners of war from their compound at Cowra in New South Wales which left 231 prisoners dead and more than 350 wounded. Their object was not to escape but to die in honour, defying the enemy to their last breath.

Another tragic observance of bushido followed the capture of ten survivors from an Australian and British raiding party of 23 aboard a 'hijacked' fishing junk, who had made a gallant attempt to blow up several vessels occupying Singapore Harbour in September 1944. These men were treated with respect and even admiration by their Japanese captors, and were subsequently placed on trial. In the records of the prosecutor's closing address, it is clear that the code of bushido was 'generously' applied to the prisoners:

When the deed is so heroic, its sublime spirit must be respected, and its success or failure becomes a secondary matter. These heroes must have left Australia with sublime patriotism flaming in their breasts, and with the confident expectation of all the Australian people on their shoulders. The last moment of a hero must be heroic, and it must be dramatic. Heroes have more regard for their reputation than for anything else. As we respect them, so we feel our duty for glorifying their last moments as they deserve, and by our doing so the names of these heroes will remain in the heart of the British and

Australian people for evermore. I consider that a death sentence should be given to each of the accused.

The ten men were executed on 7 July 1945, just seven weeks before the capitulation of the Japanese nation on 28 August.

Those three years and nine months since the Japanese entered the Second World War had been a period of immeasurable anguish and torment for the more than 22 000 Australians who fell into their hands. By the time Japan surrendered, nearly a third of that number, set by historians as 7777, had died as a direct result of starvation, disease and maltreatment. Of this number, 27 are said to have been executed for attempting to escape, and a further 193 for other reasons.

The majority of Australians who became prisoners of the Japanese were taken in the fall of Singapore on the afternoon of 15 February 1942. That morning the British Commander, Lieutenant General Arthur Percival had received advice from Churchill that he was agreeable to a surrender, and had set the process in motion. With the signing of the Japanese terms of surrender shortly afterwards, nearly 130 000 Allied soldiers, including 16 000 Australians, became prisoners of war and all British troops were ordered to congregate at Changi.

At first the Japanese placed no real restrictions on these weary captives so long as they remained in the area designated as a POW enclave, and they were permitted to wander around the eastern end of Singapore island. Things changed abruptly on 12 March when the Japanese ordered the prisoners to wire themselves in and declared the area separating the prison camps from the mainland a no-man's land. The perimeter was now patrolled by Japanese guards as well as some Sikhs who had volunteered to serve their captors. These

renegades quickly earned a reputation as being even more demanding and brutal than their masters.

In August 1942 most of the senior British and Australian officers,
including Lieutenant General Arthur Percival, were shipped off to
Japan. Major General Shimpei Fukuye, together with a large staff,
was brought in as Commandant of all POW camps in Malaya and
given responsibility for organising and administering the large POW
camp located at Changi.

Soon after he arrived four recaptured prisoners were brought
to the camp. Two had been on the loose for five months, having
managed to escape from Bukit Timah and paddle a small boat
more than 250 kilometres before being caught. Two of the men
were British (Privates Harold Waters and Eric Fletcher), and
two were Australians – Private Victor L. Gale from New South
Wales and Corporal Rodney E. Breavington from Victoria. The
Japanese administrators promptly issued a decree on 30 August
that all prisoners in Changi were to sign a statement which read:
'I, the undersigned, hereby solemnly swear on my honour that I will
not, under any circumstances, attempt to escape'.

The senior British officer, Colonel E.B. Holmes, and the
commander of Australian POWs in Malaya, Lieutenant Colonel
F.G. Galleghan, 2/30th Infantry Battalion (known affectionately to
his men as 'Black Jack' Galleghan), countered by declaring that the
prisoners were not permitted to give any such undertaking and that
all officers and men would refuse to do so. For the next two days an
uneasy silence gripped Changi. The Japanese reaction, when it came,
was swift and brutal.

On 1 September Fukuye ordered the prisoners at Changi,
including 1900 Australians (with the overall exemption of those in

hospital), to assemble at the military barracks square at Selarang. The events concerning what became known as the 'Barrack Square Incident' have been faithfully recorded by Stan Arneil in his book *Black Jack* (Macmillan, 1983).

> The barrack square was 8.5 acres in area and was surrounded by five buildings of two floors each, making a total standing room of 11 acres. The crush of troops in the hot sun was unbearable, particularly as there were little or no amenities. Latrines were dug through the bitumen of the square, rations of rice were cut by two-thirds and worse. Water for the 15,000 troops was available from two drinking taps only.
>
> The crowded conditions resembled a milling ant heap and the danger of an outbreak of dysentery was high. Fukuye called for another meeting with Galleghan and Holmes requesting once more that they order their troops to sign the 'no escape' promise. The two leaders refused to alter their stand and Fukuye then told them that they would be required to attend the execution of four prisoners, two Australians and two Englishmen, who had all made an abortive attempt to escape from Singapore in May 1942.

The execution, under Lieutenant Okasaki, could only be described as inhumane. The site was changed several times and the condemned men were dragged from one place to another until Okasaki was finally satisfied. Corporal Breavington meanwhile kept pleading unsuccessfully with Okasaki and Colonel Makimura for Gale's life, stating that the 23-year-old private was simply following orders. As a passage was read from the New Testament by one of the witnesses, Breavington shook hands with the other three men. One final time throughout the term of our captivity, I was disappointed to find that our officers, instead of encouraging us to attempt to escape or to defy, at least covertly if not openly the Japanese authorities, actually urged us to co-operate with them and not to attempt to escape. Their logic was simple. The Japanese took terrible vengeance on any attempt to defy their authority, and attempts were certainly doomed to failure and meant certain death for the would-be escapees with possible repercussions against those remaining in captivity. Our officers, therefore, bearing in mind the welfare of the majority of the captives, encouraged us to co-operate, and despite the fact that this was the best course overall, it irked many of us.

Groups of prisoners began leaving Changi from January to mid-April 1942 for unspecified destinations. In May 3000 Australians in the so-called A Force left by sea under Brigadier A.L. Varley, destined initially for airfield construction work at Tavoy in Burma, then in October to Thanbyuzayat, the Burma base of the proposed railway to Siam (later Thailand). In 1943 more groups left for Ban Pong, at the head of the Gulf of Siam, to begin work at the other end of the railway. These groups comprised 17 760 British, Australian and Dutch POWs.

On 18 April the ill-fated F Force, comprising 3334 British and 3666 Australian servicemen departed for Ban Pong. Then followed H Force (1411 British, 670 Australians, and 588 Dutch), and two smaller parties of medical staff of mixed nationalities, known as K and L Forces.

Initially, the men of A Force found their accommodation and conditions poor but tolerable. They received better rice and food rations and the Japanese were lenient towards any prisoner caught outside the wire trading with natives. But when word of these minor escapades reached the ears of the higher Japanese authorities they issued blunt warnings that any prisoners caught outside the wire would be shot.

Encouraged by the attitude of their guards and friendliness of the Burmese people, several prisoners turned their minds to the prospects of escape. In June, eight men from the 4th Anti-Tank Regiment led by Victorian Warrant Officer Matthew W. Quittendon made a short-lived attempt to escape to India but were quickly recaptured. A notice that they were to be executed was issued. Brigadier Varley and the Australian leaders protested the severity of the sentence – particularly one handed down without any pretence of trial – but their objections were ignored. Sid Marshall (8th Division Signals) was present when the escapees were brought back:

> A small party of men, of whom I was one, were separated from the main working party at the Tavoy aerodrome and taken to a place quite some distance from our POW camp. On arrival we were set to work digging eight holes which were to be two metres long, one metre wide, and two metres deep. It did not take us long to realise that these holes were meant to be graves, and for whom they were intended. The Nips kept at us to hurry the job; we in turn tried to hasten slowly in the forlorn hope that this may in some way stave off the inevitable. Unhappily it was not to be.
>
> The holes were less than two metres deep when two trucks arrived. One carried the eight escapees (four of them well known to me), the other Brigadier Varley, Colonel Charles Anderson, and a padre. Posts were put in the ground at the head of the holes and the eight men, arms tied, were brought to the scene. Brigadier Varley requested

camp in Fukuoka. He was recaptured soon after, beaten and brutally murdered, and his body returned to the camp inside a corn sack. In 1948 three members of the Imperial Japanese Army implicated in the killing were hanged. Sometimes, justice prevailed.

2

FROM THE CLUTCHES OF THE KAISER

HENRY LAMERT (MERT) THOMAS WAS born in Orange, in the central western region of New South Wales, on 17 October 1897. The area's orchards produce mostly apples and cherries but, as Mert Thomas knowingly recalled, his birthplace was named for the Prince of Orange, later King of Holland, and it was to then-neutral Holland he fled in one of the truly dramatic escapes of the Great War of 1914–18.

Mert's family moved to Toronto, near Newcastle, when he was young and he started work as a junior clerk in a wholesale warehouse when he was fifteen. With the threat of hostilities in Europe, trade diminished to such an extent that he found himself sitting behind a desk with little to do. On 4 August 1914 the chief clerk of his department told Mert he might as well go outside for a walk, rather than looking bored and doing nothing. He strolled around the streets for a while and was just about to head back when he noticed a group of people crowding around a news bulletin which had just been posted outside the *Newcastle Herald* building.

In those days important news was posted in this way, then followed up as soon as possible by special editions of the paper. Mert fought his way to the front of the crowd, read that England had declared war on Germany, and hurried back to the warehouse with the news. A few moments later the manager of the firm, Lieutenant Colonel Paton – one of the senior military men in Newcastle – strode up to young Mert and asked him exactly what the bulletin had said. He was so surprised that a junior clerk had heard the news before him, he forgot to enquire why the lad had not been at his desk.

Australia's enthusiasm for aiding in the war effort was almost unanimous. The Prime Minister, Andrew Fisher, offered England the use of its navy and a force of 20 000 men, while the recruiting offices were deluged by thousands of eager young volunteers. The landing at Anzac Cove on 25 April 1915 brought with it increased pride in being an Australian soldier.

Compulsory military training was in operation but Mert, living in Toronto, was too far distant to be included in the training call-ups. Determined not to be excluded from helping in some way, he offered himself as a cadet in Newcastle and was accepted. Now seventeen, he began putting pressure on his parents to allow him to enlist, which could be done providing the volunteer had proof of parental consent. After a considerable period of what Mert called 'softening up', his father finally gave in.

Why did I go to war? The reason had its roots in my school days. We were intensely loyal subjects of the King and very proud of being part of the British Empire. On Empire Days, May 24, the schools united in displays at the Newcastle Showground and we sang songs of various parts of the Empire. With this love for the

Empire came enmity for Germany, which we regarded as a power whose aim was to supplant England as the leading nation, and take over its empire. We had an inherent belief that war with Germany was inevitable, and when it came the event was looked upon as something in the nature of a relief – it had come at last. Germany's invasion of Belgium was looked upon as a cowardly act which merited punishment. England's declaration of war as the result of the Belgian invasion gained unqualified approval.

Mert was accepted into the army and became an infantry gunner with the 30th Battalion, attached to the ill-fated 8th Australian Brigade. In due course his unit was shipped to Egypt, where their first camp was at Tel-el-Kabir on the site of an old 1882 battlefield. From here they were sent to an isolated outpost east of the Suez Canal, where it was believed a Turkish attack might take place. Once this threat had diminished, some of the outposts were withdrawn back to the canal.

It was here that the first Anzac Day commemoration took place on 25 April 1916. Sir John Monash, in charge of the AIF, ordered that every man who could be spared from actual defence duties should attend a short religious service, followed by a 'Last Post' for fallen comrades. This was the first of all Anzac Day commemorations.

Soon after, the 30th Battalion embarked for France. Arriving at Marseilles and following a three-day train journey, the men were marched to billets in ruined farmhouses near Armentières. Then began a series of marches with full equipment for days on end, until finally they were deployed into trenches in what they were told was a quiet place on the front. No sooner had they arrived than they were subjected to a violent bombardment by German field artillery.

On 1 July 1916 the first Battle of the Somme began. A week of intense bombardment of German positions gave ample notice of Allied intent and the attack failed to gain an immediate penetration of the German defences.

The 5th Division, of which the 30th Battalion was part, was ordered to attack at Fromelles, north of the Somme river, as a diversionary tactic. On 19 July the men were told they would be going over the top that night, their immediate objective being two lines of trenches. When the signal to begin the attack came, a tide of soldiers surged out of the trenches.

Until we reached the German front line we came under severe machine-gun fire and artillery bombardment. The wire had not been cut by our own artillery fire so our casualties were increased because we had to find the passages in the wire and go through in single file.

We jumped over the German front line, according to instructions we had previously received, and ran on in search of the second line, but failed to find it. Instead, we found a drain as wide as a trench with water in it, about two feet deep. I have since found out from the war history that this was indeed our objective, but we could not stay there. We still went on to try and find a second line, but only succeeded in finding a communication trench. There were no Germans, and somehow we became split up into small groups with no officers or NCOs. Darkness set in and we did not know what to do, so we spent the night where we were, under severe artillery fire.

The Germans kept out of the way until first light when we found them behind and in front of us, and on our flanks, trying to drive us out with hand grenades. There was nothing to do but try to get back to our own lines, even though the small group I belonged to did not know in which direction we should go. There were about half a dozen of us, so over the top we went again. The machine-gun fire was so heavy that we took refuge in a large shell hole.

After a while the fire ceased and we found the place swarming with German soldiers. We were rounded up and taken prisoners. I had a wound in the leg, but it was not serious. We later learned that in our sector the order was given during the night to fall back to our own lines, but we were so far forward the order did not reach us.

On just one terrible night in that bloody conflict, 5533 Australians from the 8th Brigade had been lost, including 400 taken prisoner. It was the highest loss sustained by any Australian division in any one day during the entire war. Mert Thomas' battalion lost 352 men – over a third of its strength.

Following their capture the badly wounded were placed in hospitals for treatment, the officers were sent directly to Germany, and the rest were taken by train to Fort MacDonald near Lille, where they were joined by other recently captured prisoners. After a short, uncomfortable time in the cells at Fort MacDonald, the men were sent to prison camps.

Mert Thomas, his wound considered too minor for hospital-isation, was part of a large contingent sent to Dülmen camp in

At Duisburg-Meiderich the two men were in a position to develop their escape plans. Getting out of the camp presented few difficulties, but the task of crossing the Rhine, travelling through a thickly populated part of the country and sneaking past the frontier guards into neutral Holland was a different proposition. As they soon learned, many prisoners had managed to get away from the camp, but none had reached the frontier. A successful escape would call for careful planning, and a few essential items.

The list Thomas and Holmes drew up was short, but difficult to fill. They were aware that any escape would be virtually impossible without a good map, a reliable compass and clothing which would not attract attention. On arrival at Dülmen they had been kitted out in dark uniforms with bright yellow ribbons around the sleeves and down the outside of each leg, but these conspicuous outfits could be modified with little trouble. The map and compass would prove difficult to secure, but fortune soon began to smile on them.

Mert Thomas had been learning French, and his studies enabled him to form a friendship with a French prisoner who happened to possess a detailed railway map of western Germany. The fellow lent the map to Thomas, who persuaded another of his French friends to make a copy of it while on night work at the factory. The Frenchman finally produced a postcard-sized map, showing the ground they had to cover to reach the Dutch frontier.

Securing a good compass was a more difficult job. One of the French engineers had secretly manufactured one, which he generously gave to Thomas, but tests proved it to be quite unreliable. However, Mert Thomas soon noticed that a German youth in the factory had a small compass dangling from his watch chain. A little bribery managed to secure the compass, but further disappointment was in store when an accidental jolt knocked the needle from its bearing. Another option was to induce one of the factory hands to purchase a compass for them. One fellow agreed to do this for five marks, and soon after told them he had been successful. It did not take the wisdom of the pharaohs to guess the purpose for which the compass was intended, and the worker stubbornly demanded another five marks before he would hand it over. Holmes and Thomas paid the additional sum with reluctance, knowing the compass would eventually prove to be well worth the price.

Obtaining suitable civilian clothing was the next obstacle to be overcome. A little secret tailoring on their prison suits made them less military in appearance, while it was a simple matter to unpick the thread of the yellow ribbons on their sleeves and trouser legs. The brass buttons were replaced by more conventional ones. Despite their clumsy stitchwork, they felt the converted uniforms would pass muster on a dark night.

By international agreement, prisoners of war employed in civilian industries were entitled to receive a wage for their labours. After working hard for a couple of months Mert Thomas had saved sufficient money to purchase a collar, cap and tie from another factory worker. The map, compass and civilian clothing were then hidden in the ticking of their beds. Thomas and Holmes had worked in such secrecy that none of their immediate friends knew of their plans. However, these were complicated when it became apparent that a Russian prisoner had learnt of their intended escape, possibly from the worker who had sold them the compass, and demanded to be taken along. As any refusal on the part of the Australians could have resulted in their betrayal, the two friends talked it over, bowed to the inevitable, and reluctantly agreed to take the Russian.

Waiting for the big day would now become a more harrowing experience as they feared the unreliable Russian might tell some of his friends. However, he kept his own counsel and the plan proceeded.

The tar distillery at Duisburg-Meiderich was a large concern, fully enclosed by a high fence, and directly across the road from the prisoners' camp. A wide canal ran around three sides of the camp, while the front was patrolled by sentries. To a great extent, any plan for escape was governed by the time between the break and its detection by the guards. Given the layout and situation of the camp, the easier escape option was from the factory, although this could not be attempted in daylight. The best plan, Thomas and Holmes determined, was to break out of the factory grounds at around 6 p.m., when darkness had begun to set in. The main problem was that their absence was certain to be noticed within two hours. They then fixed the date of the attempt as 26 October.

Thomas and Holmes had foreseen that one of the essentials for success lay in having themselves regarded as a pair of dimwitted oafs with no thoughts of escape. One afternoon they deliberately walked through the main gates of the factory in full view of the workers and guards, and ambled quite nonchalantly down the centre of the road towards the camp. The incident caused considerable excitement among the guards and the two prisoners, feigning surprise at all the fuss, were berated for disregarding strict regulations on where and when they could go. Apparently humbled, they protested that they had not entertained any thoughts of wrong-doing. The Germans came to treat the two as witless and harmless drones. For the next few weeks they kept very much in the background and worked hard at their menial tasks.

The two friends now had to determine the best means of exit. The factory site was completely surrounded by a high fence of iron netting, the top of which curved inwards. Sentries also patrolled the fence on a deliberately irregular basis. Eventually Thomas and Holmes realised that the problem of the wire had actually been solved for them. Although the Germans had constructed the fence in such a way that it could not be scaled, recent heavy rain had loosened the earth beneath it. Very little effort would be required to scoop out some of this dirt on the night of the break. The only problem they now faced was finding some means of remaining in the factory after their work detail had ended.

The knock-off whistle blew at 6 p.m. each day, following which all the prisoners had to walk down to a large locked gate opposite the camp, where they were counted. Once they were in the camp another group of workers would be assembled for the short journey over to the factory. The sentries were under orders to remain at their posts around the perimeter of the fence until the count had been completed, but there had never been a successful escape and they had become quite lax, sauntering off towards the gate as soon as the whistle blew. If the Australians were to hide in the factory grounds near the wire at six o'clock, the fence would be unprotected long enough to allow them to dig a hole and get away. The count at the gate would probably reveal a shortfall, but this count was usually a perfunctory one and the only effect any irregularity might have would be to hasten the full rollcall, which was held two hours later.

On the morning of 26 October 1917 Mert Thomas and Hec Holmes rose at five and put on their civilian clothes. Over these they pulled their dungarees, and then their heavy overcoats. As the weather was beginning to turn cool, most of the prisoners wore similarly bulky attire. The map, compass, food belts, collars, ties and caps were stuffed into the pockets of their overcoats.

and their position was becoming quite grave. They knew the town of Wesel was not very far away, but the prospect of venturing through another heavily populated area was a daunting one. Then, around midnight, their spirits at a low ebb, Holmes cried out with relief. He had spotted a rowing boat, although it was sitting well down in the water. Suspecting it might leak, they dragged it ashore and tipped it to one side. The dark water gushed out and they anxiously scanned the bottom for any holes, but those they found were minor. With fingers crossed and prayers in their hearts they refloated the boat and watched as it bobbed up and down.

There were no oars to be found, but a house stood nearby, and they decided to have a look around. Mert Thomas found some feeding tins in a fowl yard which he emptied out, knowing they would come in handy for bailing out the boat as they crossed. Nearby, the other two had found a crop of runner beans planted at the foot of some stout rectangular poles which would do as oars. The three men then returned to the shore and stepped gingerly into their boat. Once they'd settled down there was barely an inch of freeboard.

We then pushed off and started on what we afterwards admitted was one of the most confused hours of our journey. The Russian had never handled an oar. We showed him what to do, and he and Hec Holmes were to row while I steered and gave the boat as much way as possible from the stern. The river was flowing at the rate of about five kilometres an hour; ten metres from the shore we became caught in an eddy, which turned us round and round, and began to take us back to the shore we had just left. I changed places with the Russian, and we two Diggers managed to get the boat pointed in the right direction. We set off again, and after some time learned

55

that by steering diagonally across the river we could make the fullest use of the current. Our progress was painfully slow – the bean sticks were poor substitutes for oars. We were soaking wet, and the fear of detection had our nerves on edge.

The boat was leaking badly but the Russian kept working with the feed tins, and after battling for an hour the three escapers set foot on the west side of the river and set off for the frontier. As they had travelled so far north, it was decided they should now proceed south-west, towards the frontier between the small towns of Walbeck and Straelen.

The countryside between the river and the border was bristling with German patrols. Several times they had hair-breadth escapes, and on the second evening they camped in a wood. Just as dawn was breaking, and for no apparent reason, Hec Holmes became uncomfortable with their position and they decided to shift elsewhere. They subsequently discovered that their earlier position had been in the centre of a gamekeeper's beat. This gamekeeper actually passed them several times during the day, as did a number of people on their Sunday stroll. The bad weather undoubtedly saved them from discovery, as comparatively few people were out and about.

On Sunday night we were kept in a graveyard near Issum for two hours by bicycle patrols continually moving up and down the road. Later, on the same night, we had to dive into a roadside ditch half full of water to avoid another patrol. On yet another occasion we were held up in Issum, between the bend in a river, a railway junction and a continually patrolled road. Three hours elapsed before we finally crossed the river by a railway bridge, but in the meantime we had been badly cut on the hands, and had our clothes torn when escaping from a dog over a barbed-wire fence.

On Monday, with the weather clearing, they camped in a hedge near Walbeck, about fourteen kilometres from the frontier. By dawn the six biscuits each of them had carried were gone and they had to depend on turnips picked from the fields for food. On one side of their hedge a farmer spent the whole day harrowing his field, often passing within a few metres of the three apprehensive escapers. On the other side, dozens of people, mainly soldiers, moved along a path between two villages, again within a few metres. Fortunately no one bothered to glance into the hedge as they passed, but it was a long and tension-filled day.

On the fourth and final evening of their journey they did not stir until darkness was well advanced. It was a startlingly clear and bitterly cold night, with a bright moon. At about nine o'clock the trio crossed the railway line which ran near the frontier, moving slowly and very cautiously, taking advantage of whatever cover they could find in hedges and coppices. To be discovered so close to freedom would be a disaster, and each of the men exercised great care as he edged ever closer to his goal.

An hour later they came across a block of huts which Thomas and Holmes believed to be the barracks of German border guards. They circled around these huts and at about eleven o'clock came upon a sentry box manned by an armed guard. Moving back into the shelter of a small wood in the centre of a field they kept the sentry box under observation, then spotted another 100 metres further on. At irregular intervals the Germans left their boxes and moved towards each other, crunching loudly over the frosty ground and only stopping to converse briefly before returning to the relative warmth of their sentry boxes.

Thomas and Holmes discussed their predicament and finally decided to crawl through the trees until they were about 50 metres from the frontier. They would watch for the changing of the guard, and then wait until the new guard became drowsy.

The decision now made, they had barely settled down when a dog patrol arrived, and the men froze in fear as the Alsatian led its handlers across the track they had recently made. The dog paused and snuffled momentarily at the frosty ground, but the cold and frost had deadened the scent and the patrol moved away. Surviving this latest in a series of narrow escapes heartened them considerably, and they needed some heartening in the hours to come, with the likelihood of spending much of the night lying undetected in a frozen field.

Three hours later they felt that the nearest guard had become noticeably less diligent in his duties. He and the other sentry spent a lot of time talking as they met during their patrols, and on one of these occasions Thomas and Holmes decided it was time to attempt the crossing. Stiff with the cold the three men slowly crawled up to the line and were within a metre of the sentry's beat when they saw him approaching. Immediately they flattened themselves beneath some trees, faces pressed against the frozen ground, hands beneath their bodies. The shadows cast by the trees saved them. The German passed by without so much as a glance in their direction, entered his box and, swearing loudly at the cold, stamped his feet to warm them up. Mert Thomas could see the other sentry further down to their right; he too was stamping his feet and grumbling.

Their moment had now arrived. On elbows and knees they crawled ahead for a couple of hundred metres until they entered the shelter of a coppice. Then they rose and, bent double, ran until they fell from sheer exhaustion. Daylight found the three escapers at the River Maas, in neutral Dutch territory, and it was here they were arrested by Dutch soldiers.

Following a period of quarantine and an injection for smallpox, the three men were handed on to the Belgian Consul at Venlo. Their Russian colleague was then taken to a different authority and Thomas and Holmes never saw him again. The Belgian Consul arranged for the Australians' passage to Rotterdam, where the British Consul took over and returned them to England in a small ship which sailed from the Hook of Holland. Holmes had seen enough of the war and was pleased to be told he would be repatriated to Australia.

While in England, Mert Thomas was awarded the Military Medal for his daring escape. Instead of accepting the fact that he had 'done his bit', he chose to return to France in 1918, and was sent to the Somme as a member of the 1st Division Field Artillery, and later the 5th Battery. Soon after the Armistice his unit followed up the German withdrawal as far as Charleroi in Belgium. Thomas remained in France and Belgium until his final repatriation. He returned to Australia in July 1919, having been overseas for a total of three years and 333 days.

Settling back into civilian life, Mert Thomas took a job with the New South Wales Railways and became the enthusiastic secretary of the Toronto Sailing Club. One windy day in 1920 he was participating in a sailing contest at nearby Lake Macquarie, and literally ran into the girl of his dreams when his yacht and another were involved in an unavoidable collision. He and his hapless crew were unceremoniously tipped into the water. There were no hard feelings over the mishap, and when everyone was safely ashore Mert was introduced to the sister of the young man who'd been sailing the other yacht. She later told him she'd 'only been brought along to act as ballast'! Mert Thomas and Nell Webb were married two years later, on 22 December 1922.

Mert and Nell Thomas lived through the harsh economic years of the Great Depression, although as Mert stated, 'It was a pretty rough spin'. The parents of four children by 1939, they were both distraught when Hitler invaded Poland and the Second World War began. 'That's why we fought in the first one,' Mert reflected. 'So there'd never be another world war. It was terribly disillusioning.'

Disappointed though he may have been, at nearly 42 years of age Mert re-enlisted. Initially rejected because of his age, he persisted and finally left Australia's shores once again for five years service in Syria and New Guinea with the 2/3rd Army Field Workshop Unit, which maintained and repaired armaments and vehicles along the front line. During this time he gained a staff commission and was twice mentioned in despatches. On his return to Australia he resumed work with the railways, and stayed with the department until his retirement.

Of his daring accomplishments, Mert Thomas was modestly succinct: 'You can do these things when you're young,' he told me. It was his brief summation of a fine and audacious escape while in the service of his country.

The Mert Thomas story is based on information supplied to the author at an interview conducted in 1986. In October 1988, Mert and Nell Thomas were presented to the Governor of New South Wales, Sir James Rowland, at Government House. Because of his bold escape during the Great War, Mert had achieved a modest latter-day fame during Australia's bicentennial year as one of the nation's group of specially selected 'Unsung Heroes'. A few days later he suffered a stroke, and a second seizure the following month took his life on 16 November 1988, at the grand old age of 91. He had survived long enough to witness the 70th anniversary of the signing of the Armistice.

3

TUNNELLING OUT OF GRUPPIGNANO

SAPPER BOB HOOPER FROM TARRAGINDI in Queensland served with the 2/7th Field Company Engineers, and was taken prisoner on 28 July 1942. Earlier that month his unit had been recalled from Palestine and, together with the 2/28th Battalion, was hurled into battle at El Alamein.

The Australian 9th Division had been ordered to attack the Miteirya Ridge and Tel el Eisa. Its General Officer Commanding (GOC), Lieutenant General Sir Leslie Morshead, had expressed well-founded concerns about the British ability to provide adequate artillery support. After heavy casualties were sustained during the first phase on 22 July, Morshead called off the action except for an attack by the 28th Battalion, which reached its objective at Ruweisat Ridge (known derisively as Ruin Ridge) but was quickly surrounded by German tanks.

The men were forced to surrender and nearly 500 Australians fell easily into German captivity. Hands in the air, still hoping for a liberating British armoured thrust, the silent, sullen men were marched off to a rocky plateau where they were herded together in the blazing heat of the Western Desert without food or water.

At around 1 a.m. on the morning of 28 July, Bob Hooper had been detailed as guard support for an intelligence officer on a reconnaissance mission to the site where the Australian troops had earlier broken through. On reaching the area they saw a German half-track containing a dozen troops about 30 metres from where they lay hidden. Hooper was all for attacking them but the officer insisted Hooper's only duties were those of observation and protection. On their return, Hooper sought out his officer and requested a detachment of six men to accompany him and wipe out the small enemy force. He was ordered to return to his post, but not before the sympathetic officer had cast a wry grin at the eager young trooper.

Disappointed at the lack of offensive action, Hooper returned to a shallow trench he had dug with brothers Tim and Arthur Jobson. Just before daylight the Germans began their counterattack. At one stage of the fierce bombardment, a sniper's bullet thudded into the soft ground by Hooper's head. Shells then began pounding the area from a different direction, which the men quickly realised were coming from their own artillery. The barrage continued until the order given by an inexperienced officer to shell the area was countermanded. The exhausted men kept firing, but reinforcements did not arrive and they soon ran out of ammunition. Shortly after eleven o'clock it was all over, and the men were ordered to surrender.

Bob Hooper slowly clambered to his feet, together with the Jobsons. In a last act of defiance Hooper stood his ground and refused to raise his hands in surrender. He cannot recall what he said at the time, but another sapper, Jim Gilson, clearly remembers the promise made through gritted teeth: 'Don't worry fellas, these bastards won't hold us. We'll escape tonight!'

For Bob Hooper and the other weary prisoners, conditions were unbearable. A relentless sun baked the exhausted men, but the rocky ground was too hot to lie on. Every so often an ineffectual breeze wafted across from the Mediterranean, but it did little more than stir the hot air. Bob Hooper was unknowingly suffering from the traumatising effects of shell-shock and concussion. Eventually a convoy of trucks arrived and transported the grateful prisoners away from the burning rock.

The first stop in their journey was the former British cage at El Daba, now in German hands and only forty kilometres west of the Allied lines. Though still badly dazed, Hooper knew his spirit alone was not enough to see him clear of the prison camp. His mouth was dry, and when a small biscuit ration was issued to each man he could not raise enough saliva to chew on it. They were each given half a cup of water, for which they were grateful, although some managed to persuade their guards to take their watches in trade for an extra ration. Those who declined to do so later regretted their decision, as the Germans eventually confiscated such valuables. The camp was very primitive, basically a section of desert encased in barbed wire, but a sweet sea breeze cooled it by night and the POWs were able to fall into a deep sleep stretched out on the sand.

The men were next crammed into large Italian trucks and trailers, crowded so tightly they were forced to stand, and taken to Benghazi by coastal road on a four-day journey. Their first stop was at Mersa Matruh, where they received enough water to slake their thirsts and their dry rations even became palatable. Several of the men were interrogated by the Germans, who found out little they did not already know. Before the tiresome journey recommenced the German officer in command apologised for having to hand the men over to the Italians, but explained that Libya was on the Italian front.

Every night the prisoners were kicked and pushed into barbed-wire pens by guards not shy in using the butts of their rifles to hurry things along. Once settled, they were given their ration of bully beef and biscuits and enough water to sustain them as they passed through Tobruk, Derna and Barce on their journey west. Bob Hooper remembers very little of this period, but once he'd arrived and recovered somewhat in Benghazi he began to look for ways of breaking away from captivity.

The dual-compound prison camp at Benghazi was a palm-covered oasis at the bottom of a steep, stony wadi a few kilometres south-east of the town. It was about 50 metres wide and 350 metres long, and because of the prolific date palms it became facetiously known as 'Palm Grove'. The smaller of the two compounds was for coloured troops and Free French, while the larger held just over 1000 British and Allied prisoners, though that number would greatly increase before long. The only permanent buildings were a cookhouse, storehouse and orderly quarters, while the men slept out in the open on top of a single thin blanket. Barbed-wire fences were strung along the tops of the wadi, and Italian guards looked down over the camp and its inmates.

There were no lights on the perimeter of Palm Grove and several prisoners managed to escape at night, but were soon recaptured. Two New Zealand sergeants by the names of Campbell and Cleverley clung to the underneath of a wood truck as it left the camp, and were free for five days. Bob Hooper decided the time had come to make his own exit and suggested to his sergeant, Jack Bollington, that they also leave beneath a truck.

When Hooper decided to escape he had no food, but a Corporal Bruce Gardiner had two little loaves of bread he was keeping. Hooper told the corporal he would give him £10 after the war if he let him have them for his escape. Gardiner agreed and handed them over. (Hooper finally met Gardiner again, nearly 45 years later, and presented the surprised veteran with a bottle of beer and a $100 note for the loaves, which his wartime friend framed and placed on his wall. 'We were so hungry back then,' Hooper said, 'I don't think I could have done what he did for me; not for a million quid!')

The following afternoon the truck hauled into the camp and, trying to appear casual, the two escapers walked beside it when it was almost unloaded and scrambled beneath when they felt no one was watching. In their weak state it was not easy hanging on beneath the chassis of the vehicle, so they were relieved when the driver eventually returned and drove off towards the main gates.

Sadly, the attempt was short-lived. At the gates swarms of uniformed men surrounded the truck and angry voices told them to get out. Reluctantly they lowered themselves to the ground and rolled out into the sunlight. The Italians were furious; they yelled and screamed at the escapees in Italian, then chained and padlocked their hands behind them.

One guard thrust his face into Hooper's. 'No escape!' he yelled. 'We tell you no escape, but you still try to get away. We will teach both of you a lesson, you and your stupid friend. We are going to shoot you to show that escape is forbidden!'

Hooper looked the excited man straight in the eye. 'Piss off, you crazy dago bastard!' was all he could think to say. As the outraged guard shoved him hard in the chest, a large company of guards moved in and took over, parading their captives through the camp and on to the Italian quarters. There they were given 'the treatment', boots and all, by the *Carabinieri* – the Italian equivalent of the SS. The men's hands were still chained behind their backs, in case they tried to retaliate. Hooper and Bollington were then dragged outside and taken to the main gates once again. With rising alarm they noticed that the Italians had brought along two lengths of rope. Hooper's throat suddenly went very dry.

Their misgivings were somewhat relieved when the ropes were tied around their wrists and the free ends thrown over a horizontal post above their heads. The two men were then hoisted up with their chained, bound arms stretched out straight behind them until their toes barely touched the ground. The pain was instant and excruciating, and they were left suspended in agony for all to see as an Italian lesson in the folly of escape.

The other prisoners began to shout at the guards but Hooper and Bollington told them to calm down. If the Italians started shooting it could result in a massacre.

It was sheer hell for the two men as they hung there in unrelieved agony, but soon after dark some Royalist Italian soldiers furtively placed stones under their feet, which greatly reduced the pain. There was no love lost between the two factions of Italian soldiers. They also gave each of the men a drink of water and fed them some grapes. In the meantime the Australians could hear the *Carabinieri* celebrating in their huts, and once again they wondered what the immediate future held for them.

Around midnight the Italian Commandant made an appearance. The two men hurriedly shuffled the supporting rocks away from beneath their feet and the pain tore at them once again. The Commandant, a colonel, cursed the two men then ordered the guards who'd accompanied him to let them down and return them to their prison compound where, to their surprise, the Royalist soldiers had given the prisoners some more grapes and cigarettes 'for the two brave men'.

The two small loaves of bread Hooper bought from Corporal Gardiner had been confiscated. The following day Hooper, his arms and shoulders stiff and aching, had the temerity to demand their return from the Commandant. The swift response to that impertinence was a hard punch to the face.

On 16 August some mixed relief reached the prisoners' ears. They were to be shipped to Italy. By now they were half-starved and ill-clad, suffering from dysentery, desert sores and numerous unattended wounds. Two freighters had been assigned to transport more than 5000 prisoners in their holds – the *Nino Bixio* and the *Franco Josi*. Hooper found himself on the *Franco Josi* and, escorted by two Italian destroyers and a cruiser, the two aged freighters set out to cross the Mediterranean towards Taranto, in southern Italy. On the second day out the *Nino Bixio* was struck by two British torpedoes, one of which exploded in a hold containing hundreds of prisoners, causing unspeakable carnage. Although the ship floundered, drowning many more of the men trapped in the holds, it did not sink and was eventually taken in tow by one of the destroyers to a port in southern Greece. Of the 2000 prisoners on board, only 300 survived the terrible catastrophe unknowingly wrought by the captain of HMS *Thunderbolt*.

The *Franco Josi* continued on to Bari, where the prisoners were bundled off the old freighter and made to march to their first prison camp on Italian soil. As they marched through Bari the people treated them with unconcealed contempt, and several women spat in their faces as they passed. Then the column was out in the countryside and walking along roads lined with vineyards. The fruit was ripe and hanging heavy on the vines, but the guards sensed the men's longing and warned that anyone who moved out of the line would be shot. Nevertheless, temptation finally got the better of Bob Hooper, who dashed across a couple of times to grab some. Later he paid the price for stealing those grapes, which were heaven going down but played havoc on an empty stomach. That night Hooper dashed around the staging camp desperately trying to find a toilet, but only succeeded in getting himself tangled in some barbed-wire fencing. He was lucky not to be shot, but unlucky in that his stomach finally gave forth and he soiled the only pair of trousers he had.

Campo PG 75 at Bari was one of the main transit camps for British prisoners taken at Benghazi. Overcrowding was a major problem which steadily became more critical. Other-rank prisoners were clustered together into an orchard and provided with bundles of straw, as well as standard Italian groundsheets for use as rudimentary tents. Others found themselves gathered in a dry canal bed just outside the camp, with absolutely no provision for shelter or sanitation.

With totally inadequate food rations, dysentery was rife in Bari, combining with a lice infestation to make life untenably wretched. A deep despair rose in the men. Several tried to escape, only to be brutally beaten when recaptured, and placed in wire manacles. It came as something of a relief to thousands, including Bob Hooper, when a large number of the Australian and New Zealand prisoners were transferred several weeks later to a larger permanent camp known as Campo PG 57 Gruppignano, surrounded by snow-capped mountains. The camp was situated fifteen kilometres from the city of Udine, in north-east Italy, and close to the border with Yugoslavia. Ten kilometres to the north of the camp were the foothills of the Julian Alps, while to the distant west and north-west stood the mighty Dolomites and the Swiss, Austrian and Bavarian alps. The camp was on a flat river plain amid this spectacular beauty, but for the 2500 POWs held there – including 1200 Australians and 1000 New Zealanders – there was very little to like about PG 57.

On their arrival at Gruppignano, the camp was represented to the prisoners by their captors as 'the best camp in Italy'. Their added arrogance in declaring the camp 'escape-proof' provided the necessary spur to many, who would quickly rise to the challenge.

The camp was divided into two occupied compounds, each containing around twenty-six newly constructed sleeping huts. These huts were of wooden construction lined with malthoid, a waterproof, bitumen-impregnated material. Heating in winter was by means of a centrally situated stove fuelled by wood and coke. Each hut housed about 80 men. Bunks were of wooden construction of two tiers, four on the bottom and four on top. At one end of each hut were two separate rooms which housed the senior NCO and warrant officer, the senior of whom was hut commander.

There was a cookhouse in each compound, a canteen of sorts, adequate toilet and ablutions facilities, and an area for washing clothes. Water was relatively plentiful.

The official history of New Zealand in the Second World War, in the volume *Prisoners of War* by W. Wynne Mason (War History Branch, Department of N.Z. Internal Affairs, 1954), says of conditions in PG 57 at that time: 'There were plenty of Red Cross food parcels on hand . . . the canteen was well stocked and parcels of tobacco were beginning to arrive from New Zealand House and private sources.' But former prisoners at Campo 57 dismiss this as rubbish. Bill Kelly of the 2/8th Field Ambulance recalls that there was only one time when they were able to buy food at the canteen: 'and that was one week when there was a local surplus of onions. The canteen catered mainly for toothpaste and razor blades.' The canteen was in fact a tiny pantry in the back-to-back kitchens of the two compounds. About two metres wide by three long, a small box-office wooden window opened to the outside. In line with the camp commandant's attitude to his prisoners, it was the smallest possible concession to the Geneva Convention. Apart from the limited supplies of onions, there were occasionally some sweet toffees available. The other items, which could be purchased using camp money, were mainly stationery, shaving gear and toiletries. Sometimes a thick syrupy wine and Nationale brand cigarettes were available, but these would be gone in minutes. Money chits, printed especially for the camp, were paid to the men weekly for use in the canteen.

Alexander Barnett from Melbourne was with the 2/3rd Light Anti-Aircraft Regiment. As he recorded for the University of New South Wales' *Australians at War* film archive in 2003:

In the winter the winds blew from the Alps and in the summer it blew from the Adriatic and all the huts were braced with huge buttresses [but] it's starting to get cold, and we've got shirts and shorts and no clothes. And they had one little stove in the hut but didn't give you any fuel; if you got some you were lucky, so because the huts were made of wood the boys whittled it so when the wind blew it was damn lucky they didn't fall down. During the winter one of the guards froze to death, and of course that received cheers and not condolences; we were subjected to a lot of electrical storms because it was ironstone country, iron and limestone country and the electrical storms that are created are fantastic when they hit, I've never seen anything like it, they moved along the road and they hit the cookhouse one day and the Italians, for their meat rations, they used to keep rabbits and the rabbits got out when the cookhouse caught on fire and the boys tried to snare them to eat them, I think they got two, and that went into the pot-bellied stove with the fur and all.

Private Garvan ('Snowy') Drew from the 2/15th Battalion was captured at Derna and spent several months in PG 57. He recalled that when he arrived there the senior officer of the camp was Major Raymond Binns, a medical officer with the 2/8th Field Ambulance – a South Australian unit. The senior warrant officer was Arthur Cottman of the 2/15th Battalion. Cottman had featured in an incident when the camp was first occupied. Camp Commandant Colonel Vittorio Calcaterra had ordered that all prisoners have haircuts and shave off any beards, but the men, including Cottman, stubbornly refused. Along with other 'ringleaders' of the revolt he was handcuffed and tied to posts overnight. Facing further rebellion the next day, Calcaterra ordered all available guards to fix bayonets, a machine-gun was set up, and small handcarts bearing loads of handcuffs were wheeled into the compound. Those who still refused to be shorn were immediately manacled and placed in the detention cells, while the rest made a mockery of the proceedings, bleating like sheep to the mounting rage of Calcaterra. Eventually all of the men were given rough haircuts, but they had certainly succeeded in enraging the pompous commandant.

Food, as at transit camps, was insufficient and almost inedible, but as Snowy Drew recalled, the Red Cross was once again to the fore.

Red Cross parcels which came at regular intervals were a great supplement to our meagre diet, which consisted mainly of a watery mess containing some sort of greens, with occasionally the addition of a little macaroni or sometimes mangelwurzels – a type of white beetroot. Everyday life was quite boring if one couldn't find some activity to occupy the time. Card games were a good pastime, the main games being bridge, euchre and crib. Once a fortnight, a hut at a time, we were taken to a bath house to have a hot shower. The only other highlights in the camp were the arrival of Red Cross parcels or the occasional arrival of new prisoners with fresh news of the war.

'Our first guards were Alpine troops, some of Italy's best,' according to Mason Clark of the 2/43rd Battalion, who had been captured after an attack on German positions in the salient of Tobruk. 'Our commandant was one Colonel Calcaterra, a sadistic fat little monster. This lovable character had a motto [placed over his desk]: "Cursed be the British but more cursed be the Italian who treats them well". He made life as miserable as possible for us, and his chief delight was "the boob" or "Bastille". This gaol within a gaol was built at one end of the camp, and the Colonel saw to it that no cell remained empty for long.'

As commandant, Vittorio Calcaterra, a strident, strict disciplinarian from the *Carabinieri Reali* ran PG 57 effectively but with an unnecessarily heavy hand. Brutality was not discouraged among the guards, and the camp had a bad record over the ill-treatment of the internees. Andrew ('Bluey') Rymer, an RAAF wireless operator/ air gunner with No. 70 Squadron, was a little more succinct in his appraisal of Calcaterra: 'He was a short-arsed, fat-gutted little shit. If you were sitting on one side of the camp and you did not get up and stand to attention it was into the boob, bread and water!'

Prisoners caught in escape attempts were killed or wounded. Calcaterra prided himself on the fact that no one had been able to breach the formidable three-metre high, double barbed-wire perimeter fencing. Early in the winter of 1942 a New Zealand infantryman, Private Arthur Birdwood Wright, was shot at close range while attempting to crawl through the wire at night. The bullet entered the base of his neck and there was no exit wound, which led to the suspicion that he was shot with a dum-dum bullet. Outlawed for warfare in the 1899 Hague Convention, these were illegally modified by cutting an 'X' into the top of the lead at the front of the bullet, allowing it to fragment and spread on penetration. When this suspicion was conveyed to Calcaterra he paraded all senior NCOs in the camp church where he pointed out that in the First World War no prisoner escaped from Italy, and that none would escape in this one. Former Flight Sergeant Eric Canning (3 and 6 Squadrons, RAF) attended the highly emotional meeting.

In regard to the bullet which killed Private Wright, and demonstrating a similar cartridge [Calcaterra] pointed out that it was a shrapnel bullet consisting of a tube of brass encasing nine cylindrical steel pellets. When fired the rifling of the barrel cut the brass into longitudinal strips, and these, plus the nine pellets, went on their roving way.

He claimed the projectile to be sanctified by international law, but it seemed to his audience that it was a considerable improvement to the dum-dum, at least at close range. He spent some time proclaiming that no one would escape from his camp, and the fate of Private Wright awaited whoever attempted it. The confidence of the Colonel stimulated ambition to prove him wrong.

Any schemes for crawling through the perimeter wire, which was well lit and heavily guarded, were regarded as both difficult and dangerous, so a small group of Australians conceived an idea for a tunnel. According to Eric Canning, the planning group comprised of himself, Tom Comins (38 Squadron, RAF), Richard (Dick) Head (2/10th Battalion) and Bill Kelly (2/8th Field Ambulance). Canning recalled:

In digging a sewerage pit in No. 2 compound the deep soil was found to be heavily compacted alluvium – far too hard for tunnelling – and it wasn't until a new compound was opened up to house prisoners taken in the battle of El Alamein that we were able to sample the earth under the hut closest to the wire, when it was found that the alluvium at a depth of about twelve feet was friable enough to enable a tunnel to be commenced.

Lance Sergeant Noel Ross (2/13th Field Company), a bridge contractor from Queensland, was in charge of the actual tunnelling. The tunnel, driven out from a vertical shaft, was to be about 80 metres long, starting under the floorboards beneath a central bunk in an empty hut in No. 3 compound. This corner was well away from any barracks or administrative buildings outside the wire, so escaping prisoners had a reasonable chance of getting away unde-tected. On the other side of the wire, an Italian farmer had grown a patch of maize, and it was planned to slope the tunnel up gradually to the surface, with the exit hole in this patch.

The steady influx of new prisoners to the compound upset the normal search routine, and the work went ahead unhindered. The tunnel team had earlier managed to steal a short-handled pick, and tin hats were used as shovels. The spoil was placed in boxes which were hauled back to the exit shaft, lifted out, and spread over the 60-centimetre gap under the floorboards of the hut, or surrepti-tiously over dirt pathways and a cricket pitch being prepared for the new compound. The tunnel itself was about 75 centimetres high by 50 centimetres wide.

Mason Clark and two fellow prisoners were amazed when Eric Canning and Dick Head told them of the tunnel, and that it had been under way for several weeks. As Clark observed:

We were told that only the men actually working on the tunnel knew of its existence. Secrecy was a must, as there were some eighty Cypriots in the camp, and some of them could not be trusted. Once they knew of it, our Italian captors would soon be told. We had been picked as likely escapees, and because we were known to keep ourselves fit, with as much exercise and boxing as the meagre rations allowed, we would be handy as workers in the tunnel. Fit men were needed for the work; it was very arduous and dangerous. We three new recruits were quite excited that evening meeting our fellow escapees. The tunnellers were all Aussies and New Zealanders with the exception of two British-born 'Aussies', Arch Noble (2/24th Battalion) and Scotty King from the 2/1st Pioneers.

We learned that our fellow escapees had all formed groups of two or three, and several were going alone. All had made careful plans and had been saving some chocolate from the occasional Red Cross food parcels. Bill Thurling, Johnny O'Hearne and I had to start from scratch, but we eventually agreed on a plan to strike out for Yugoslavia once clear of the camp. Several of the others intended to do the same, hoping to meet up with the very active Yugoslav partisans. Some of the others intended making the long hike across northern Italy to Switzerland. As we were situated north of Trieste, and close to the Yugoslav border, we thought the partisans our best bet.

Supplying fresh air to the tunnellers was a continuing problem, especially as the tunnel grew longer and the diggers moved further from the vertical shaft. As described by Clark, the initial solution proved to be moderately successful.

We stole tubing and conduit from some of the toilets and washrooms, and made a pipeline from the surface deep into the tunnel. Bellows were made by some handyman, and so a new air supply was born. A man on the surface worked the bellows which pumped air through the pipe to the air-starved men in the black tunnel. Then too, flex and wire was stolen, the electric light globes taken from the centre of the hut, and light was introduced into the lengthening tunnel. We couldn't use lights down there during the day, unfortunately, as the power was switched off.

Once the tunnel reached a length of about five metres, the system for supplying air to the work face became ineffectual, due both to the small diameter of the conduit, and the fact that the diggers continually separated the taped joints while moving backwards and forwards.

The men then hit on the idea of inflating volleyball bladders to supply fresh air, as recounted by Noel Ross: 'They were pumped up at the mouth of the tunnel and then we would hold it in front of our face against the wall and let the air out. Due to the routine of the camp we couldn't work too long each day. Half an hour was the maximum time we each spent digging.'

Several cave-ins occurred during the tunnelling, but nothing too serious. Progress was slow, especially when clay was encountered. The men at the face worked hard in the mud caused by gradually rising water, the long drag back to the shaft with the spoil becoming slower all the time. They either worked naked or in some quite putrid old clothes kept down the hole; it was their choice, but they had to exit wearing their ordinary camp clothes. Fighting claustrophobia, muscle cramp and exhaustion, the men toiled away in the darkness, struggling to inflate their lungs in the fetid air, which caused them blinding headaches. Bathed in perspiration, their lacerated knees deep in the dirt and slop, their backs bloodied from continually scraping the roof of the tunnel, they drove on with grim determination. Each afternoon at a certain time tools were collected, boxes, bellows and buckets placed in the tunnel, boards lowered, and all dirt on the floor carefully swept away before replacing the heavy bunk. The retching, half-blinded diggers dragged clothes over their naked, dirt-covered bodies. Singly and in pairs the men then slipped out of the hut and returned to their own compound. After a quick cold-water clean-up in the wash troughs, it was time for the afternoon check parade. Then, as explained by Mason Clark, a new complication arose.

Prisoners from the bitter El Alamein fighting began to arrive, and one evening a batch of new men were allotted to our escape hut. They were men of the 2/28th Battalion – all West Australians who had fought out from El Alamein, being eventually cut off and surrounded by hordes of German infantry and tanks.

Our Sergeants visited these men the following day, and they were told of the tunnel that reached out from under the floorboards of their hut. They were asked for their co-operation, which was eagerly given, and sworn to secrecy. These gallant men proved dinkum Aussies, helped us in the work in the tunnel and sentry duty, and dirt disposal. With the added help the work speeded up and the tunnel was finished on time.

In fact the men of the 2/28th, gaunt and in poor physical condition from earlier ill-treatment, went to extraordinary lengths to ensure the success of the tunnel. Bob Hooper was one of those captured with the 2/28th at El Alamein who arrived in PG 57 with the tunnel well under way. As he had already been involved in an unsuccessful tunnel at a previous camp, he was asked if he would apply his skills to the completion of the tunnel. 'So they took me in with them.'

The newly-recruited prisoners stopped all visitors at the door of the hut with the excuse that items had gone missing from the hut, and the person being called upon would be sent out to see them. The four men sleeping in the double-decker, side-by-side bunks over the hidden entrance to the shaft did so knowing that they would be liable to the harshest of penalties if the trap was discovered, but this did not deter them. 'Of course they were all for it,' recalled Noel Ross with pride. 'They wanted to be in it, but the tunnel would only hold nineteen, and their health also ruled out their participation. They were in poor condition and looked like scarecrows.' In all, the tunnel took six weeks to dig.

Bill Kelly remembered one terrible fright towards the end:

'Pud' Poidevin, who would be first out of the tunnel, decided to make a visual check as to where from the end of the tunnel it would break. While we watched out of the hut window he poked a thick stick up through the ground from the end of the tunnel. But we couldn't see the stick, so the message to poke it higher was passed down the shaft. We still couldn't see it, so again a message was sent along the tunnel. Suddenly we saw this stick waving away about thirty feet across from where it was meant to be. We had a few anxious moments as the word was hurriedly sent down for him to pull the stick back down!

The escaping team, meantime, had undergone some changes. Mason Clark, weak with dysentery, was unable to escape, and his two friends would not go without him. Noel Ross, too, had to give up his plans of getting out: the Italians had found his reserve of escape food, and he was under observation. Bill Kelly, one of those who had first conceived the idea of the tunnel, reluctantly but gallantly gave up his place in the escape. Bill, an RAASC driver attached to the 2/8th Field Ambulance, had been given word that an exchange of non-military personnel was imminent, and he did not wish to jeopardise the chances of other men in his medical unit for repatriation. He had previously escaped from captivity twice, and felt this tunnel presented a marvellous chance for freedom, so it was with the greatest reluctance that he informed the escape team of his decision.

'One of the most courageous and wonderful men I have ever known,' said Dick Head by way of tribute to his friend. Two of the helpers from the 2/28th, Corporal John Costello and Private Stan Long, were given places in the escaping team.

In the early planning stages the escape leaders decided not to break the tunnel unless it was raining. They believed the guards would be less alert and seek shelter from the rain, and the searchlights would be less effective in delineating objects. But with the tunnel virtually ready to break the troops involved in the escape expressed their keen desire to go, irrespective of weather conditions. 'Their resolve was clear' according to Dick Head. 'Good or bad conditions, we can do it. There was an unspoken feeling – the greater the challenge the greater the incentive.'

On the afternoon of the break, Bill Kelly and Noel Ross placed a mushroom baffle made from wood and an Italian groundsheet beneath the thin ceiling layer of dirt and grass at the end of the tunnel, and using a bayonet cut an exit hole around the baffle while carefully planned diversions were taking place to distract the guards. This was then cautiously lowered. 'I stuck my head and shoulders out for a look around,' said Bill Kelly. 'It was a beautiful feeling; the air just seemed so much fresher that side of the wire. I felt very jealous of the blokes who were going out.' The mushroom baffle was then replaced.

That same day, South Australian Kevin O'Connell requested an urgent audience with Dick Head, Tom Comins and Eric Canning. He told the escape leaders of a twice-recurrent nightmare, in which he was trapped by a searchlight after leaving the exit hole. He was so genuinely concerned his dream might become a reality that he offered to withdraw rather than spoiling it for the remainder.

The three men appreciated his concern, and in order to reassure O'Connell, who had been a hard worker in the scheme, they arranged for him to be one of the last out.

Mason Clark, whose illness precluded his own escape from the tunnel, described the successful breaking of the tunnel on the evening of 30 October:

> The escape was set for a moonlight night before the cold weather set in. The day before the escape we had a fright. An Italian appeared in the patch of maize and started to cut it. We watched him in anguish expecting him to disappear down our hole at any moment. To our relief he left the patch without stumbling on the hole.
>
> On the day of the escape, the last earth was removed and the tunnel was now ready. That evening Bill Thurling, Johnny O'Hearne and I went to the tunnel to make sure that no one 'jumped the gun' with their provisions. They looked a motley crew as they came in, some with old hats and berets, and an assortment of clothes. We lowered them one by one into the tunnel; they then crawled forward to the front of the tunnel.

The escapers had to be in the tunnel, closed with boards down, and the external helping team back in their huts by 'lights out' at 9 p.m. It was a time of nervous tension, but finally the nineteen escapers, plus the seven opening and closing helpers were all in the tunnel, stretched out uncomfortably in the cold water and mud. Although he was not supposed to know of the escape, a Catholic padre, Father Lynch, had made his way to the hut and blessed each man as he lowered himself through the floorboards. The occupants of the hut were singing lustily to drown out any noises, while outside the hut 'stooges' were posted to warn of any approaching sentries. Several men were watching the nearest sentry. If he happened to notice any prisoners emerging from the tunnel behind him and made to shoot, the team, under Bill Kelly, would throw stones at him to distract his aim. In the darkness of the hut nearest the machine-gun and search-light other men were posted with stones, ready to similarly distract the post if they opened fire. Mason Clark continued:

When all was ready, word was passed along the tunnel and the first group crawled up and out into freedom. We all held our breath, but not a sound was heard. At intervals the others slipped out and away, to reform in their groups and slip away into the darkness. At last they were all away, and the tunnel closed and we were back in our huts for 'lights out'. The beds of escapees were made up. The guards and *Carabinieri* strolled through the huts and then lights went out. It was a success – after weeks of work, this was a thrilling moment. We laid [*sic*] sleepless, thinking of the boys making their way to freedom.

Kevin O'Connell's recurring nightmare almost became a reality. As he exited the hole he was caught in the beam of a searchlight. Fortunately he recalled his infantry training: when trapped in a searchlight you 'freeze' to avoid a long moving shadow. He froze, his skin prickling, waiting for the first shots to ring out. Then the searchlight swept on, and he moved off undetected.

The dullness of everyday life at Campo 57 was shattered the following morning when word was passed around of the escape, and the wise took food with them on the early morning parade in anticipation of being there for some time. The Italians counted the men on parade, and finally they came to realise what most prisoners already knew – there were quite a few absentees. Parades in both compounds were subjected to a multiplicity of counts. The enraged Italians screamed abuse, but did not quite know what to do. Finally, they formed a squad of guards in a ring working around the barbed wire. Eventually they found the tunnel outlet and a guard, with obvious trepidation, crawled back through it. Mason Clark recalled:

We were held on parade all day; our belongings were searched, and all other huts torn apart for signs of a tunnel. We had no food that day, and anyone who smiled was rushed to the 'Bastille'. However we cheered occasionally and booed whenever someone was marched to the 'Bastille'. The air was electric as prisoners became more rebellious, and the guards fingered their rifles more itchily. One act of violence could have caused a general charge at the guards and the wire. We were eventually herded back to our huts.

Activity was tremendous during the following days, as search parties of police and guards came to the camp, were briefed and sent away. Planes were overhead in the search for the escapees, and we were told that the whole countryside was alerted to watch for the dangerous *Australianos*.

From a distance the Julian Alps, thickly wooded to the snowline, appeared to present a reasonable refuge, but were in fact heavily populated. In addition to alerting local residents, the police and three divisions of Italian troops deployed in the region were notified of the mass break-out. The first two escapers were recaptured the following day, followed by others at various intervals. To make matters worse for the prisoners, it began to rain heavily. The lightning and thunder in the mountains was frightening, every clap of thunder had a thousand echoes. The rain was like an aerial river. 'It was like someone standing on a roof and throwing buckets of water over you,' Bob Hooper reflected.

The nineteen POWs who had managed to escape through the tunnel were:

Australia
CANNING, Flight Sergeant
    Thomas E. (RAAF)
COMINS, Flight Sergeant
    Thomas B. (RAAF)
COSTELLO, Corporal John D.
COTTER, Private George
DWYER, Private John A.
HEAD, Sergeant Richard L.
HOOPER, Sapper Robert St Q.
KING, Lance Corporal David
LANG, Private Stanley J.
LIND, Lance Corporal Charles

NOBLE, Warrant Officer
    Archibald
O'CONNELL, Private Kevin F.
POIDEVIN, Sergeant Gordon C.
WILLIAMS, Sergeant Albert

New Zealand
BOULT, Warrant Officer Leslie F.
NATUSCH, Sapper Roy S.
O'BRIEN, Private Hector A.
O'BRIEN, Sergeant John F.
SLOAN, Private William

Two days after his escape, wet through and shaking uncontrollably, Hooper was discovered in the passageway of a farmer's home in Primulacco, five miles from Udine. Some domestic fowls ('the place was a bloody menagerie!') had set up a strident rumpus, and the owner confronted him with a trembling shotgun. The farmer, soon convinced that his sick captive presented no danger to him and his wife, led Hooper into the kitchen by the fire, where they drank coffee and ate chestnuts while his clothes dried. The owner, with abject apologies, then handed his prisoner over to the local police.

The odds were greatly stacked against the escapers, who were rounded up one by one; the last two were sent back to Campo 57 on the fifth day after the mass break-out. The decision to escape in their uniforms, which made them all the more conspicuous, was certainly a big factor in the rapid recapture of the escapers, but in formulating the escape plans, the men had been worried that if they were captured in civilian clothing they might have been shot. The escape committee certainly did not want a massacre of recaptured prisoners to occur. As it turned out, the weather actually proved to be the biggest factor against them, undoubtedly shortening their freedom. Heavy rain caused the already cold rivers to run quite swiftly, and guards had been mounted on the bridges to prevent the men crossing.

Tom Canning, Tom Comins and Dick Head were fortunate in that they escaped the near-mandatory beating when recaptured by some Italian troops. The colonel in charge of the unit had himself been a successful prisoner escaper in World War I, and he sympathised with the three prisoners. He ushered them into a small village inn and gave them some food and drink until the *Carabinieri* arrived to take them back to the camp. The colonel offered his sincere apologies as he handed them over. Manacles were applied, and the men were loaded into a waiting truck.

All nineteen escapers were eventually returned to the camp, most of them in a relatively unharmed condition. On arrival, however, they were stripped naked or semi-naked, beaten, and locked in the camp cells for a month, where they were forced to exist on a starvation diet of bread and water. Afterwards they were placed into a hut in an unoccupied compound well away from the other prisoners and put to work carrying large rocks, which were set in a circle around the guards' barracks.

At least, as Mason Clark recalled, they were recaptured 'mercifully without loss of life':

We had achieved something, however. We had accepted the challenge of the 'escape-proof' camp. Our tunnel had done wonders for the morale of the camp; boredom was broken. We had shown defiance and spirit, even though we were wired in. Some of the information gained from those who had escaped helped the rest of us who were fortunate enough to escape later, so the long weeks of work in the tunnel and the escape had not, after all, been in vain.

Mason Clark was later transferred to a work camp, from which he escaped and got clear away across northern Italy to Switzerland and eventual freedom.

Eric Canning agreed with Clark's thoughts. 'The escape finished as most such episodes do, by recapture of the participants,' he mused, then adding with some satisfaction, 'To the best of my knowledge our effort had the distinction of being the greatest mass break-out in Italy.'

Colonel Calcaterra was fortunate enough to have been away on leave when the break-out occurred, and he managed to apportion the blame among his staff when he was summoned back to take command of the camp. He imposed severe restrictions on the prisoners, and made their lives more of a misery than before. Searches of the huts and the men's belongings became an almost daily affair, but he was certainly closing the gate after the horse had bolted.

'It probably didn't do his chances of promotion much good,' declared Eric Canning. 'But he only had a short time to live, as word has it that he was shot by the partisans shortly after Italy capitulated late in 1943.'

Normal life resumed at Gruppignano, but under far tighter security. Red Cross parcels were opened upon distribution and all cans punctured by the Italians, both to prevent food hoarding and hinder their use in any escape attempts. As an immediate consequence, all perishable food had to be eaten straightaway.

While daily counts in most Italian camps were relatively lax affairs, in PG 57 the counts were a full military parade. Battledress had to be worn in the heat of summer, and in winter the icy wind sweeping down from the Dolomites and Julian Alps was bitter. Another wearisome exercise took place every two or three weeks, lasting a whole day. This entailed the complete contents of each hut being taken out, the double-decker beds dismantled, and all bedding and personal gear removed. The hut floors had been laid in sections and these were all pulled up in turn while the guards checked to see that no tunnels were being dug.

'Bluey' Rymer shared some unfavourable comments about the conditions they continued to endure in PG 57:

Two things I remember most about Udine were the lice and the lice. The lice got into the lining of your clothes and laid their eggs.

You had to pick them out and kill them between your fingernails. The bloody Sikhs in the compound next door used to pick them out and drop them onto the ground – they would not kill them for religious reasons!

Wintertime was bad, especially at the 0600 parade. Blokes already ill from beri-beri used to pass out when it was really cold. It was so cold that the sentries on duty, in their half-closed sentry boxes on stilts, could not last more than two hours' duty; they stamped and screamed with the cold. It was the most goddam cold place I have ever been in my life. We were in a windy hut, and all we had was one worn-out blanket. It was even too cold to go to the toilet; some hardy souls managed to make it to the door to urinate, others did it in the aisles. Have you ever been so cold and desperate that you simply pissed yourself in bed?

Acts of barbarism still occurred at the camp. On 20 May 1943, 41-year-old Corporal Edward W. ('Socks') Symons (2/32nd Battalion) from Kalgoorlie, Western Australia, was shot dead when he refused to accompany a *Carabinieri* guard to the detention cells. Symons, a capricious and knowledgeable lecturer at the camp, and a difficult man to beat in a debate, was a cool-headed stretcher bearer who had distinguished himself by his unselfish heroism in Tobruk. During an attack on S.7 Post by soldiers from the 28th Battalion on 3 and 4 August 1941, a truce was called on the second morning to collect the dead and wounded. Socks wandered too close to the German lines, and was asked to tend some of their casualties, but having done this, the Germans took him prisoner. From the prison camp at Derna he gravitated to Italy, first to PG 66 (Capua) and then Campo 57.

On that fateful day, with *Carabinieri* guards patrolling among a noisy group of spectators watching a cricket match organised between two POW teams in No. 2 compound, Symons was cheering lustily as his 'E' team prepared the pitch for a long-awaited match against the 'A' team. 'You should have seen them rolling the wicket,' Noel Ross recalled. 'Solemnly walking up and down, pulling a jam tin filled with sand!'

After saving his camp money for several weeks, Symons had purchased a small bottle of Italian beer at the canteen (just one per cent alcohol), and by the time the match started he was enjoying the proceedings. Suddenly, one of the guards, Corporal Marinello Sodini, appeared in front of the spectators and began yelling and waving his rifle about. He was apparently motioning Symons to accompany him to the cells.

The next few seconds shocked everyone, according to eyewitness Noel Ross. 'We all stood up. Socks was a bit unsteady and the guard seemed to pick on him. A couple of chaps were steadying him when this *Carabinieri* stepped back a pace, brought his rifle to the shoulder and shot Socks through the chest. The bullet picked Socks up and threw him ten feet where he fell on his face, rolled over and said, "The bastard shot me!" How he said it I'll never know, but I was within ten feet of him.'

Bob Hooper, who also witnessed the shooting, said there was no reason at all for the guard to fire. Arch Noble, meantime, had bravely confronted the guard responsible and told him in Italian to put his weapon down or there would be trouble.

'I didn't see the shooting, but everyone knew what had happened,' added John Foxlee of Brisbane, formerly a corporal with the 2/15th Battalion. 'It was just cold-blooded murder. So far as I know, no one was ever punished for the death of Socks. I only knew the guard who shot him as "Strawberry Neck". None of us knew his real name.' (The guard was later identified as Marinello Sodini. Postwar, in March 1946, Sodini was sentenced to death for his crime. The following month this was commuted to life imprisonment, and then he was paroled in December 1950.)

The outrage following the mindless shooting was not the only reason why so many former prisoners from Campo 57, including Noel Ross, remember the incident so clearly.

'The Commandant had promised a sum of 1400 lira and fourteen days leave for anyone who shot a prisoner in the course of any pro-vocation or escape attempt,' he recalled. 'Well, the *Carabinieri* got his leave, and Socks' official record shows "Death due to pneumonia".'

Shortly after, some of the prisoners were moved to south-eastern Austria, and a camp known as Stalag XVIIIA, Wolfsberg. The town was situated in a wide green valley, beyond which towered snow-topped mountains covered in pine trees. Due to long neglect and unsanitary conditions, the camp itself had a severe problem with vermin when the first Allied POWs moved in, and they had to undergo a strict 'delousing' process in a tented quarantine area before being registered and allowed to enter the main area. As new arrivals poured in, the settled inmates were assigned to work details outside the camp to make room for the new occupants. In late 1943 Hooper was put to work in a brick factory at a place called Trieben.

The prisoners at Trieben were generally well treated and given the status of 'permanents', which allowed them to receive their weekly Red Cross parcels. By means of a small, hidden radio they were able to listen in to the BBC news broadcasts, and so knew a lot more about the true course of the war than their captors. An alcohol still was soon in operation, producing a semi-lethal brew from raisins, prunes and other assorted contributions.

Arch Noble, one of Hooper's fellow escapers from Gruppignano, was with him and they befriended a mysterious chap named Eric Oliver. Eric, as he later confided, was a German Jew who had escaped to Israel and joined the Israeli commandos. It was this group which had attacked Rommel's headquarters in the desert but missed the Field Marshal by less than an hour. With capture inevitable Eric had discarded his clothes and was taken wearing only his underclothes. Arch Noble suggested they give him an Australian Army number and dummy unit.

It seemed Hooper and Noble were the only Australians in Trieben at that time. The factory in which they worked made bricks from material brought down from the mountains by a continuous line of hoppers on an overhead cable line.

The three men were given the task of loading bricks into enclosed railway waggons. After Gruppignano, escape from the work detail at Trieben seemed remarkably easy, and it wasn't long before they had planned an escape to France. Eric Oliver decided to join the two Australians in their bid, although he was well aware that recapture would mean far more than the month's term in cells the others could anticipate.

They decided to wait until the waggons were being loaded for France. When loaded, the doors were closed and wire seals attached before they were shunted onto the rail siding. Each had a small wooden window located high at each end, which could be locked from the inside. The men's idea was to jam one of the windows closed with a piece of wood so it could be pushed inward from outside. As they waited for a suitable day light snow began to fall.

On the afternoon of the escape they rigged one of the windows and all was in readiness. It was still snowing and they dressed in as much warm clothing as they could muster.

That evening they managed to change shifts so that all three were on once again. They tossed their food haversacks over the wire into a snow drift at the back of the camp, intending to pick them up once they had passed safely through the gates. However, they were challenged by a guard as they sneaked around to the rear of the camp. The previous plan of escape was now history, and Hooper decided on an improvised do-or-die attempt.

'Run, you two!' he cried. 'Head for the hills!'

They set off, running as hard as they could as the guard yelled for them to stop. As the three men ran through the snow that lay thick on the frozen ground they could hear the sounds of pursuit behind them, but knew that the guards would find the going just as tough. Near the hills the snowdrifts were sometimes up to their waists, but they managed to lose their pursuers and circled back down to the rail waggon. Quickly opening the small window they clambered through onto the stacks of bricks bound for France. Even as they locked the window and recovered their breath they heard guards approaching, arguing and obviously still looking for the escapees.

When the Germans spotted their quarries' tracks near the rail waggon the station master was called over to open the sealed door, but he dug his heels in. He had personally sealed the door and the fragile wire seal was still intact. He also informed the guards that the train was scheduled to leave within the hour and he was not going to delay it with a futile search. His authority won out and the guards moved on. Eric translated the goings-on outside the waggon.

Not long after, the waggon was hitched up to a goods train and the trio were on their way to France, where they hoped to link up with the Resistance, or the French underground. After several frustrating days of stop–go travelling and shunting, and at one stage becoming the target for some Allied bombs, the men's meagre ration of food was gone and they were becoming a little desperate. Finally their waggon arrived at Dornbirn, just south of Bregenz on Lake Constance. Peering through their little window they could actually see the lights of the Swiss border.

The following day the three men scrambled out through the window and headed off across the snow, walking south-west as hard as they could. They planned to cross at the Liechtenstein frontier, as they felt the Germans might not be quite as active in that area. It was still light as they neared the border, so they hid beneath a small bridge until it became dark. Despite the thick clothing they had on they were still cold, and hunger gnawed at them.

That night the men eagerly crawled out from under the bridge and headed towards another, which they had worked out would take them across the frontier. When the bridge was finally behind them their spirits rose with every stride they took. They were free at last. Then, just as Hooper was about to embrace his friends, a dog patrol hove into sight.

'*Hande hoch!*' screamed one of the dog handlers, while the rest covered the three startled men with their rifles. One moment the elation of liberty, the next the disheartening jolt of capture. They simply couldn't believe it. Surely they were home free? Sadly it was not to be, and the three of them reluctantly raised their arms.

Confused and angry, they were marched off by the guards and placed in some cells in Feldkirch, which they knew to be on the

German side of the border. The Germans had quickly established who the men were, and during that almost sleepless night in the cells Hooper, Noble and Oliver kept trying to work out where they'd gone wrong. Morning brought even further frustration for the men; they could see Swiss workers as they went about their day's labours, ploughing in the fields of freedom beyond the frontier.

'Switzerland, so close!' The voice at the cell door startled the men. It was a guard who had stopped to gloat. 'I am afraid you English prisoners are not so clever,' he continued. He was out to tease the men, and did a good job. 'You know, if you had chosen instead to go half a kilometre down the river you would by now be free men – you could have just waded across in the shallow water.'

Two days later they were sent to the interrogation centre at Landeck. Here they were stripped and a methodical search included running a comb through their hair and inserting a pencil up their anus to make sure nothing had been lodged there. They were then ordered to open their mouths, and the same pencil was used to probe under the tongue and around the mouth. They spent two weeks at Landeck being questioned about the escape, living in cells that were little bigger than their bunks back at Trieben. The game was apparently up for poor Eric Oliver; he was separated from the two Australians, and his fate was never known. Meanwhile, persistent efforts were made to find out the route they had taken, where they had received shelter and how they'd obtained food, but Hooper and Noble had nothing to say. They were returned to Stalag XVIIIA at Wolfsberg, where they spent another month in solitary confinement. A sentence for attempted escape could not exceed 28 days by the terms of the Geneva Convention, but their previous confinement at Landeck was not taken into consideration. Their food ration over a four-day period would comprise just bread and water; on the fifth they would be given normal camp rations. After this punishment they were placed in the Stalag's *disciplinaire* compound – a *disciplinaire* being a prisoner who had escaped or committed some offence warranting a gaol sentence.

The Kommandant in charge of this section at XVIIIA was Hauptmann Steiner, who turned out to be a reasonably fair person. Steiner had been severely wounded in the Great War of 1914–18, so at times he demonstrated a little sympathy for his *disciplinaires*. He allowed them to remain in their quarters during rollcall on particularly freezing days, and even permitted them to receive Red Cross parcels – a lifesaving comfort denied those in several other disciplinary camps. As the winter of 1944 began to settle down, the escaping urge grew stronger in Bob Hooper.

The next stop along the POW road for him was Camp 7010 GM near a small railway village known as Gross Reifling. Hooper describes this as 'the toughest punishment camp of them all', while his fellow *disciplinaires* called it 'the second front'.

It was quite a small *arbeitskommando* camp. The prisoners occupied a three-room hut with two rooms allocated to sleeping quarters, while the third room, ostensibly a kitchen, was padlocked. The two rooms allocated to the men each had a functional stove, for which a reasonable supply of firewood was obtained by foraging prisoners. The German guards turned something of a blind eye to the practice. This small comfort made up in some small way for other annoyances the men were forced to endure, including the bed bugs and lice. In this camp as in others, some men took to placing the legs of their beds into tins of water in the hope that the bugs would not crawl into their bed, but it was a futile exercise. If nothing else, killing the despised lice and bed bugs occupied many of the longer, quieter hours.

Outside the hut sat shower and toilet huts, as well as the guards' quarters. Despite the barbed wire and prevailing grimness of the camp, it was nestled in a picturesque valley through which the Enns River meandered, sharing a narrow corridor of tenable land with a road and railway line. The village itself boasted a hotel, a smattering of well-kept houses and a few stores. The hotel had an outdoor water sprinkler system that was used to manufacture ice which was sawn into blocks by the prisoners and stored, packed in straw, in the cellars. Other small villages were dotted along the banks of the river, and in the distance lay the high glacial country. However, the temperature in Gross Reifling sometimes dropped to −16°C.

The prisoners' principal duty was to maintain the railway track and sidings, and to cut deep trenches in hillsides to prevent rocks from falling onto the tracks. They were also employed in shovelling snow from points and transferring coal from waggons at the sidings. Another, less agreeable job, was to maintain the tunnels. As trains swept through, the men sheltered in recesses where they were covered in soot, steam and ash.

Allied POWs knew better than to refuse such arduous or filthy work, which was in fact permitted under the terms of the Geneva Convention. Refusal could lead to sentences of up to four years in gaol. Better, they soon realised, to do the job at a much reduced pace and suffer some occasional light punishment for loafing.

Bob Hooper joined in the work on the railway, but he and others managed to keep up their war effort with a little sabotage. When munitions trains came through they secretly poured ashes into the grease boxes on the axles, hoping they would suffer a hotbox and break down. The food was far better here, and when combined with some exercise it wasn't long before Bob Hooper started thinking about a fourth escape attempt. In a rather forlorn attempt to keep escape activity to a minimum, the prisoners' boots and trousers were locked up by night in a small room in the corner of their barracks, but the men quickly became adept at springing the padlock.

In discussing the layout of the camp with some of the longer term inmates. Hooper found out that two prisoners had begun a tunnel under the floorboards near his bed, but it had been discovered and loosely filled in by the Germans. He decided to reopen the tunnel and found a ready co-conspirator in Victorian Ron Hinton.

A gap of twenty centimetres beneath the floor of the hut and the ground meant that disposing of the spoil was relatively easy and safe. Hooper managed to open the shaft and made good progress. He did most of the digging by night, hacking away at the work face with a screwdriver and scooping the dirt into a bag. He always worked with a string tied to his big toe. Ron Hinton kept watch and gave the string a sharp tug if any guards moved into the vicinity. Two tugs gave the all-clear.

When the tunnel reached the area beneath the wall of the hut Hooper encountered a concrete footing which extended a metre and a half into the ground. A downward diversion took care of this minor obstacle, and it meant he was nearing the end of his task as the wall served as part of the camp perimeter. Within days the tunnel had been scooped out and was ready for the break, but an irrepressible Bob Hooper was still having fun with the Kommandant, known to the prisoners as 'Two-Gun Pete', who claimed the Australian was malingering.

If the prisoners worked hard they could earn small rewards and privileges, one of which was shoe polish. The Kommandant would continually deride Hooper for not working hard enough to be able to polish his boots.

'If you are not going to work for this polish, then why don't you simply borrow some from your friends?' he asked one day.

'No chance,' replied Hooper. 'We Aussies don't bludge off our mates!'

The Kommandant sighed. 'You seem to be doing much less work than the others,' he observed. 'Forget about the boot polish. If you do not share the work then too bad, it will be the cells for you!'

'I do my share,' Hooper growled. 'But if you're not satisfied with that, then just open the gate and let me go!' The Kommandant gave a short laugh, and Hooper put his hands on his hips. 'You won't have to worry about me much longer,' he continued. 'I'm going to escape from this hole!'

'So the Hooper is not happy here,' the German said, a wry smile on his face. 'You must let me know when you are escaping and I will make sure I give you some extra bread and sausage!' The Kommandant laughed again and strolled off across the compound.

One of the guards at Gross Reifling had acquired the nickname 'Gold Teeth'. He was about 40 years old, had been wounded in battle in North Africa, and was a bit of a larrikin. One afternoon he confronted Bob Hooper in his barracks and in lowered tones told the Australian that the Kommandant knew he was going to attempt an escape and had warned all the guards to keep an eye on him. Gold Teeth suggested that for 200 English cigarettes he would turn his back at the appropriate moment to allow the escape to run its course.

'Sorry old mate,' replied Hooper, slapping him on the shoulder. 'I'm not about to escape. Thanks, but no thanks!'

The night before they made their break. Hooper was polishing his boots when Two-Gun Pete came to lock up the dormitory and stuck his head in.

'What is mitt the Hooper?' he asked.

'I am getting ready to escape,' Bob replied, and looked up. 'What about my extra bread and sausage?'

'Oh no, Sapper Hooper, no need for that. There is much work to be done before you are finished.'

'I'm afraid it has to be soon,' Hooper continued, baiting the German. 'The moon is getting full and I'll be able to see my way over the mountains. I must say I am disappointed you have not kept your promise with the extra rations!'

The German laughed derisively and strode to the door of the dormitory, peering up into the night sky. He then looked back. 'I think I will be seeing you for this full moon and many others, I am afraid.' With that the door was closed and bolted securely.

The following night the two men readied themselves for their escape. Hooper was a little concerned that the larger Hinton would become jammed in the exit, but decided they had to go. He crawled to the end of the tunnel and carefully broke through the thin crust of dirt. After sticking his head out of the exit hole and looking around, Hooper carefully hauled himself out, turned to help his friend, and heard a low curse.

'Shit, I'm stuck!'

Ron Hinton was jammed in the narrow opening, his head and shoulders protruding and his arms jammed uselessly by his side. Just as Hooper bent to help his wedged companion, a guard strolled around the corner of the hut, saw what was going on and called out. As the German frantically unshouldered his rifle Hooper placed his hands under Hinton's armpits and hauled him upwards with all his strength. Hinton popped out of the hole like a cork as the guard fired a wild shot into the air. The two men ran for their lives towards some cover, but went sprawling over a trip wire 50 metres out from the camp. The bundle containing their food tumbled away, but they were not about to waste precious seconds in gathering it up again. They ran on until they reached a creek bed, where they concealed themselves just as the pursuing Germans hove into sight and then crashed past.

That night they climbed a mountain covered in snow, and just before dawn crawled into a hayshed to hide. When daylight came they found themselves looking straight down on their camp, not 400 metres away. Without realising it they had climbed up and down the same side of the mountain.

Around 3 p.m. a horse and cart carrying an old man and a girl pulled up outside the barn, causing the two escapers to burrow deeper into the hay. They had not chosen their place of concealment very wisely, as they realised when the girl swung down from her seat and took a pitchfork from the empty cart. With a hefty lunge she impaled a good-sized wad of hay, carried it outside and tossed it into the rear of the cart before returning for more. Following another hearty lunge Hooper decided enough was enough. He leapt out of the diminishing pile to the astonishment of the girl, who cried out in alarm and ran to the old man.

'It's okay,' said Hooper, holding his arms palm-outwards away from his body in a gesture of friendship.

The girl choked back a sob and hugged the old man's arm. 'Are you the escaped men they are all looking for?' she asked in German. Hooper had by this time picked up a reasonable amount of German and acknowledged that they were.

'My brother came home a while back from the Russian Front', she said, with tears forming in her eyes. 'It was so terrible – he had lost both of his legs.' She squeezed the old man's hand. 'Our family is not very happy with this war. If you want I will travel into the village to find out if the soldiers are still searching for you.'

They looked at the girl and her father, and then at each other. Hooper shrugged. They had no option but to trust her.

Several hours later the young girl returned, rattled on the barn door and called out '*Yo Ho, ich rufen!*' ('I'm calling!') The Australians clambered out from beneath the pile of hay, wondering if she had turned them in. To their relief she not only stood there alone, but had brought some boiled eggs and hot coffee. As they ate, the girl told them that the search had been called off. They thanked her for her kindness and promised to leave the area that night.

At midnight they stole out of the barn and began to cross the mountain. As dawn was approaching Hooper and Hinton blundered straight into the path of a hunter armed with a shotgun. Realising he'd stumbled across the escaped prisoners, the surprised hunter covered them with his gun and demanded that they put their hands in the air. He then marched them several kilometres to a local village, where they were handed over to an equally surprised local police-man, who locked them in his cell.

The following morning a guard arrived from Gross Reifling to escort the prisoners back to the work camp. The guard, whom they dubbed 'The General', had been wounded in battle and was terrified that he would be sent off to the Russian front if his charges escaped. He told Hooper they would be placed in the local prison at Gross Reifling, and said he might be able to do things for them if they promised not to escape en route. Hooper and Hinton agreed, and once they'd arrived at the prison they asked their guard for a pencil and some paper, to test his part of the deal. The man was as good as his word.

The prison contained three cells, each of which held five men behind wooden doors with peepholes. As a further precaution the passageway leading from the cells was secured by a massive timber door. The prisoners had food delivered by men from the camp, and that afternoon two of his colleagues arrived in company with the cooperative guard, bearing some bread and a large pot of sauerkraut. Hooper asked the affable German if he would deliver a letter to a senior ranking British officer back at the camp. The note asked if some little items could be smuggled in to him, buried in the sauerkraut. These 'little things' were a screwdriver, a set of pliers and half a hacksaw blade, all of which he'd previously concealed at the bottom of a half-barrel which was used as a urinal when the men were locked in their dormitory at night. As an afterthought, he reminded his mate to give them a good wash before putting them into the sauerkraut pot. The guard stuck the note in his pocket.

The door of the cell would not present too much of a problem, Hooper had decided, but the door in the corridor was far more daunting. When closed, it could be secured using three solid beams, which dropped down into steel brackets on the outside and could be padlocked into place. Fortunately for Hooper's escape plans the German guards had become lax about securing the beams, only slipping the central one into place. The following evening the sauerkraut arrived containing all the requested items, and Hooper and Hinton made another bid for freedom. The lock on the cell door was easily sprung using the screwdriver, but the task now in front of them was a formidable one. There were 32 bolts and nuts holding the main door to its hinges, and as each was undone the men said a little prayer of thanks. But the more they managed to undo, the more nervous they became.

Hooper and Hinton were joined in the escape bid by an Englishman from the Queen's Royal Regiment named Bob Gardiner. He was none too well after a recent escape and subsequent capture by German land forces, but he was keen to make another break. The other two prisoners in their cell declared they were too ill to try.

Once all 32 bolts had been unscrewed the three men were able to prise the heavy door outwards at the bottom, creating just enough room for them to squeeze through. Hinton became jammed once again and Hooper and Gardiner had to drag him free.

The three men quickly put some space between themselves and the cells, heading for the mountains once again. By the time they reached the foothills, Bob Gardiner apologetically explained that he was too ill to tackle the arduous climb, so they gave him half their loaf of bread and wished him well. (Gardiner was captured some days later when a policeman and members of the *Landwache* searched the Italy-bound train he was hiding on at Heiflau. In 1945, when his new camp fell into Russian hands, Gardiner escaped once more and was able to link up with the liberating 8th US Army.)

Meanwhile Hooper and Hinton crossed the snow-capped mountains. During their two-day trek they continually heard the howling of wolves and saw paw tracks in the snow, but none was sighted. They found themselves in a valley, close by the village of Rottenmann. Hunger and cold were now their most immediate concerns and both men tried eating snow, but Hinton became ill as a result. Calculating that they were only a few kilometres from the camp at Trieben. Hooper decided to contact the prisoners for some food.

They laboriously made their way to the brick factory and hid in an abandoned shed nearby. That night Hooper approached the factory and asked one of the men for some food. The fellow promised he would talk to the Camp Leader and see what could be spared.

The next day passed slowly for the two escapers. Ron Hinton was still weak with his illness, and both were anticipating a meal of sorts to give them the strength to keep going, but there was a galling disappointment in store. When Hooper contacted the fellow that night he said they had held a meeting to discuss what to do for the escapers.

'Look I'm sorry Hooper,' he stammered. 'But the majority of the men decided that as you'd escaped from here before, and they were punished by not being allowed to play soccer for six months, they just can't help you!'

Hooper could hardly control his anger. 'You tell those effing sods back in the camp that it's a bloody disgrace,' he hissed through clenched teeth. 'I'm going to report the whole bloody lot of them once the war's over. Pack of bastards!'

'Let me talk to them again,' the man replied. He then hauled three biscuits out of his pocket and passed them over. 'Sorry, that's the best I can do for the moment.'

Bob Hooper returned to the shed and told Hinton what had transpired. The biscuits were quickly devoured, but hunger still gnawed at them and Hooper next approached a group of young Ukrainian women who also worked in the factory. They were far more sympathetic and handed over some bread and other small items of food. They told Hooper to come back the following night and they would have some more food. Evidently there'd been a change of heart at the working camp and when Hooper met the women the following evening they handed him some food the prisoners had put together out of their Red Cross parcels.

After three days Ron Hinton's health had improved, so Hooper stole a pushbike belonging to one of the German factory workers and doubled his friend towards Innsbruck. Before reaching Innsbruck they changed direction as planned and made their way to the south of Graz, near the Yugoslavian border, but here their luck ran out. For an unknown reason a small force of American Fortresses decided to drop their bombs on the forest area in which the two men were hiding. German troops appeared from everywhere to survey the damage, and the two men were quickly spotted. So ended another little tourist trip, and the escapers were sent to Landeck for interrogation and a term in the bunker. They were then returned to the disciplinary compound and spent another 28 days in the bunker at Stalag XVIIIA.

At this time in XVIIIA permission was granted to a New Zealand Anglican chaplain named Johnny Ledgerwood, also a prisoner, to visit the men at their working camps. In addition to conducting religious duties he involved himself in welfare work and became something of a spokesman for his fellow prisoners. Bob Hooper sought his counsel and told Ledgerwood what had happened at Trieben, and how the Camp Leader and his men had refused to help them. ('I believe he went there and gave them a good old dressing down!') The men on the working *Kommandos* were grateful to Ledgerwood for his invaluable help, not only as a visiting padre, but for the ready assistance he gave in camp activities both within the Stalag and at the outlying *Kommandos*. He was later awarded the MBE for his endeavours on behalf of his fellow prisoners.

After five escape attempts the urge to be free still pressed strongly upon Bob Hooper, so when he found himself on a train bound for another disciplinary camp at Leizen (for further insubordination) he was determined not to complete the journey. Unfortunately Ron Hinton was not on the train, but Hooper found another escaping ally in an artillery private from New South Wales by the name of 'Snowy' Schultz.

Of all the means of escape employed by prisoners of war, one of the most harrowing and certainly most dangerous was train-jumping. The escaper would leap from a train – sometimes when it was travelling quite fast. If it was night time he had to take his chances with railway stanchions and posts, rocks, and any number of utilities along the way. Many POWs died train-jumping; it took a bucketful of luck and a momentary madness to attempt the feat.

Bob Hooper had decided to play the odds and scramble out through the window that afternoon. The window was of the lift-up type and he figured that the two of them should just be able to squeeze through, one after the other. Their small compartment, containing nine prisoners, was under the watch of a single armed guard, and as the train drew to within a few kilometres of Leizen at around 4 p.m. the men knew they had to go.

'Now or never, Snowy,' Hooper whispered, watching carefully as their bored guard turned around for one of his customary looks through their compartment doors and down towards the far end of the carriage. The noise of their escape would hopefully be drowned out by those of the train. 'Just don't let the bastard shoot me when I'm halfway out!'

'No worries, Bob', Schultz replied. 'If he comes this way I'll just grab you on the balls and you'll fair rocket out!'

Hooper grasped the lower part of the window and shot it up as high as it would go. He then thrust his head and upper torso through the narrow aperture and levered himself out. To this day he doesn't know quite how he did it, but after squirming and pulling desperately he was suddenly out of the window and had leapt clear of the train. His feet hit the ground with a bone-jarring impact and he felt a sharp pain in his left ankle as he rolled away from the train tracks and tumbled down an embankment. He came to rest and sat quite still for a few moments as he recovered from the terror of the past few moments. After going over his aching body he felt there was nothing that would not heal in time and began to call out to Snowy.

No one answered his calls, and he followed the tracks a short distance until he came to the conclusion that Snowy just hadn't been able to get out of the window. Hooper hoped the kid was all right and, deciding he'd better make himself scarce, he headed off for some hills he could see in the distance. He hid in a wheatfield until nightfall before continuing his journey.

Coming across a small creek Hooper took off his shoes and immersed his ankles in the cool water. His left ankle was still sore, but not enough to seriously restrict his movements. After resting by the stream for a while he decided to follow the path of the railway line and eventually came across an area where the engines had their boilers refilled from a water tank. A train marked with a destination sign for Innsbruck had pulled up at the water tower, so Hooper clambered aboard and concealed himself in a brake cabin at the rear of one of the waggons.

On arrival at Innsbruck Hooper waited for an opportunity to leave the brake cabin unseen, but the place was crawling with railway security police, who were moving along the train, checking every truck for unpaid guests of the German railway system. He decided not to wait for the inevitable discovery and leapt from the van, running as fast as he could. Behind him he heard the security police shouting and giving chase, but eluded them by dodging between carriages in the goods yard. The station master's well-tended vegetable garden offered temporary refuge, so Hooper dashed in and lay face-down among the sheltering plants, gasping for air. He remained there throughout that night and well into the next day, feasting on snow peas and sweet green beans.

When night began to fall he moved on, deciding to take for the hills once again, and moving in a southerly bearing towards Yugoslavia. He travelled by night and hid in any convenient shelter during the day. At one time he encountered a man working in a field and decided to approach him for food. The fellow did not look German, so Hooper took a chance on him being a sympathetic foreign worker. As he approached the man looked up.

'Good evening,' said Hooper. The man nodded without expression. 'I wonder if you have any food you can spare me?'

The worker looked Hooper up and down, and to his relief answered with a thick French accent. 'I have some,' he stated. 'You are English, no?' Hooper nodded and the man walked over to a nearby bag, from which he extracted a small loaf of bread which he handed over.

'You are perhaps an *aviateur* – a *flieger*?'

'No, but thank you for the food. You are most kind.' The two men shook hands, and as Hooper walked off the Frenchman called out '*Monsieur!*' He turned, and the man was holding up his hand in farewell. '*Bonne chance!*' he cried, and Hooper waved back.

The following day Hooper's luck ran out once again when he was picked up by a group of soldiers on training exercises with a Hitler Youth group. He was taken back to Landeck for interrogation, and found himself flanked by two brutish-looking guards in front of an SS officer who seemed far from pleased with the Australian's escape record. He riffled the papers in a folder on his desk and looked briefly at the prisoner in front of him.

'Why were you in the hills?' he demanded.

'I was trying to head for Yugoslavia,' replied Hooper quite truthfully.

'You have escape contacts there?'

'No one at all.'

'Maybe you had some friends in the hills then?' When Hooper did not reply immediately the officer sat back in his chair and pulled out a silver case of cigarettes. He extracted one, which had a smart gold band at one end, and tapped it on the case.

'Perhaps you wanted to join the partisans?' He lit the cigarette and blew a thin stream of smoke towards the ceiling.

Involuntarily, Hooper laughed. 'You've got to be bloody kidding!' he blurted out. 'I don't know a flaming soul between here and England, and I'm not about to ruin a perfectly good escape by running around some forest with a bunch of bloody bush cowboys.'

Even the German had to smile at that. 'So tell me, Sapper Hooper, why were you found in the hills? What were you doing there?'

Hooper's voice took on a conspiratorial tone and he leant towards the officer. The two guards tensed a little. 'Well . . . if you *really* must know, I was looking for some Alpine snow flowers – edelweiss!'

The German nearly choked on his cigarette. When he'd recovered his composure he closed the file in front of him. 'So, you escape, and you spend your time looking for edelweiss, is that correct, Sapper Hooper?'

'Close as I can recall.'

The officer looked at the two guards standing behind Hooper and muttered something about all British prisoners being crazy. Hooper chose not to let on that he'd understood. The interrogation apparently at an end, the German pointed at the two small Australian rising sun badges pinned to Hooper's lapels. They were not standard issue, but had been made for him by a Russian prisoner at an earlier staging camp.

'I would like to have those, Sapper Hooper. You understand – a little souvenir of our chat.'

As the officer reached out to examine one of the badges, Hooper lunged at the German's jacket, intending to seize his medals by way of retaliation. The guard to Hooper's left hit him across the hand with his rifle, while the other clubbed him in the back. As Hooper fell in agony to the floor he heard the officer screaming something, and through his pain he recognised the word *fertig* (finish). For a moment he thought the guards had been ordered to finish him off, and his immediate thought was for his mother, and how heartbroken she would be if he was killed. But the officer was actually chastising the guards for hitting him. When Hooper had regained his feet the officer offered him one of his fancy cigarettes. The blow had broken a bone in Hooper's hand, and it was exceedingly painful. (It remained painful for the ensuing twelve months, and he still has a large lump on the back of his hand.)

The interrogation now at an end, Hooper was taken back to the disciplinary compound at Stalag XVIIIA, and to another 28-day term in the bunker for his latest exploit.

Hooper's escape file had been growing thicker with the passing months, so it wasn't a complete surprise to the Australian when he was called before the Kommandant of XVIIIA and informed that, as an inveterate escaper, he could no longer be trusted in working camps.

'You won't stop me from trying,' Hooper replied. 'It's a soldier's duty to escape and to cause as much trouble as possible.'

The German sighed, but looked at the Australian with a little more respect. 'Of course it is your duty, just as it is mine to prevent any of my prisoners from escaping, and to keep you from causing trouble. It has been interesting to observe you and the others. Do you know if we'd had soldiers – *disciplinaires* – of equal conviction in the last war Germany might have won?' It was a remarkable thing to hear from any German, and particularly the Kommandant of a prisoner of war camp.

Restriction to the confines of the Stalag was not unwelcome. For the first time in quite a while Hooper could look forward to receiving a regular supply of Red Cross parcels. However, inactivity did not sit well with the Australian and after a month of this sedentary lifestyle he'd had enough. By keeping an ear to the ground he had learnt that a group of *disciplinaires* was being sent to the Leizen *Strafelager* (punishment camp) and he quickly devised a means of joining in with the group. By making furtive enquiries among those going to Leizen he managed to find one who would agree to a substitution, remaining at XVIIIA while Hooper took his place. The two men memorised each other's name and service number, and the game was afoot. Hooper had no definite plans beyond leaving the Stalag, but the day the working party left the camp Hooper was nestled in their midst, staying well back and answering when his newly adopted name and number were called out.

At Leizen the prisoners found themselves digging out dirt and rock for extensions to a factory, but their mood of resigned indifference changed to one of anger and rebellion when they discovered that it was a munitions factory. They pointedly refused to do any work which might aid the German war effort, which they correctly claimed was contrary to the terms of the Geneva Convention, and went on strike. Twenty ringleaders, including Bob Hooper, were thrust into an underground cell, where they were kept for four days without any food or water. Decent sleep was also denied the men, as German guards deliberately and continuously ran their bayonets along the upright bars of the cells, making a hideous racket. They would also taunt the thirsty prisoners by calling out '*Wasser wasser!*' ('Water, water!'). When the men were released, they all had a renewed loathing for their captors. The game now was to harass and annoy the Germans by doing as little work as possible, and to practise small acts of sabotage where and if they could.

One little ruse developed by Bob Hooper and two others was to give each other a dabbing-down over the chest and back with a cloth soaked in Dettol antiseptic liquid, which left a red patch closely resembling a rash. The men presented themselves to the German doctor, who examined them with obvious puzzlement.

'You have had this rash before?' he asked.

'Yes,' Hooper replied. 'It's quite common in the other *arbeitskommandos*, and the doctors refer to it as "Egyptian eczema". Prisoners get it a lot when they don't receive proper food or showers. I'm sure you've treated it a lot of times.'

'Yes of course,' the doctor said, 'but you will excuse me while I check on the preferred treatment.' He walked out of the room as the three men stifled their laughter. They wondered what he would do when he couldn't find the disease in his medical books, but when he returned it was obvious that he'd decided to bluff it out.

'I will keep you from working details for a few days,' he declared. 'Keep away from others in the camp and drink a lot of fluids.'

The Dettol caper was only a temporary ruse, and it could not be milked for too long, so Bob Hooper began looking for other means of avoiding work. He knew that finger-breaking devices existed in most camps, but he was reluctant to lose the full use of his hands and opted for an alternative – a broken little toe. A none-too-willing friend was talked into doing the gruesome job and a suitable piece of water pipe was located.

'Make sure you do it right the first time,' Hooper growled as he pulled a sock over his foot. 'I'm not going to stand here and let you hit it twice!' The fellow took his advice, but if anything was a little over-zealous. The small toe was smashed and was a real mess. Hooper yelped and bounded around on his good right foot, clutching at the area of his agony before he was taken limping off to the doctor, where an accident was recorded. The medico sent Hooper to a German hospital at Rottenmann, where a Polish doctor responded sympathetically to his circumstances by encasing the leg in plaster from toe to knee!

When word reached Leizen that old Hooper was resting comfortably in the hospital, one of his New South Wales friends by the name of Ken Livingstone decided to join him in his protracted convalescence with a similarly painful exercise. Since two instances of broken toes would have raised German suspicions, he opted to have part of the top of one of his fingers removed. Having gone through with the painful process he saw the camp doctor and waited to join his mate in Rottenmann.

But once again Bob Hooper had landed himself in hot water. A belligerent German soldier visiting the hospital had become offended at the sight of an enemy soldier resting comfortably in a German bed and his vituperation was too much for the Australian. He leapt out of bed and told the German to do impossible things to himself, at which the enraged soldier lashed out, kicking Hooper squarely on his good leg. Hooper decked the cowardly fellow with a savage punch. That was the end of hospital care for Hooper. A complaint to the Kommandant at Leizen soon disclosed that the patient was not who he claimed to be, and a call to the Kommandant at Wolfsberg revealed his true identity. Flanked by two stern guards, Hooper was marched off to the railway station. A long walk on a bitterly cold day through deep snow, with his leg still in plaster, resulted in a painful touch of frostbite.

The hospital subsequently refused to take any more prisoners from the Leizen working camp, so Ken Livingstone unhappily missed out. Hooper was placed in the small camp hospital at Stalag XVIIIA.

Having been through so much in such a short time, Hooper was run down and developed a severe dose of bronchitis. He was still very weak and non-comprehending in hospital a week later when the camp was galvanised into panicky action as a group of six American Flying Fortresses flew overhead. The pilots were apparently unaware that prisoners were held at the camp, as they unleashed their load of bombs from low altitude.

When the noise and conflagration had settled down, several Germans and prisoners were dead, including two doctors and three prisoners suffering from tuberculosis, who had been waiting to be sent to Berlin for repatriation home through Switzerland. In his semi-delirious state Bob Hooper did not know much about what had happened and was unaware that his name was recorded as one of those killed. When the shaken hospital staff mistakenly assumed Hooper to be one of the surviving TB sufferers, he was placed on a train to a hospital transit camp at Chemnitz, near the Czechoslovakian border and 100 kilometres from Berlin.

Hooper fell into line with the mistake the German authorities had made. After all this time, it seemed it might be bungling German administration that saw him back in England. His convalescence was not aided by a massive injection, intended to prevent his contracting typhoid, which sent him spiralling back into a weakened state for nearly a week. But as Hooper began to grow stronger once again it soon became obvious to the medical staff that their patient was not suffering from tuberculosis. One day the doctor walked in, and as he took his patient's temperature he calmly stated: 'By the way, we have been told that your real name is Hooper, and we are to keep a good eye on you until they decide what is to happen with you!'

In time, Hooper was put to work in the hospital, washing dishes and cleaning the floors in the officers' and doctors' mess. He was rewarded with reasonable amounts of nourishing food, and at one stage was even allowed to partake of some alcohol.

After two months he was transferred to another nearby hospital camp, together with an Australian infantryman, Jerry Woods, and a Scot from the 11th Parachute Battalion called Bill Broadhurst, who had been wounded and captured after literally falling into the action at Arnhem. Further moves to other small hospital camps took place over the next few weeks.

By this time it was January 1945. Throughout Germany and Austria massive numbers of despairing citizens were fleeing for their lives in the middle of a freezing winter as the Allies continued their thrust into the heart of Hitler's rapidly crumbling Third Reich. Prisoners of war from dozens of camps were being sent on ill-conceived death marches, numbly crisscrossing enemy territory in a vain attempt to keep them out of the hands of the liberating American and Soviet forces. Thousands of prisoners and their dispirited guards died in this futile exercise, starving or freezing to death in sub-zero conditions.

Hooper and Broadhurst decided to make an escape to link up with the Allied forces, but as they formulated their plans the Germans decided to split up the hospital. Bob Hooper's name was among those destined for transfer, but Woods volunteered to change identities with him so the escape could take place as planned.

A few nights later they decided the time was ripe to make this final bid for freedom. Security among the crestfallen Germans was almost non-existent, so Hooper and Broadhurst had little difficulty in slipping away one night and heading towards the Allied lines. They didn't worry this time about hiding when they saw any German troops; in fact they often saw uniformed Germans running for their lives in the opposite direction.

Eventually they spotted a despatch driver in a jeep and waved the man down. The remainder of the story is told in Bob Hooper's own words.

I guess our liberation was something of a disappointment to me after three years in the bag. After all those attempts, and all those disappointments, to be driven by jeep to freedom was something of an anti-climax. I can't recall being excited at the time, but of course relief was the predominant emotion, and we could relax, enjoy the ride, and chat to our friendly liberator.

He took us to an American unit at Charleroi in Belgium and wished us good luck. We shook hands and officially handed ourselves over to the Americans from the 67th Tactical Reconnaissance Group.

We remained with the American unit for about ten days; they and the Belgian people gave us lots of white wine and food. As a matter of fact we felt at times, with our hangovers, that we might have been better off if we'd stayed in the prison camp, as we were quite run down in health and certainly not used to unlimited quantities of food and numerous booze-ups! The Yanks then told us that the railway line to Brussels would be repaired in a day or so, and planes would be flying into the airport with supplies from England. Soon after we jumped on a train, this time as legitimate passengers, and went to Brussels. Here we were interrogated, debriefed, deloused, and given papers to say we were ex-prisoners of war. We then boarded an empty Dakota aircraft and were flown back to England.

Now this was okay for my mate Bill, as he was back in his own country, but they didn't quite know what to do with me. Eventually they placed me with an army unit in Surrey and gave me a clean English uniform and some money. Real money. But I didn't have to go on parade or anything like that – the only place I could go was the local pub, and as Australians were then very popular it was hangover time once again. Eventually word came through that Lady Blamey had arrived in England and was taking over guesthouses and hotels on the south coast in places such as Brighton and Eastbourne for the use of ex-POWs when they came back. I was sent down to tell the Pommie cooks what the men would like to eat when they got back, which really was quite a stupid bloody exercise. But I told them what I thought the men would want, and to include plenty of meat, and I then enjoyed a four-month holiday in England. On VE Day I was at a little village called Snodland, about ten kilometres north-west of Maidstone in Kent. What a party that was!

I came home by ship through the Panama Canal, then via Hawaii and New Zealand to Brisbane. Shortly after my arrival the war with Japan also ended.

When the Australian Intelligence officers interrogated me after the war I found to my amusement that I had actually been a subsidized 'tourist' around Germany during my escapes. For every day I was out, I was paid the grand sum of five shillings. Australian Army officialdom being what it was, I wasn't about to confuse the issue by telling them that I hadn't spent a single penny during any escape. So I took their money and fled!

At war's end Bob Hooper was repatriated back to Australia where he was reunited with his fiancée, Gloria Setter, and resumed working in Brisbane as a customs agent for Dalgety and Company. The following year he and Gloria, whom he had met at Dalgety's, were married. They would have a son, Mark, who became one of Australia's finest classical pianists and music teachers. 'Perhaps I was meant to make it back home just so Mark could come along and give the world his beautiful music,' Hooper said. 'The funny thing is that he has a German agent and now spends most of his time travelling to Germany for concert performances. Me, I was always trying to get out of the bloody place!'

In 1947 Hooper travelled to Port Moresby with Gloria after being offered a job as a customs agent for BP (British Petroleum), but later quit and over the next six years was involved in several occupations, including tough and dangerous salvage and survey diving work. On their return to Australia he tried numerous jobs such as taxi-driving and bookmaking with mixed success before opening a used car yard which he ran until his retirement in 1986.

Three years earlier, he had travelled to Sri Lanka with the Australian Cricket Team as assistant to manager Bert Rigg, and later to England for the Prudential Cup with manager Phil Ridings, then Chairman of the Australian Cricket Board. Here they were invited to Buckingham Palace, where he enjoyed what he describes as one of the most memorable moments of his life – the pleasure of meeting Queen Elizabeth II and Prince Philip.

Following his retirement, the good-natured but indomitable character who defied and harassed his enemy captors until he finally achieved his goal, settled into a life of peace and contentment with Gloria in Tarragindi, Queensland until he passed away on 5 June 2006.

4

PATIENCE, PERSISTENCE AND GUTS

ANY ESCAPE FROM THE JAPANESE during the Second World War was fraught with danger; their policy concerning the treatment of recaptured prisoners became abundantly clear soon after the outbreak of hostilities. Curiously, however, they respected those who dared to escape and even paid homage to their soldierly courage. This was unfortunately of little comfort to those recaptured, many of whom later suffered execution under the sword, bayonet or bullet.

In discussing escape there doubtless were, and are, many under-lying determinants in any prisoner's philosophy, but the true escaper generally nurtures a driving need to get away because he is rebellious by nature, ill at ease with the frustrations and uncertainties of incarceration, and refuses to have his needs and liberties – and even his life – subject to the whims of a captor he loathes. One aspect of escape which is sometimes overemphasised is the prisoner's sense of duty, but in the case of Lieutenant Bill Jinkins the motive for his daring escape was a desire to raise a force which might help liberate the men who shared his captivity.

William Thomas Lloyd (Bill) Jinkins, MBE, Bronze Star Medal (US) was born on 29 November 1912 and spent his early childhood in the Melbourne suburbs of Elwood and Hawthorn. He studied building construction and architecture, and during his leisure hours he was involved in the Scouting movement and joined the Boy's Department of the YMCA. At sixteen he was indentured for five years as a carpenter and joiner. In 1934, in order to keep up his sporting activities, he joined the local 3rd Military District's CMF unit, in the 39th Battalion at Hawthorn. In 1939 he was promoted to lance corporal.

On the evening of 2 September 1939 Colonel Jackson, the Commanding Officer of the 39th Battalion CMF, called up the unit and announced the formation of a Prisoner of War Holding Unit at Wirth's Park in Melbourne, under the command of Lieutenant Fred Atman. Three of the circus's four entrances were wired up, and floorboards laid over the sawdust of the central ring. The tiered seating remained. As Jinkins recalls, over 250 internees passed through the depot.

Eventually the 39th Battalion was relieved by another unit from the 10th CMF Brigade, the 14th Battalion, under the command of Lieutenant Colonel Leonard N. Roach, MC, ED (1st AIF, Captain 5th Battalion, Indian Army), a soldier who was to have a great impact on the life of Bill Jinkins, the new QM Sergeant. Roach requested that Lieutenant Frank Pitman and QMS Jinkins be taken onto the strength of the 14th Battalion, thus retaining administrative continuity of the unit. On 15 November, the internees were transferred elsewhere and the Holding Depot closed down. Colonel Roach arranged Jinkins' transfer to the 14th Battalion's Kooweerup Company, where he had a vacancy for a sergeant. In January 1940 the battalion went into camp at Trawool for three months' training.

Jinkins was sent to the Officer Cadet Training Unit in Seymour for an eight-week course and emerged as a lieutenant.

Len Roach needed to assemble officers for a new unit, which was to become the 2/21st AIF Battalion, and on 1 July 1940 Bill Jinkins and Lieutenant Noel Thomas were summoned to Victoria Barracks to organise the officer interviews for him. The nucleus of the battalion was formed and assembled at Trawool that month where the men were given six weeks' initial training. From here the unit marched to Bonegilla near Albury for a further five months, and in March 1941 they were sent by train via Adelaide and Alice Springs to a tented camp at Winnellie, eleven kilometres from Darwin. Because of delays caused by floods north of Alice Springs and an inadequate transport system they did not arrive until the following month. It was then that Jinkins' knowledge of building and engineering offered him a sublime challenge.

We had arrived at the start of the wet season to live in well-used army tents with wooden floors above the high water flood level. Colonel Roach was very concerned for the men's comfort and the effect on the morale of his troops. He arranged with the Northern Territory's Senior Engineer Officer that the battalion would undertake the erection of a permanent camp if materials were delivered to the site. There had been plans for the construction of a permanent camp, but it had not been contracted, so it was agreed we would undertake the task.

Jinkins' Pioneer Platoon supervised the work schedules. They built six 'Sidney Williams' huts of steel tubular framework with corrugated-iron roofs and walls, which were mounted on thick concrete floors. There was one hut for each Company, and two comprising separate officers' and sergeants' messes. A fenced beer garden, run by a committee appointed by each company, supervised the canteen and the running of the five licensed gambling games under strict self-discipline and equally strict hours. In a mighty effort, the new camp was completed in just seven weeks.

The move to Darwin caused many of the men to feel that their ultimate destination would not be the Middle East. However, the development of a new camp diverted their attention from speculation and the facilities provided by Roach for his men were a winner. There was no longer any need for the men to take their leave in Darwin, where many had become involved in brawls in the notorious blood-houses. The Transport Platoon had even erected and serviced fish traps at the mouth of a creek entering Darwin Harbour, so a bountiful fresh fish meal became a weekly anticipation.

Over the next eight months, the men read of the war from which they were seemingly excluded, and like other units spent their days waiting to get into the action overseas. In the meantime they were preparing for a possible defence of Darwin and were assigned to work on the wharves, under strict instructions to avoid any confrontation between themselves and the striking wharfies. They soon became tired of the continual wet conditions, and sick of life in Darwin. To give the unit something to keep them out of trouble, boxing tournaments, cricket and football matches were organised. Their waiting finally came to an end on 7 December 1941 when Japan attacked the American fleet at Pearl Harbor, and the United States entered the war.

For a time it seemed that the Japanese army might be unstoppable as hordes of victorious troops boasting superior naval and air support swept relentlessly across the islands to the near north of Australia, encountering surprisingly little resistance throughout the Netherlands East Indies, Malaya and Singapore. As a result of these well-planned campaigns the Japanese gathered in many thousands of Australian prisoners of war from such battle fronts as Timor, New Britain, Bougainville, and the small, cleft Indonesian island of Ambon.

Ambon is a rugged but impressive, heavily wooded island with spectacular mountains rearing dramatically from the sea. Frequently enshrouded by fog and mist, its name comes from the Indonesian word for 'cloud'. A mere speck on a map of Indonesia, it sits in the centre of the Spice Islands, south of Ceram in the Molucca Archipelago and 1000 kilometres to the north of Darwin.

Only 48 kilometres long, the island comprises two main bodies of land, separated for most of their length by the deep blue slash of deep-water Ambon Bay and connected through a narrow isthmus at Paso. The larger northern part of the island is called Leihitu while the smaller, arrowhead-shaped southern portion is known as the Laitimor Peninsula. The depth of the water in Ambon's bay allows ships to wharf with little difficulty. while the high terrain to either side affords ideal protection from the wind or rough seas.

At a conference held in Singapore during February 1941, well before the commencement of hostilities with Japan, the Australian government held urgent discussions on the steadily worsening situation in the Pacific, and particularly the defence of the strategic islands north and west of Australia, Ambon and Timor. It was finally agreed to send Australian troops to these islands in the likely event of war with Japan. The first step was to place an 8th Division AIF Brigade, the 23rd, at Darwin in preparation for rapid deployment

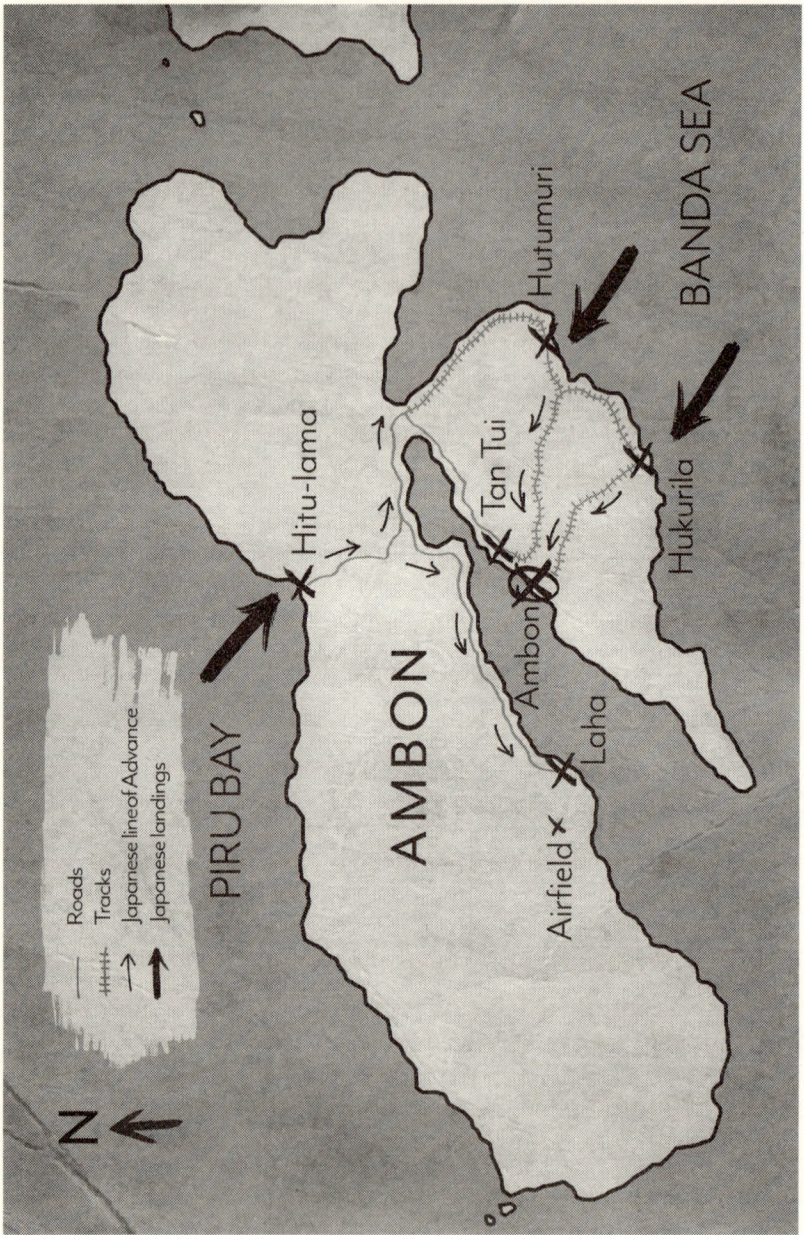

Roads
Tracks
Japanese line of Advance
Japanese landings

BANDA SEA

Hutumuri

Tan Tui

Hukurila

Hitu-lama

PIRU BAY

AMBON

Ambon

Laha

Airfield

N

should war be declared. The 23rd Brigade comprised the 2/21st, 2/22nd and 2/40th battalions.

With the outbreak of war against Japan these three reinforced battalions were shipped out of Darwin. The 1090 troops of what had become Gull Force headed for Ambon on three small Dutch mailboats, arriving on 17 December 1941. The 2/22nd (Lark Force) were sent to Rabaul, while the men of the 2/40th (Sparrow Force) steamed towards Timor. The men were apprehensive, but excited to be heading for the action, as Bill Jinkins recalls:

> None of us had been told exactly where we were going at the time of embarkation, although we knew it was somewhere up that way. On board and en route we found out we were going to a Dutch island, and then we began to receive lectures on Ambon from a Dutch officer – its topography, customs, languages, religions and population – and were strongly advised never to eat red berries on the island!

Virtually from the moment he set foot on Ambon the commander of Gull Force, Lieutenant Colonel Roach, was a deeply concerned soldier. He had made two reconnaissance trips to Ambon that year, and things had not improved. His men were fit and eager, but had not been trained for guerrilla combat, and were both ill-equipped and poorly supplied. He transmitted strongly worded messages to army headquarters in Melbourne complaining about the futility of attempting to repel any large-scale Japanese assault on the island. Unless extra supplies of armaments arrived he did not feel his men of Gull Force, however gallant, could hold back a large landing force for more than a day or two, pointing out a complete lack of naval and air support. Concerned that he and his men had been 'dumped' on Ambon with little regard to the consequences, he recommended an immediate evacuation of his troops.

Bill Jinkins was in complete agreement with Roach.

We just didn't know the problems our CO was having in his discussions with the Dutch Commander. The difficulty was in our instructions that we were there to support the Dutch, who were regarded as the prime force responsible for the safeguarding of the island. This was the cause of Roach's requests for more weapons. He'd realised that our role would in fact be far greater than that of just supporting the Dutch – ours was going to be the major defensive role.

Roach's view was shared by his superior in Darwin, Brigadier E.F. Lind, together with the senior RAAF officer on Ambon, Wing Commander E.D. Scott (AFC, No 1 Squadron) and Roach's own officers. The response to Roach's request, when it came, was swift and decisive. He was relieved of his command and recalled to Australia, his place being taken by the staff officer of the Directorate of Military Operations and Plans, W.J.R. (Jack) Scott, who had recommended that Roach be relieved of his command. Scott arrived on Ambon on the evening of 16–17 January 1942. It was certainly not a popular move among the troops in Gull Force, particularly as Scott had no previous experience of command of battalion units, the men of the 2/21st, or the Ambon terrain. Fortunately Roach's second in command, the well-respected Major Ian Macrae, retained his position.

European and Indonesian troops (who were poorly armed and only cursorily trained) were already on the island under the leadership of the Dutch commander, Lieutenant Colonel Joseph Kapitz, but of these 2600 men fewer than 50 were Dutch soldiers, and this number included just eight officers. With the arrival of Gull Force he had a total garrison of nearly 4000 men. As agreed earlier, Kapitz assumed seniority over Scott in the emplacement of the Australian forces.

The attack on Ambon was not long in coming. In December, several Australian Hudson aircraft operating out of Ambon and nearby Buru island were attacked by Japanese fighters. As indications developed of a massive invasion force of 27 ships preparing to leave the Celebes, the remaining Hudsons were evacuated south to safer ground and the Japanese forces were soon heading for Ambon.

Lieutenant Colonel Kapitz predicted that the Japanese could not land at Hukurila, Hutumuri or Baguala Bay. He split Gull Force into two separate forces, each independent of the other, deploying 300 Australians to defend Laha airfield on Leihitu. Only light native Dutch forces were located at Hukurila and Hutumuri. The bulk of the remainder of the combined forces were positioned west of Ambon town on the western end of the Laitimor Peninsula, while Kapitz established his headquarters at Paso, well to the rear of the projected battle fronts.

Following a sustained attack by carrier-based aircraft the Japanese launched an amphibious assault on the night of 30–31 January, landing at Hitu-Lama, on the northern shoreline. Kapitz's combined forces were set in the wrong defensive zones and the Japanese surged onto the island towards Paso virtually unimpeded. The principal landing by the Japanese was at Hutumuri, on the south-east coast of the Laitimor Peninsula, and they advanced west across the island to the rear of the 'B' echelon defence. They then spread further west, to the rear of the Amahusu line and the Benteng British fixed artillery defences.

The Dutch resistance at Paso crumbled and fell all too easily as the Japanese forces moved steadily on toward and onto Laha airfield. The Hutumuri land force moved to Ambon town, meeting no resistance from the native force and defeated the Battalion HQ defenders of 'B' echelon in the hospital area.

The Australian troops valiantly attempted to repulse the invaders at several sites, but the situation by the morning of 2 February was clearly forlorn. The Dutch had surrendered virtually without resistance and the Japanese were in full control of the Laitimor Peninsula. South of Ambon, the Australians could see Japanese ships sitting at anchor in the bay, while enemy aircraft came and went overhead with impunity. The following day they observed the Rising Sun flying over Laha airfield. Desultory gunfire still rang out across the bay, but the defence of Ambon was virtually over.

Bill Jinkins' 26-strong pioneer platoon had been posted to the top of the Nona plateau on 10 January. The steep-sided plateau, rising 500 metres above Ambon town, provided Jinkins with a good observation position. Battalion headquarters and 'D' Company under Captain Clive Newnham occupied a 2700-metre defensive line stretching from the plateau to the beach of Amahusu, between Eri and the town. It had been deemed strategically important that Jinkins' 5 Platoon occupied the plateau before enemy forces could reach it, and when the platoon reached the top of the mountain they found machine-gun bunkers in place, very well set up and camouflaged. The only problem was that they faced the wrong way.

The unexpected directions of the Japanese attacks took the Laitimor Peninsula defences by surprise and by 1 February they had rapidly advanced down the road from Ambon town to threaten the rear of the Australian positions in the Amahusu line. These men were forced to readjust and defend from the rear. Throughout the day the sea-level positions to the left of the line came under repeated attacks which were repelled, but to the right of the line, and about a third of the way up Mount Nona, the Japanese thrust broke the back of the defence and the Amahusu position was abandoned.

Towards dusk on the previous evening, Jinkins had sent Sergeant Bruce Kay and a fighting patrol of six men to the north-east perimeter of the plateau to check on the action in the direction of Ambon town. When the patrol returned Kay reported that 'around two hundred' Japanese troops could be seen making their way up the lower slopes of Mount Nona. Two of his men had been despatched to inspect the south-east lip of the plateau and look down over a different area. One of them, Private Jack Lewis, was hit in the chest by a mortar shell and wounded. Jinkins quickly reported the enemy assault to battalion head-quarters by field telephone and requested immediate reinforcements.

If the Japanese attacked Jinkins' position, 17 Platoon under Lieutenant Sam Anderson was to come up in support, and it was confirmed that the platoon was being despatched – 'ETA 2000 hours'. Dusk fell quickly on Ambon; it began around 5.30 p.m. and within thirty minutes it would be dark, so it was imperative that Anderson and his men reach the plateau quickly. That was the last time Bill Jinkins was able to communicate with battalion head-quarters. Apparently a Japanese soldier stumbled over the telephone wire, which was quickly severed. All communication was lost with both headquarters and 'Don' Company.

Jinkins and Sergeant Kay were conducting an inspection of all the posts in their perimeter defence when they heard Private White issuing the first challenge, 'Halt! Who goes there!' The attack was on. The two men ran towards Private White's position, with Kay on Jinkins' right. Suddenly Jinkins heard a bullet whizzing past his face and Kay fell dead, shot through the left temple.

At the same time his men opened fire with submachine guns on the Japanese soldiers as they tried to advance on his position, and Jinkins quickly returned to take charge. The Australians lobbed 3-second grenades down the slope as fast as they could. The fierce attack continued throughout the evening.

> They were so close we had to be sure they could not pick up the grenades and throw them back at us, so I ordered the men to pause for a second before they threw their grenades. We then opened up with creeping fire using rifle grenade launchers with rifles almost vertical, until we were aiming at a 45-degree angle, using them in controlled fire. This way we were able to drive the attack to the upper lip of the plateau.

Finally, they could make out the enemy troops retreating over the lip of the mountainside. They would later learn that their platoon had accounted for 25 Japanese dead, with only one fatality (Kay) among the defenders. Jinkins was becoming increasingly concerned that Anderson and his platoon might have been in the vicinity during his heavy grenade action against the Japanese advance: 'After we'd driven [the Japanese] back, the only way I could find out if Sam was anywhere about was by calling out his name. After some time I heard him answering my call.'

However, Anderson was badly wounded in the shoulder and the back of his right knee. Together with Corporal Hand, and well ahead of his platoon, he had been climbing towards the prepared perimeter defence when they became the target of Japanese hand grenades 65 metres from Jinkins' position. Feeling he was done for, Anderson instructed the corporal to do the best he could for the platoon. Hand returned to the rest of the platoon and told them to retreat to the line. When they reported back to a platoon commander their ignorance of the true situation led Captain Newnham to believe that Mount Nona was in Japanese hands, and formed part of his and Scott's decision to evacuate all Australian troops from the Amahusu line to Eri.

Despite coming under heavy machine-gun fire, Jinkins and two volunteers applied field dressings to Anderson's wounds. Private Harry Wakeling and Jinkins hoisted Anderson's unconscious body onto their shoulders while Private Archie Buchanan kept a lookout. They then dragged and pushed Anderson up the slope while Buchanan followed, walking backwards, covering them from the rear. Once they'd safely reached their defensive position Anderson was placed on a stretcher. Rallying for a time, he told Jinkins that the fighting was all but over down below. His comments were interrupted by another fierce Japanese assault, accompanied by loud yelling and shouting. A pitched battle ensued, with hand grenades and small-arms fire from the perimeter, and Japanese mortar fire inflicting further casualties. Once again the Japanese were driven back, but Jinkins decided his men couldn't sustain another attack in this position.

He gave his men the necessary orders, and they evacuated with Anderson to an alternative defensive pill-box position 150 metres west, down the edge of the plateau. At 11 p.m. Jinkins saw a green flare go up – the prearranged signal that the Australians on the Amahusu line were being evacuated to Eri. Prior to this he had despatched runners to battalion headquarters to inform them that the reinforcements had not arrived, but the men did not return. By early morning they could make out hundreds of enemy soldiers milling around 30 metres above them, but the Japanese began to withdraw.

Meanwhile Lieutenant Anderson's condition had deteriorated so much that Jinkins decided to have him carried by stretcher to the Japanese lines. Once again Privates Buchanan and Wakeling stepped forward without being asked, but Anderson insisted they leave him where he was. The two men were equally adamant he needed urgent care, so Anderson finally agreed to be carried back to their former defensive position. They encountered a large group of Japanese soldiers about to head for the Benteng barracks, who agreed to escort the three men. Two of the soldiers even carried Anderson's stretcher for the final part of the journey.

In the interim, Jinkins' platoon had made a perilous descent down the almost-vertical, treacherously muddy side of the mountain, and as expected found Amahusu village empty. They took up a defensive position, knowing the Japanese would come their way sooner or later. Elsewhere, as Jinkins recalls, things were rapidly falling apart:

While all this was going on, Macrae was to lead a fighting patrol along the south coast of the island under instructions that if they met the enemy they were to engage them. If they didn't meet the enemy they were under orders to attempt to leave the island, get back to Australia, and report. Unfortunately Macrae who was in charge of the party ate a berry off a bush, and within a few minutes was under its influence, suffering badly from a violent attack of dysentery. It was so bad that stretcher bearers had to be sent for.

When they arrived, which was on the morning of February 3rd, they told his party that things were at an end; the troops were surrendering and the fighting had ceased. Macrae told his second-in-command [Lieutenant W.A.M. Chapman] to escape if possible and get back to Australia so that information could be given about the position in Ambon.

While Jinkins was settling in to defend Amahusu, a nervous Ambonese told him that the Japanese had captured Eri and driven the Australian defenders to the toe of the peninsula. When the wounded Private Jack Lewis was despatched to Eri for medical aid he encountered a Dutch officer who said he'd been ordered to take a note from Lieutenant Colonel Kapitz to Colonel Scott, but had been unable to find him. The note said that the Dutch had surrendered, and Scott should do likewise.

Despite his injuries, Lewis decided this should be reported. He slipped away from the Dutchman, returned to the place where his platoon was in yet another defensive position and reported the existence of the letter to Jinkins, who decided to take it directly to Scott. A bicycle was secured and he rode off towards the Benteng barracks, but he soon ran into a Japanese roadblock. Jinkins boldly used his extremely limited knowledge of the Japanese language to demand 'to be taken to a shogun – someone in high authority'. A runner was sent off, and soon an English-speaking officer was found who told Jinkins he would take him to see a Major Harikawa. When Jinkins asked after Lieutenant Anderson and the two stretcher carriers the officer escorted him to a hut where he found Anderson receiving proper treatment, while Buchanan and Wakeling were being well treated. The Japanese held them in high regard for looking after their officer before themselves. Major Harikawa in turn decided Jinkins should see Major General Takeo Ito, the commanding officer of the 38th Japanese Division.

Jinkins was taken by car into Ambon town, where Japanese headquarters had been set up in the Governor's house. Then things got a bit sticky.

I was made to kneel down on the beautifully kept lawn in front of the Japanese headquarters and place my hands behind me. I told the chap with me – I don't know who it was – that I was only there to pick up the surrender note, but he said I was there for interrogation. There were Japs everywhere. He asked me a couple of questions to which I answered with my army number, name and rank. Every time he shouted a question I would count ten seconds before replying with the same answer. He was becoming pretty hostile. Finally I heard him withdrawing his sword, and he shouted 'Why don't you answer my questions?' and I'd had about enough of this. I said 'I can't understand you because you don't speak bloody good English!' I wondered if I'd gone too far this time. After a long pause – it felt like five minutes – I finally heard the sword being sheathed and someone marching away from me. After a while I began to very slowly turn my head and look around, but there was no one near me. I got up, a bit unsteadily, and after a few minutes I walked over to the verandah of the residence.

Finally ushered in to see a high-ranking officer (possibly Ito), it was decided that Jinkins should speak directly to Kapitz, who wrote a second note and ordered Jinkins to deliver it directly to Scott. Major Harikawa then drove the Australian back to the Benteng barracks, provided him with a captured AIF motorcycle and escorted him to the forward outpost to ensure he got through without further hindrance.

Bill Jinkins made it back safely to Amahusu, located Scott at Eri and reported to him, only to find his CO had already been in touch with the Japanese and was in the process of surrendering his troops. Jinkins was stunned at this capitulation and confirmed that his men were still holding a firm position at Amahusu. The response came as an unexpected and numbing shock; Scott ordered him to bring his men back immediately and surrender.

Jinkins was aghast; his men had already acquitted themselves with determination and great courage. He now had to tell them to meekly lay down their arms and surrender, to obey an order he personally found repugnant. With a heavy heart he passed on the onerous news and received the expected howls of protest. They'd already repulsed the enemy; didn't Scott know that? As they slowly and reluctantly came to accept the iniquitous order a deep bitterness against those in command set in and festered. They had been sold out after endless months spent in waiting and training to fight the enemy. It went against the grain and Jinkins knew their anger and frustration only too well. He swore to himself that he would somehow make it up to them. Fighting down his bitterness and anger, he formed his men up and marched them towards Ambon town and captivity.

Their misery on reaching the town was exacerbated by the gleeful hordes of Japanese photographers and publicists now on the scene, recording the surrender. As Jinkins' group marched by, a Japanese soldier spotted Australian-born Chinese Alec Chew in their ranks, moved in and began belting him in the back with his rifle butt, shouting '*Cheena, Cheena!*' Jinkins rushed over and placed himself between Chew and the attacker, demanding the man stop his cowardly actions. Just as an ugly scene was beginning to develop a Japanese officer wandered over and ordered his soldier away. The cameramen continued to click away.

As soon as his men were safely in their hut an angry Jinkins sought out Macrae and asked to be paraded before Colonel Scott. Macrae, still quite ill, asked if there was anything troubling Jinkins. 'No trouble, sir,' he replied. 'I just ask that you parade me before the CO and I'd like you to stay with me.' Macrae did as he was asked. Bill Jinkins knew exactly what he was going to say, but was trembling with barely suppressed anger as he saluted his CO. 'What can I do for you, lieutenant?' Scott demanded.

Jinkins took a deep breath. 'Sir . . . you ordered me to march my platoon into the prison camp, and I have obeyed your order. But I must now report that I have taken my very last order from you. You ordered my platoon to surrender without further resistance. You may try to give me more orders but do not expect me to obey them. I intend leaving this camp and getting back to Australia at the earliest possible opportunity. That's all I'm prepared to say.'

Fully expecting to be torn to shreds for such gross insubordination, Jinkins stood his ground, staring straight ahead. Beside him he had noticed Macrae tensing with each word. Scott's reply, when it finally came, was entirely unexpected. His expression softened into one of almost sadness, and to Jinkins' surprise he stretched out his hand. 'Good luck, son,' he said with sincerity, as the handshake was returned. 'And I'm sorry for all that's happened.' He looked at Macrae and his voice was a little more authoritative, 'Jinkins' will be the first official escape party from this place,' he said. Then the two officers were dismissed.

Earlier, the Japanese had called in their air and naval forces to mop up the remaining but diminishing resistance on Ambon. With the capture of Laha airfield and the meek capitulation of Colonel Kapitz's forces, surrender had become inevitable in the opinion of Colonel Scott. On the afternoon of 3 February the Australian commanders contacted their Japanese counterparts to negotiate a total surrender. Lieutenant Colonel Roach's fears had been sadly vindicated. The only aspect he had underestimated was the fighting spirit and determination of his men, who had held out against over-whelming odds for longer than he had anticipated.

From the moment he and his men were forced into an unwill-ing captivity Bill Jinkins' resolution had become clear. Now he had delivered his men into enemy hands, he would somehow escape from Ambon, bring pressure to bear back home and return with a force dedicated to liberating the men of Gull Force. It was a vow he was determined to keep. He owed it to his men.

Before the surrender Lieutenant W.A.M. Chapman, who had been second in command to Major Macrae, succeeded in escaping from Ambon with eighteen other members of the 2/21st Battalion. According to Chapman:

> About midnight 2–3 February 1942 I was out with a fighting patrol [under] Major Macrae. The next morning [he] became ill; I think it was a violent attack of dysentery. Stretcher bearers were sent for . . . they arrived about 0900 hours [and] told us things were at an end. The troops were surrendering and fighting had ceased.
>
> Major Macrae was very ill indeed. I had a conversation with him

and suggested we might try to escape and asked for his permission to do so. [He] told me to escape if possible and get to Australia so that information could be given about the position in Ambon. I then spoke to the rest of the party which comprised about 24 personnel. I told them that fighting had ceased and the troops had surrendered but I was going to try to escape with authority from Major Macrae, and any of them that wished to do so could come with me or alternatively they could return with [him] and surrender. The rest of the party remained with me. Major Macrae was writhing in agony and had to be strapped down to the stretcher. He could not possibly have made every effort himself to escape.

The same day at about 1930 hours we reached Seri Bay where we found a native sailing vessel and got away. We eventually reached the island of Ceram. We made our progress to Australia as best we could and on occasions had to split up, but when we arrived at Dobo the party was intact, and we were there joined by six other AIF troops from Ambon.

On the Dutch-controlled island of Dobo, Chapman decided to split the men into separate parties. One, under Warrant Officer L.C. Warren, embarked on the sailing ketch *Gloria* while Chapman's group set off in the auxiliary motor ketch *Arcadia*. They were joined by several Dutch civilians as well as the six Australians who had arrived there on 12 March. According to Private A.T. Cofield, one of Chapman's escape party aboard the *Arcadia*:

We set off for Thursday Island, keeping together for two days, on the afternoon of the second day towing the *Gloria* for some distance. During the time when the *Gloria* was being towed it was reported that someone on that boat was ill and Lieutenant Chapman went over in the small boat to see what was wrong, returned to procure medicine and took it back. The wind became stronger and the *Gloria* caught up with us, and apparently it was arranged between the two boats to cast off, though I did not hear any of the conversation between the two boats. I think it had been decided to go to Merauke [New Guinea] as we had heard on the wireless that Thursday Island had been bombed.

When night fell I saw the last of the *Gloria* [and] she was out of sight in the morning. On the way to Merauke we were stuck on a mud bank for some days. During this time some of our men went ashore to a native village to secure more food, as our rations were practically finished.

On 22 March, after a week of restless inaction, it was decided that five men would make the long trek down the coast to Merauke, as the villagers themselves were running short of food, and bring help to free the *Arcadia*. On 4 April they arrived in Merauke and a rescue party was despatched in a motorboat. The *Arcadia* was towed free of the mud bank and reached Merauke on 6 April. Here the men learned that the *Gloria* had arrived two weeks earlier. With considerable relief they and 22 Dutch civilians boarded a captured Japanese lugger and, towed by the RAN motor vessel *Paloma*, finally reached Thursday Island on 12 April, nearly ten weeks after leaving Ambon.

They did not know the men on the *Gloria* had almost starved on their desperately slow journey south. After eating and recuperating somewhat at Merauke they decided they'd had enough of being at the mercy of the winds and commandeered a diesel-powered motor boat. Three days later, on 31 March, the men reached Karumba on the southern Gulf of Carpentaria, from where they were airlifted by flying boat to Townsville.

Back on Ambon, the reluctant capitulation of the Australian defenders was to have some immediate and tragic consequences. If the men of Gull Force taken at Laha airfield had expected clemency from their captors they were sadly mistaken, and those who were captured across the bay did not learn of the tragic fate which befell more than 300 of their comrades until the end of the war.

The Japanese commanders' attitudes to prisoners had become ominously apparent when ten Australians captured at Laha airfield on the morning of 1 February were bayoneted to death at a place called Sowacoad. According to a later statement made by the local Japanese commander, this was done 'lest they become a drag upon the movement of [Rear Admiral Hatakiyama's] forces'.

On 4 February, the day after the surrender, 51 Australian prisoners captured in the vicinity of the airfield were also proving 'burdensome' to the Japanese. When a couple of the prisoners managed to escape, Admiral Hatakiyama sent an order to the local commander of the naval forces, requiring him to eliminate all remaining POWs under his jurisdiction. Lieutenant Commander Kenichi Nakagawa, given the responsibility for carrying out this terrible massacre by his commanding officer named Hayashi, presented the following graphic evidence at the end of the war:

In compliance with this order I took about 30 petty officers and men to Sowacoad. In a coconut plantation, about 200 metres from the airfield, we dug holes and killed the prisoners of war with swords or bayonets. It took about two hours. The way in which the murder was carried out was as follows: I divided my men into three groups; the first for leading the prisoners of war out of a house where we had temporarily confined them; the second for preventing disorder on their way from the house to the plantation; the third for beheading or stabbing the victims.

They were taken one by one to the spot where they were to die, and made to kneel down with a bandage over their eyes. The members of the third troop stepped out of the ranks, one by one as his turn came, to behead a prisoner with a sword, or stab him through the breast with a bayonet.

The prisoners were all Australian, and their number included four or five officers, one of whom I am sure was a major. All the corpses were buried in the holes which we had dug. I was the only Japanese officer present. When it was all over I reported its completion to my adjutant.

On 17 February Hayashi issued orders that all remaining POWs were to be summarily executed. Three days later Nakagawa marched a further group of around 90 horrified prisoners to a coconut plantation near the scene of the earlier massacre. His evidence continued:

I divided my men into nine parties; two [squads] for the bloody killings, three for guarding the prisoners on their way to the place of execution, two for escorting out of the barracks, one to be on guard at the spot where the prisoners were to be killed, and one in reserve for emergency.

The prisoners were brought by truck from the barracks to the detachment headquarters, and marched from there to the plantation. The same way of killing was adopted as before, that is, they were made to kneel down with their eyes bandaged and they were killed with sword or bayonet. The poor victims numbered about 220 in all, including some Australian officers.

The whole affair took from 6 p.m. to 9.30 p.m. Most of the corpses were buried in one hole, but because the hole turned out not to be big enough to accommodate all the bodies an adjacent dug-out was also used as a grave.

Elsewhere on Ambon, troops decided they would sooner attempt to reach Australia than lay down their arms. Remarkably, many of them succeeded, and after epic adventures moving progressively south by sea in a series of sailing and motor vessels, steadfastly leapfrogging from one island to another, they finally reached friendly shores.

Having sustained heavy losses in a gallant but ultimately futile defence of the island, a surviving total of 791 Australians were rounded up and taken to Tan Tui barracks, their former quarters, three kilometres north-east of Ambon town. There they were interned with 300 Dutch prisoners, although the two nationalities were separated inside the barrack compound by a barbed-wire fence. The prisoners were later joined by a group of fourteen Americans who had been captured on nearby eastern New Guinea following an escape attempt from the Philippines.

For those first few weeks food was quite plentiful and the prisoners remained in relatively high spirits. Due to the strategic importance of Ambon they fully expected a large Allied counter-attack, but this assault never came. However, they were permitted to grow their own food and raise poultry for eggs, while trading flourished quite openly between POWs and the local natives and also with their guards. After the first months of internment, and with little to do, several men even volunteered to go on Japanese work parties both to maintain their fitness and to indulge in food scrounging and trade activities.

Fretful and bored with this life of inactivity, some began to weigh the prospects of escape. After all, it was only 1000 kilometres to Darwin, although a circuitous route would have to be taken.

Although several members of Gull Force fled Ambon before they were taken prisoner, the first to actually escape from Japanese captivity were in a group of four men from the 2/21st Battalion under the determined leadership of Corporal Frank Redhead.

It was originally Private Don Johnson's idea to slip out through the wire at Tan Tui and locate a suitable native sailing craft. Together with Private Bill Dahlberg he made his way out of the camp one evening on a pre-escape reconnaissance mission and located some friendly Ambonese villagers who were not only willing to furnish the escape party with a suitable outrigger prau, but promised to supply some food and water for their voyage.

It was raining hard when they returned to camp and they managed to slip back under the wire without incident. Shortly after they recruited Frank Redhead and Private Bert Goodall into the escape party. According to Redhead: 'A party of us formed a plan of escape which we discussed with the CO [Scott] and 2 i/c [Macrae]. We were given every assistance in the matter of food, and on the night of 9 March at 2300 hours we made our way through the barbed wire and across the hills to a friendly village on the coast.'

Once here the native people lived up to their earlier promises, supplying an outrigger prau and a couple of men to row them across to Ceram, as well as the agreed provisions. Before long, Redhead's escape party was under sail on the first leg of the long voyage home.

According to reports later submitted by both Johnson and Goodall, the journey south was 'uneventful', apart from the sighting of a Japanese reconnaissance aircraft, as they island-hopped from Assilulu to Amshi on Ceram, Geser, Tual and Dobo. Here they were joined by a group of five men led by Corporal H.S. Kitson who had evaded capture at Laha airfield. These five were accompanied by two American naval airmen, Lieutenant Hargreaves and Petty Officer Nelson, the only survivors of an eight-man Catalina aircraft shot down over Ambon on 5 February. Two Dutch artillerymen had also joined his group.

The Dutch Administrator on Dobo, a Mr Wolfe, agreed to find a seaworthy vessel large enough to transport all of them to Dutch New Guinea. An old double-master was soon located resting on its side in a creek. According to one of Kitson's party, Private Stan Shaw, it had 'a smelly old bilge' but it was relatively seaworthy. Once it had been checked for leaks Wolfe arranged for a motorboat driven by a native youth to tow the craft away from the island. Five other natives from Dobo were recruited to help sail the old double-master. Shaw continues:

He [the native boy] towed us all night, out to a group of islands . . . there was this channel leading way out eastward [to] near New Guinea. He said to us before he left: 'The monsoons are going to change any tick of the clock; you'll have a headwind, but now you've got a tail wind. You might get to Merauke quickly. It has been done in four or five days.' Anyway, after he dropped us off the winds changed; we had to tack zigzag into the wind all the way. It took us 26 days to get to Merauke!

On arrival the men quickly contacted the Dutch Controller, who sent a radio message to the Australian military base on Thursday Island. A week later a naval boat arrived and transported the men to Thursday Island, where they arrived on 7 May. A few days later another boat took them down to Townsville. From there they caught a train to Melbourne and, after reporting in, they went home.

Ben Amor and Ron McPherson never intended staying long as unwilling guests of the Japanese. Even before they were taken prisoner they'd agreed to rest up for a short time, prepare and kit themselves and then escape from Ambon.

Ben Amor had joined the Signal Platoon of the 2/21st Battalion when it was formed in 1940, while Ron McPherson became dry ration storeman for the battalion before transferring to the Signal Platoon in Darwin in May 1941. Here they served as two of the three despatch riders, with Amor promoted to lance corporal in August.

Once things had settled down at Tan Tui they began to check the strength and alertness of the guard company, and noted a small dip under a section of the perimeter wire which could be breached with little difficulty. The two men then began scrounging around for any escape supplies and useful equipment. Amor took on a job repairing boots and was able to purloin some rope, a pair of pliers, a torch, a knife and some clothing. 'Every waking moment became precious,' McPherson recalls. 'We found an old *Women's Weekly* with a map of an air route the Japanese were planning from Japan to Australia. They had not told the magazine about the bombers that later used that route to bomb Darwin! From this rough map we estimated routes and distances from Ambon.'

Much to their disgust, the two escapers found themselves up against an insidious new enemy – their own officers and some of their colleagues. According to McPherson, it was well known within the camp that a team of officers were planning to make their own break, and Scott vowed he would not tolerate any escapes by other ranks (ORs) which might jeopardise the attempt. Had his men respected him more they might have heeded these words. Only a few troops remained unquestioning in their allegiance to Scott's position of command, but Amor and McPherson soon came in for their unwanted attention.

The two men needed to have an idea of the terrain over which they would have to walk by night, so whenever they left the camp on working details they would cast their eyes about, later comparing notes and formulating plans. Their next problem, as McPherson relates, was to put together a small supply of food:

Our only hope of getting food finally came down to an isolated hut within the POW camp guarded at times by an armed sentry. We raided it and got a haversack of tinned stuff – too dark to see what it was. But where do you hide food in a hungry prison camp? I scooted under the wire and up the hill to a position where I could plant the haversack, and which I could find on a dark night.

Ben Amor considers the daring 2 a.m. raid on the guarded hut, which took two hours to accomplish, as 'the most nerve-racking [part] of our escape'. It was with considerable relief that he returned quickly and quietly to his bed that night.

Their first escape attempt early in March was foiled – not by the Japanese, but by a member of their own platoon ordered to keep an eye on their activities. To their consternation they were literally dragged back under the wire. It was an act of betrayal both men remember with a mixture of sadness and outrage to this day. The following morning Colonel Scott announced that the names of any men carrying out escapes not authorised by himself or Major Macrae would be given to the Japanese. This only served to make the ORs more hostile, and several began to formulate escape plans. Amor and McPherson were secretly informed that the officer escape party would soon be making its break. Since security would be dramatically tightened after such an escape, they realised they would have to go soon. As it turned out, Frank Redhead's group beat them to the punch.

The break-out by Frank Redhead's escape party reinforced the two men's feeling that they too could make a clean getaway, especially with the help of the local people. They set themselves for a break the following night, and made sure this time they were not being watched.

At 10 p.m. on 10 March, Amor and McPherson slipped under the wire for the final time in company with Don and Vic Findlay from 'A' Company. The two brothers, who were late starters in the scheme, had already assembled and hidden some escape provisions of their own. The two teams were to collect their gear and meet at the top of the nearby hill. After crawling under the wire they hastily rearranged the shrubbery around the small dip, so their place of exit was not distinguishable, should others wish to use it. The men then went off to their supply dumps, but the Findlays failed to make the rendezvous. After a long and anxious wait until one o'clock, Amor and McPherson decided they couldn't afford to hang around any longer. Amor recalls:

When they didn't turn up we just kept on going, and headed towards Hutumuri on the other side of the island. Once we were out we just had to risk travelling by day as well [as night]. The terrain back then was very thick – not like it is today – but we just headed across to Hutumuri, up and down the hill which formed the backbone of the island.

At the end of the war they found out that the Findlay brothers had gathered their escape gear as planned, but had taken the wrong path, ending up in Ambon town. They returned to the camp and their plans to try again at a later date went awry when they were shipped off to another camp on the island of Hainan. Meanwhile, back at Tan Tui, Colonel Scott was infuriated by the latest escape and reported the men's absence to the Japanese, who were reasonably philosophical about the escapees' chances.

As Amor and McPherson neared the coast they realised they were being shadowed by some local Ambonese, but as they were not attacked they assumed the men to be Christians. They'd heard of Muslims who worked for the Japanese, and who would return escapees for a reward, so it was with relief they realised these friendly people were actually guiding them onwards. Finally they encountered a lithe Ambonese who regarded them with great interest, smiled and indicated they should follow him. They did as he suggested and were led down to a small village near Roetang where the women cooked up a delicious and welcome meal of eggs, fish and rice.

From this small village, Amor and McPherson were paddled south along the coast until they reached Hutumuri. Once again the friendly native inhabitants saw to their comforts as the escapers scoured around looking for a suitable boat over the following days.

Their good fortune held. Some villagers offered to take the men to the neighbouring island of Huruku for 20 guilders, to which they agreed, and they took their leave of Ambon aboard a native prau. After battling strong headwinds for six hours they pulled in near Paso and recruited three more native paddlers.

Unhappily, Amor bore a debilitating legacy from Ambon – a dose of tropical malaria. Together with the elation of leaving the island behind came the first effects. By the time they reached Oma on Huruku he was weak and trembling, and had to be helped ashore. The uncle of one of their accompanying helpers made Amor comfortable and sympathetically tended his illness.

During Ben Amor's convalescence the officers' party which had escaped from Ambon (and whose story is told later) arrived on the island. On learning of the presence of Amor and McPherson a local boy was despatched by the officer in charge to ask the two men to report directly to him. Ron McPherson made the ten-kilometre hike and told the officer Amor was ill with malaria. It was a terse conversation; McPherson was still quite hostile towards those in command on Ambon, while the officer in charge reiterated that the two men had escaped without permission and could be shot for disobeying a direct order. The two men parted with ill-feeling, but as McPherson passed by the others in the officer's escape team they shook his hand, wished both of them well and each gave him five guilders to help them on their way.**

Ben Amor still had a high temperature when McPherson returned, and was perspiring freely under a pile of blankets. By morning, however, he felt much better and his temperature had gone down, although it continued to fluctuate over the next few days. A poultice made of green leaves covered in shredded coconut was applied to his back after a particularly bad attack, and this seemed to do the trick. With Amor's slow recovery came the realisation that it was time to move on.

The islands around Ambon were not only visited by Japanese patrols, but some of the local people were quite unsympathetic towards the Australians. Threats of terrible reprisals against those caught harbouring fugitives were known to be rigorously applied by the Japanese, and many fearful villagers had to be regarded as untrustworthy. There were also those who could not resist the large cash bounty placed on all escapers. It was therefore just a matter of time before the presence of the two men on Huruku became known to the Japanese, and it was suggested they leave the island as quickly as possible. Amor continues:

Our friends took us across to the next island [of Saparua]. They were Christians, these people, and they'd hand us on to other friends on

---

** The author has been in touch with both protagonists, but will not argue the rights or wrongs of the issue. The officer, no great friend of Scott's, was nonetheless adamant that the two men's 'unauthorised' escape should have been cleared with the CO, while McPherson's chief frustration was that those in charge at Tan Tui had actually impeded their first escape bid. Though the larger party was certainly better provisioned and funded, the two friends were determined to make their own way home. 'Ben and I had almost nil funds and relied on help from the local people whom I must add . . . were wonderful,' was McPherson's proud claim.

the next island and so on; we were wholly dependent on them. This way we sailed on to Ceram and Geser, then down to the Kai Islands, where we knew there was no Japanese occupation. At this point we began to feel safe at last.

The two men left Saparua on a two-masted sailing boat in the company of the Dutch Controller of the island, together with his wife and two children. On 17 April the escape party arrived at Tual in the Kai Islands, where they met a pair of Australians who had fled Ambon at the news of the surrender, Privates McIntosh and Johnston. They decided to leave as a group the following day. McPherson recorded their departure in his diary:

18th April. There are twelve in the party due to leave today. Four Australians, four Dutch soldiers and the Dutch family. Boat is a two-masted job similar to the last but is very old.
19th April. Got away okay at 1700 hours from Toeal [Tual] last night. Rounding bottom of Little Kai Island at 0800 hours. Boat is a leaky old tub. 1200 hours, seas rough, wind steady.

Despite McPherson's misgivings about their boat, they docked at Saumlaki on the afternoon of 24 April. Here they once again encountered the officers' escape party and were told they had secured the use of a 40-tonne trading schooner for the final run across the Arafura Sea to Darwin. With only 300 kilometres to travel to Darwin and with the most perilous part of their journey behind them, they decided, albeit with some reluctance, that this was the easiest and quickest way to get home, so they too sailed for Australia on the good ship *Griffoen*.

The crossing, although rough, was accomplished without incident, and on 4 May 1942 the schooner sailed into Darwin Harbour.

Besides those who managed to evade capture and make their way home, thirteen men actually managed to break free from Japanese captivity on Ambon. Of these, Amor and McPherson probably faced the most difficulties in breaching the wire and making good their escape. Their indebtedness to the kindly Ambonese people who assisted them extends to the present day.

Throughout February and March Bill Jinkins meticulously planned his escape from Tan Tui, leading food and stores recovery parties and burial details in order to establish contacts and to determine the best route away from the camp. He needed a group of resourceful and willing colleagues with skills in sailing, marine engines and navigational techniques, but he wanted to maintain the utmost secrecy in their selection. Colonel Scott had authorised an escape party comprising no more than seven men, so Jinkins began to seek out those most suited to the task.

On one of his outside forays he made contact with Peter Gaspersz, the younger brother of Bill Gaspersz, whose father at that time was the Raja (King) of Galala District, Tan Tui, and the Dutch Chief of Police on Ambon. The oldest of three brothers, Bill Gaspersz and his wife Barbara had been forced to evacuate their lovely old Dutch home and live a simple life among the peasants in a nearby hillside village. Bill was under Japanese surveillance for his outspoken and seditious view of the invaders (for which he was later gaoled), so their clandestine meetings were always carefully organised. He was keen to assist in the escape and reported back to Jinkins whenever certain arrangements had been made. His mother was Rani of the village of Naku on the south-west coast of the island, which they determined would be the best place from which to embark on the sea journey. He would provide nine men to paddle the boats, and his native servant Peter would act as escort.

In a stroke of luck the Japanese had requisitioned Jinkins' Pioneer Platoon to build a barbed-wire fence around the compound at Tan Tui. When this was erected he made sure there was a small but negotiable area beneath the wire in a small gully near the camp hospital. This was the hole the other escapers had used, each of them carefully replacing the grass and a bush so the escape route remained undiscovered by the Japanese.

It was now time to assemble his escape team, and the first person Jinkins invited along was his trusted friend Alec Chew, who was delighted to accept. He then spoke to another close colleague, Lieutenant Gordon Jack from Bendigo. Once again he received a positive response.

I suggested to Macrae that there ought to be an education scheme started so the fellows would have something to occupy their minds, and he wholeheartedly agreed. I nominated the subjects of commercial law and geometry, and he soon found two willing teachers. The whole purpose behind the education scheme was in fact to allow me to find the rest of my escape team. I needed to find one fellow capable of handling diesel engines, and at least one other who knew how to handle sailing boats, so in the geometry class we got the men talking about astronavigation, and it was sufficiently camouflaged so that the Japs (and even the men) could never detect what it was really about.

I wasted considerable time with one fellow who had operated his own pearling lugger in Darwin, but he turned out to be totally uninterested in getting back to Australia. Then I found [Corporal] Cliff Warn, who used to operate a supply boat for the author Zane Grey when he was marlin fishing off the New South Wales south coast near Bermagui. Cliff had been sailing since he was quite young, and had been out with supplies for Grey many times. When I approached him he agreed to join the team, and was sworn to secrecy. Gordon Jack nominated another fellow from his platoon, [Corporal] Arthur Young, so I arranged to accidentally bump into him and we had a bit of a yarn together. I was pleased with Gordon's selection, and Arthur was willing, so he too was invited to join us.

[Private] Harry Coe was a Wonthaggi district farmer who'd operated and maintained a diesel-driven milking machine on his property, and he was our next recruit. At this stage Cliff Warn informed me that his platoon commander [Lieutenant] Rowland Rudder used to sail skiffs around Sydney Harbour, so I approached him and after a while asked him if he was game to escape. He said he was. Rudder was the seventh recruit, and we now had our whole escape party.

With everyone fully briefed, and outside arrangements in place, it was almost time to go. Jinkins found a school atlas and copied a useful map of the route to be taken. Unfortunately it was on a scale of 1:250 000, but it at least gave his navigators something to work by. He had kept Macrae informed on the progress of his plans, and he in turn liaised with Scott. In the meantime Corporal Frank Redhead had somehow learned of Jinkins' plans and requested permission of the CO to join the escape team. Scott told Redhead that he was mistaken – no one was permitted to escape. When the corporal had gone Scott mentioned to Macrae that the cat seemed to be out of the bag.

A few days before he planned to go, Jinkins was called before Colonel Scott, who handed over his leather briefcase, which was locked, with a request that he deliver it to Military Operations back in Australia. Jinkins was asked to give a firm oath he would not under any circumstances open it. Two days before his planned break Jinkins was once again summoned to appear before Jack Scott.

The CO appeared a little ill at ease, and the reason soon became apparent. 'I believe you're going tomorrow night, lieutenant?' he asked. Scott looked him in the eyes. 'I've given it a bit of thought, and I've decided to come with you.'

Stunned, Jinkins was unable to answer for some time. He asked Scott to excuse him for a few minutes while he considered this new twist to his carefully arranged plan. He finally decided Scott had to be dissuaded – not because of any personal dislike for the man, and not because he felt he should remain with his men, but for another very good reason which Scott did not suspect was already known to Jinkins. He quickly sought out medical officer Bill Aitken who was playing poker and asked to speak to him in confidence. Soon the two men were walking the compound, engaged in deep conversation.

'I can't give you the reason for my questions, doctor,' Jinkins began, 'but it's terribly important that you be frank with me. Just how is the CO's health? Would you say he is fit?'

'Far from it,' Aitken replied. 'He's suffering from a rather bad case of piles.' Jinkins pursued the matter. 'Would he be capable of walking far – say half a mile?' Aitken smiled. 'No man in his condition could walk that far.' Jinkins was satisfied. 'Would you be prepared to tell him that to his face if I were to ask you?' Bill Aitken replied that he would, and the two men made their way back to Scott's office. When Jinkins asked Scott how he was, the CO became noticeably tense but replied that he was quite well.

Jinkins beckoned Aitken forward. 'Doctor, I've been talking to the CO about his health, and I wonder if you could tell me whether he's fit at this time.' Aitken, surprisingly, did not look at all uncomfortable as he made his reply. 'No, as a matter of fact the colonel is quite unwell.' Jinkins came straight back at him. 'I don't need to know the nature of his illness, but is he capable of walking half a mile without stopping?' Aitken was nonplussed. 'No, not half a mile.' Jinkins looked across at Macrae, who had said nothing, and then back at Aitken. 'Well, over a short distance then, would he be without pain?' The doctor shook his head. 'No. He would be in considerable pain the whole distance.'

At this Jinkins directed his attention back at Scott, who was looking most uncomfortable. 'I've asked Dr Aitken all the questions I need answered,' he said. 'Do we need the doctor any more?' Scott shook his head slowly. Once Aitken had departed, Scott's voice had a sharp edge to it. 'I don't know how you found out about my little problem, lieutenant, but I suppose you now feel justified in refusing me a place in the escape?'

'Sir,' Jinkins replied, 'if my escape is to be successful I need to know every little step I'm taking. I'm not prepared to take you, but I am prepared to take Major Macrae.'

Scott knew he'd been upstaged. 'No,' he stated with resignation, 'I need Major Macrae here. I can't do without him.'

Jinkins had heard enough. 'Thank you sir, I believe we've discussed all we need to discuss at this time.'

Once outside Scott's hut, Jinkins walked with Macrae. He was still shaking with outrage. 'That bastard was prepared to leave you to look after the camp. Did you know about this?'

Macrae was in a sombre mood. 'No, I didn't, but I've had a funny feeling he was up to something like that.'

The next problem Jinkins had to deal with concerned their pending absence from the camp. Manipulating head counts was not a real problem with the lower ranking men, but the disappearance of three officers would soon be noticed, so three men from the ranks were picked and happily elected to fill in for Jinkins, Rudder and Jack. This subterfuge was to prove successful although two of the men, Private G. Waring and Sergeant C. Wilson, later died in captivity and were buried under the names of Jinkins and Rudder – an anomaly which was corrected at the end of the war.

The first escape attempt was postponed for two days following the news that Frank Redhead's party had gone under the wire. The following night Ben Amor, Ron McPherson and the Findlay brothers made a hasty exit. Scott was furious, but Bill Jinkins calmly set his group's escape for Tuesday night, 17 March. Their provisions, money, clothing and even some weapons were waiting for them at Naku, and he felt sure their flight from Ambon would go as planned. There was just one change Jinkins wanted to make. He had decided in secret that Ian Macrae should join the escape party.

Conditions on the evening of the break-out were ideal; the skies were overcast and it had rained off and on all day. Just after seven o'clock the escape team and Macrae assembled at the break site on the northern side of the camp and began sliding out under the wire. As the last of them crawled free, Bill Jinkins turned to Macrae. 'Okay sir, it's your turn!' Macrae was taken aback, but Jinkins was adamant.

'Sir, Colonel Scott can look after the men; it should be you who reports back to Australia.'

Macrae was unmoved. 'No, Jinkins. I'll say my goodbyes to you here. I'm not all that well myself, and my place should be here with the men. Good luck though, and I hope to see you back in Melbourne before too long.' Deep down, Jinkins knew the major was right. They shook hands and Jinkins slid out under the wire. A couple of the men then readjusted the bushes at the point of exit and they made their way up the hill in the drizzling rain. After a while they reached the Gaspersz house, where they met up with the six porters who would assist them along the way to Naku. Their helpers had brought along lengths of bamboo filled with coconut oil to light their way, as well as some of the Tommy guns, rifles and grenades Jinkins had found and concealed on earlier forays. These armaments were supplemented by 150 rounds of ammunition. Just after 8.30 p.m., as Jinkins recalls, the party set off on the next stage of their journey.

The men carrying the torches kept them alight as we crossed over the mountains, and would only extinguish them when we had to pass by inhabited villages.

On arrival at Naku we were given a nice hearty meal and then we descended down to the water level. When we finally reached the water the four praus were waiting, already loaded up with our three kitbags filled with food and clothing. After an hour we pushed off, at about two-thirty in the morning. We had a native paddler in the front of each prau, one at the back, and one prau had another in the middle. Our group occupied three of these praus, the fourth carried our kit bags and tucker.

PATIENCE, PERSISTENCE AND GUTS

After two hours a sudden but brief squall known as a Sumatra blew in, with strong winds whipping up white caps on the waves. They headed back to shore and beached at Hutumuri, where they found a small abandoned hut and lit a fire to make a tin of tea and allow the men to dry off. Fortunately the rain began to ease and Peter, one of Bill Gaspersz's servants, insisted they had to go on despite the rough seas. Arthur Young managed to record the events of the escape in diary form, and he tells of the ensuing events:

> Dawn broke soon after leaving Hutumuri. Weather improved with the dawn and sunrise was calm with scattered clouds. Experienced no trouble and saw no sign of Japs while passing across Baguala Bay. Very worried when crew wanted to stop on shore for breakfast, eventually got them to go on and crossed from north side of bay to island Huruku. Arrived there 0930 hrs. Crowd of very inquisitive natives and very friendly natives (men, women and children) greeted us.

The escapers were taken into the reception hall of the Rani of Huruku, where they were given some fruit and other foodstuffs. Their paddlers felt they'd done as much as they could and asked for permission to return to Naku. The Rani said she would arrange a suitable vessel and some paddlers for the next stage of their journey, so Jinkins gave them a little money and let them go. Young continues:

> Arranged for large prau (*orambai*), and nine rowers to take us to Ceram, our next stage of our journey. Promised them 125 guilders if they got us there in less than a day and a half. Peter said goodbye to his brother and father, he deciding to come to Aussie with us,

and to this we agreed. Heard of two Aussies staying at a village six kilo[metres] from here, probably McPherson and Amor. Have sent boy to contact them and ask them to come here and see us.

Mac has just arrived and informed us that he is making a very leisurely escape. Amor did not come as he had an attack of malaria. Both doing well and quite satisfied, much better than Tan Tui! Left Huruku 1830 hrs, sailed to island of Saparua, weather fairly rough, some rain.

By morning they had reached the north side of Saparua, but still had to cross to Amahai on the south side of the large island of Ceram. But progress was slow and tensions were high. The winds had dropped off and the paddlers were exhausted by mid-morning. The Australians were disguised in wide-brimmed conical native hats, but the agonisingly slow journey still made for a nervous few hours.

When they finally made landfall at Amahai after fourteen hours they met the Dutch Controller of Ceram and his wife, who put the men up in their house and the local hospital. The owner of the *orambai* was not prepared to go any further, so he was paid off. As luck would have it Jinkins heard of a Chinese estate manager at the far end of Amahai Bay who owned a 10-metre diesel launch. Alec Chew and Harry Coe set off with some money in their pockets; after an inspection of the craft they returned with the good news that the owner was prepared to let them use the vessel, providing it was returned at the end of the war.

The escape party had soon victualled the launch with food and water, made their goodbyes and motored east along the coast towards the island of Geser. One last-minute passenger they carried on board was a local schoolteacher who had asked if he could have a ride down the coast to his brother's village. They headed out at dusk, and turned east in fine conditions.

About 150 kilometres down the coast they came within sight of Turuhu Bay, where the teacher wished to disembark. To Jinkins' amazement, three canoes had pulled alongside within five minutes to take the teacher ashore. 'How did they know to expect you?' he asked. There were no telegraph or radio facilities to this remote village, and a man running from Amahai could not have covered the distance in the time. The teacher shrugged his shoulders. It all seemed perfectly natural to him, but it had certainly astonished Bill Jinkins.

It was the first time I'd actually seen telepathy work, and let me tell you there was no way in the world his brother could have known he was coming down – well, no conventional way. I still chill when I think of it. Anyway it all worked out well, as they'd brought out some food for us, and everyone was in a happy mood.

After a brief stopover they struck out for Geser once again. Along the way they picked up two Australians from Ambon named Johnston and McIntosh. As well, they agreed to take some Dutch servicemen with them. The crew now consisted of nine Australians, four Dutchmen and one native (Peter). The Dutch Controller was still in Geser, together with his 'very pregnant' wife. They asked the two if they wanted to accompany them to Australia, but the Controller felt it was his place to stay – at least until the Japanese came. 'We said goodbye to both of them', recalls Jinkins, 'boarded our boat, and then spent two days trying to get the engine started!' Arthur Young continues:

March 29. Went to motorboat early – still cannot start engine. Have decided to take praus and leave motorboat. Controller has arranged the two praus. Party will be split into two parties of seven. Original party from Tan Tui sailing in one prau, 1700 hours. Heavy rainstorm; departure held up. 2000 hours – meal at hospital – rice and fish. We have had three meals of rice and fish per day for five days, and have enjoyed them all. Rainstorm abated – no wind now. Returning to boat from hospital after having said goodbye to the Controller, heard Chinese orchestra playing 'Beer Barrel Polka' and 'South of the Border' at a wedding feast. 2040 hours. Good wind has arisen – hoisted sails and left. Prau smells somewhat, but must put up with it.

The prau, named *Java*, was roughly three metres in the beam with a shallow draught, a small jib and a mainsail. A Malay seaman had been hired by Peter to handle its tiller. The following evening they caught a fine breeze which carried them along quite nicely, but by morning they were becalmed. They heard the sound of aircraft engines around nine o'clock, but did not see anything. By afternoon a breeze had sprung up again and they began making headway towards Tual. The Malay trailed a fishing line, and soon two good-sized fish had been welcomed aboard. Some sharks were sighted around the prau but Jinkins fired his rifle at them and they soon dispersed. That evening they cooked up the fish and ate them.

Late on the morning of 1 April they sailed into sight of Tual, hoping that it was not under Japanese occupation. By afternoon they found themselves becalmed once again, but their spirits were heightened by the sight of the other prau, and soon the two were being paddled slowly towards Tual. Eventually they had to pole their way along the shore in order to make any headway, but the

Australians soon forgot about the dangers of their situation. They were fascinated by spectacular coral formations and colourful fish passing beneath them in the clear waters.

At Tual, they were greeted warmly by the Assistant Resident, the Controller, and the Chief of Police, fed and bedded down in the hospital. After a discussion the next day, the original seven escapers from Ambon decided to make their way to the island of Saumlaki, while those in the other prau headed for Dobo. The following day, Good Friday, the Australians purchased the *Java* for 225 guilders and hired a crew of native paddlers. It was raining as they set off, but with every kilometre they knew they were that much further from the Japanese and that much closer to home. However, it was not all smooth sailing, as Arthur Young states in his diary:

At Tual we acquired the service of three natives – a skipper of Papuan descent with an asinine laugh, and possibly of a long line of missionary-munchers, whose apparent good humour kept us amused while our sense of humour lasted, but after two or three days of bumping about, the cackle of the skipper and his habit of not giving us direct answers to our questions made us ready to throw the crew overboard. When we asked, 'Berapa djam Ridol?' (how far to Ridol) he would say 'Kalau angin baik' (if winds good) or 'Angin tidak baik' (winds no good), to which we would answer anything sufficiently descriptive in pure Australian. Once I showed the old man a map of the Banda Sea, correctly oriented, feeling he was not quite acquainted with our position at that moment. Twas then that I realised that he could neither read nor write, and he explained that he never used a map, but could sail the Banda Sea by the mass of knowledge he had in his head!

It was a most unsatisfactory arrangement, and Bill Jinkins did not share the fellow's miscreantic confidence in his navigational ability.

We were many miles off course, sailing and being drifted toward the middle of the Banda Sea. Late that afternoon Harry Coe happened to look over the stern and sighted a speck of land on the horizon. We quickly went about to find we had passed Pulu Molu, which we then made after three hours. It was a close thing; we had nearly ended up out in the open sea with very little idea as to our whereabouts.

According to Arthur Young's diary they were about 40 kilometres west of their course after three days sailing from Tual. They were then obliged to sail south-east into the wind to reach Ridol on the island of Larat. In all, it took them five days to sail from Tual to Ridol.

At Ridol we waited only a few hours in order to restock food, and replenish food and water supplies. We dismissed our very unpopular crew, choosing to sail the *Java* ourselves with only a native guide. At about 1745 on April 9 we sailed out through the strait between the islands of Larat and Jamdena to the east coast of the latter, and into an unfavourable south to south-easterly wind. It would be a hard and long journey to Saumlaki.

Bill Jinkins was becoming increasingly puzzled by Rudder's lack of sailing skills, so at Ridol he asked him about his supposed sailing ability. 'It was then that I learned that Rudder's sailing experience on 18-footers was as a bailer boy; he had never sailed a boat before!'

It was a difficult, exhausting journey, but the rookie crew were determined to overcome the vagaries of the round-bilged prau without a stabilising keel or centreboard. Despite the strong winds, their combined skills and exertions finally carried them to Saumlaki, on the south-eastern end of Jamdena. It was a close thing; just as they reached the jetty at Saumlaki the rotor on their rudder broke, but luck was again on their side. The resident Dutch official, Controller Leenartz, greeted them with his wife, and over the next few days they were looked after in royal fashion. The men grew quite fond of the Dutch family and the Controller's two children were in friendly awe of Jinkins, who by now sported a red beard.

Soon it was time to consider making the last burst homeward and Jinkins elicited Leenartz's help in locating a suitable vessel, finally persuading the Controller to allow him use of the government's 250-tonne diesel-powered motor vessel *Aleida*. But the ship's crew flatly refused to take the escape party to Australia. Eventually Jinkins gave in, but first he asked the crew members to give him and his men a run around the harbour to familiarise them with the vessel. Bill Jinkins said his crew soon felt confident they could handle the big MV.

The only trouble was that it only had enough fuel to travel about 250 miles in calm water the same distance from Saumlaki to Bathurst Island. We would still need to go about another 80 miles to reach Darwin. As there was no more diesel to be found we decided we had to go anyway. We felt sure by conserving fuel and travelling at about eight knots we could travel the 250 miles, and we felt sure we would be spotted by the RAAF Hudsons which flew overhead every second day. It was all very chancy, but we were determined to press ahead and chance our luck that we would be picked up.

The escape party boarded the *Aleida* on the afternoon of 21 April in driving rain. The ropes holding the lifeboats had become swollen, making it very difficult to raise the boats. Then the engine refused to turn over and they had to postpone their departure until the next day. In the interim they would organise an engineer to start the engine. This settled, they had tea on board and played poker until three o'clock. On reflection, Arthur Young said this late-night game was pure folly. 'We did not know what test our endurance [would] be put to in the next few days.'

Everything seemed to be in readiness by mid-afternoon. The engineer came aboard and the motor kicked over, running smoothly. However, a strong southerly gale had been building up and they sailed out of the harbour into the teeth of the storm.

Soon the *Aleida* began seesawing in the lashing waves; the bow and then the stern smacking into the water, the boat heeling around uncontrollably on the crest of powerful waves before plunging into troughs some five and ten metres deep. They would never reach Bathurst Island at this speed and disaster now seemed inevitable as the largely inexperienced crew clung on for dear life. They returned to the harbour, but as neither helmsman had plotted the course out, they motored in through the heads and were lost until the boat suddenly grounded itself against a reef.

When morning came and the storm had abated their predicament could not have been worse. The MV *Aleida* had grounded at high tide, and as the waters abated the ship became hopelessly stranded on the reef, tilted over to a 45-degree angle with the port side deck awash and the engine room half full of water.

The crew lowered the lifeboats and filled them with food and water, but were reluctant to abandon the vessel. Eventually, after dawn, Bill Jinkins and Cliff Warn took off to row the five kilometres back to Saumlaki, where they informed the Controller of the sad fate of the *Aleida*. 'He was not very pleased at all,' recalls Jinkins. 'He was very upset.'

The vessel righted itself that morning, but she was still stuck fast. At 4 p.m. they gave up hope and set off for the village in their lifeboats. An attempt was later made to refloat the yacht by stringing 44-gallon drums together with the ropes passing beneath the ship's hull, waiting for the tide to lift her off the reef, but this was unsuccessful. Bill Jinkins was anxious to leave, but it meant finding another suitable vessel.

> Another week went by, and we were surprised to see coming up the bay quite a large craft, about 80 feet long – a very healthy craft. It arrived carrying nine women and some children, and four Dutchmen, including the Resident of the Kai Islands. This vessel, the *Griffoen*, came up and moored at the T-end of the jetty at Saumlaki. We were astounded to know that such a vessel existed, and I can well understand why the Controller was not going to let me know that such a vessel was there when we were at Tual!

Jinkins now began to press Leenartz to allow him use of the *Griffoen* to sail the former prisoners and Dutch evacuees to Australia, but the Controller was naturally reluctant to do so. Jinkins promised that if they made it to Darwin he would personally guarantee an Australian warship would be sent to Saumlaki within 24 hours to pick up the remaining men, women and children. While his negotiations were going on, a prau arrived carrying four more

Australian escapers (McPherson, Amor, Johnston and McIntosh) and four Dutch soldiers from Tual.

Negotiations continued and Leenartz began to soften his attitude following an attack on the vessel by an Australian bomber aircraft. No serious damage was sustained, but the Controller knew the ship would present an inviting target from that time on. That evening they heard a radio report of a large 'Japanese' vessel being bombed and sunk at the pier at Saumlaki.

Leenartz reluctantly agreed to their using the ship, but on the proviso that Jinkins leave one of his officers to guarantee he would keep his word and send help. This condition came about as a result of a meeting of the Dutch civilians, but Jinkins was outraged at this suggestion, and refused to leave a fellow officer as a hostage. Leenartz passed this refusal back to a meeting of the suspicious civilians. He was sympathetic to the plight of the Australians and asked Jinkins what he could do to help overcome this awkward situation.

I said, 'What I want, Mister Leenartz, is for you to understand that I am the senior army officer present and there's a war on. I'm going to declare martial law in Saumlaki within the hour. The alternative to that is that you call a meeting of the crew of the *Griffoen* in your public hall and enquire whether those men are prepared to sail the *Griffoen* to Australia. In the meantime we have to victual the boat to make sure it gets to Darwin.'

The first problem was that there was insufficient diesel oil on the island, so he gave an edict to all the surrounding villages to produce coconut oil as a substitute. Following this hundreds of natives were coming to us with massive bamboo stems with the centres knocked out, filled with coconut oil. This went on for four days, and as we strained the coconut oil through hospital gauze more kept arriving. We finished up with three or four 44-gallon drums to which we added some aviation fuel. The ship would be started on diesel, and once the engine was running the fuel tanks would be switched over to one containing the coconut oil.

Jinkins then attended a hastily convened public meeting in the community hall. He and Leenartz sat on one side of a long table, while the crew of the *Griffoen* sat on the other. When the crew again refused to sail the ship to Darwin, Jinkins stressed the urgent need to report vital military information back in Australia. He also promised to pay the crew on arrival, but they remained stubborn. Realising further negotiations would be futile, Jinkins pulled out his handkerchief and made to blow his nose. At this prearranged signal Alec Chew and Harry Coe, who had been standing by the doors, dropped their groundsheet raincoats to reveal submachine guns, a rifle and other armaments. Arthur Young, standing at the third entrance, drew a .32 pistol. Jinkins then told Leenartz to explain to the crew that they were being taken aboard the *Griffoen*, which they would then sail to Australia. Any man who resisted would be shot. This was carefully translated by the Controller, and the crew members reluctantly allowed themselves to be escorted down to the jetty.

With the crew on board and under close guard, Jinkins ordered the drums of coconut oil to be brought alongside and poured into the ship's fuel tanks. He then told the ship's captain he would have to navigate the vessel to Darwin, adding that if his set course deviated by more than five degrees he would be shot and thrown overboard.

The *Griffoen* sailed out of Saumlaki on the evening of 1 May, carrying eleven Australians and six single Dutchmen, in addition to the crew – 26 in all. Jinkins expected the crossing of the Arafura Sea to take around three days. Their wonderful guide Peter had decided he would return home, so he was presented with the prau *Java* in which he made his way back to Ambon. Sadly, he was later denounced to the Japanese and executed. Before leaving Saumlaki, Jinkins repeated his promise to Leenartz to send a naval vessel at the earliest possible time to pick up the other families and evacuees.

At sea a watchful Jinkins remained by the skipper at the helm through each night, keeping constant check on their bearing. Harry Coe stood guard in the engine-room but pitched in where he saw a need. The rest of the crew were told to go about their normal ship-board duties, but they knew they were being watched. Although suffering acute seasickness, Jinkins did not move from his position on the helm. During the night there was a very rough head sea, and the following morning they discovered the ship's dinghy had been ripped out of the davits and lost.

Finally they saw land, and after consulting their rough school atlas map they realised they had made their way into Snake Bay on Bathurst Island. Jinkins immediately reversed course and headed north-west. When they were clear of land by eye he changed course again to due west, and within 100 metres had hit a coral reef. This was to happen three times before they cleared the reef and headed due south. Not long after they saw an unmistakable indication that they were nearing Australia – an empty beer bottle bobbing in the water.

Arthur was the first one to identify anything around Darwin, and we were then able to steer by sight until we arrived at the boom gate leading in to Darwin Harbour. We left Ambon on the 17th of March, and on the 4th of May at five o'clock we were met by

Chief Warrant Officer Henderson aboard the *Chinampa* who was in charge of the boom gate. He couldn't believe what he saw, but asked us to motor through. In true naval fashion he then escorted us through the harbour to Darwin jetty. He'd radioed ahead that the *Griffoen* under Lieutenant Jinkins had arrived with Australians aboard, escaped prisoners from Ambon, and by the time we got to the jetty I don't think there was a single person left in the navy who wasn't there! We were given a right royal welcome by the navy chaps, and looked after magnificently.

Word was sent by Naval Intelligence down to 6th Division Headquarters in Adelaide River that we had arrived, and their response was that they wanted to see us. We were then placed in Winnellie camp, the camp I had built before we left for Ambon, so we were going home – for the first time!

Some NEI senior officers took over control of the *Griffoen*, and her crew, and as promised gave the crew their promised money. The MV was then taken into service as a defence vessel, and proved a very handy acquisition.

Although the people from the navy wanted to talk to us about what we'd done the army arrived the next day and the navy got shuffled out; the three of us, the officers, were then asked to sit down and write out full reports of the battle.

One of the first things Jinkins had done on stepping onto the wharf at Darwin was to speak to the Naval Officer In Charge (NOIC), Commander Pope, and set in motion plans for the promised evacuation of the men, women and children at Saumlaki. Pope moved quickly and the next afternoon a signal was sent to the *Warrnambool*, which was located in the Arafura Sea, telling it to proceed directly to Saumlaki and pick up all the evacuees. Two days later the *Warrnambool* came through the boom at Darwin.

A car came to Winnellie to pick me up, and whipped me in to the jetty where the Commander was waiting. He had his pinnace all ready there waiting to welcome the *Warrnambool*, which had been ordered to tie up and anchor at a buoy. Minutes after she'd been tied up we went over on the pinnace; a gangplank was lowered, and our small welcoming party went up into the *Warrnambool*. Prior to this I'd shaved off the beard I'd begun growing from my first day as a prisoner, and when I went up to Leenartz and shook his hand he suddenly woke up to who I was. I was still in tropical khaki, without a hat, and after I'd spoken to his wife, who didn't recognise me at first, I said hello to his two children, who were wondering who their mum was talking to. I took them by the hand as I'd done every day at Saumlaki, shook their hands, and said 'Hello'. They both looked at me in bewilderment, looked at their mother, and cried out something in Dutch. On Saumlaki, because of my beard, they'd called me a certain name, so when they saw me on the ship and recognised my voice they'd said 'This must be Jesus Christ!' It really made my day.

After leaving the ship Jinkins returned to Winnellie, where he was given written instructions telling him to report to the Director of Military Intelligence in Victoria Barracks at the earliest possible moment. The following day he was on a Qantas flying boat bound for Sydney's Rose Bay, in company with Leenartz and some of the Dutch wives and children. From there he travelled by night express to Melbourne.

On arrival at 9 a.m., and still dressed in his light tropical uniform, Jinkins reported directly to Victoria Barracks, where he was greeted by the ex-Adjutant to the 2/21st, Major Gary Armstrong, who was now Secretary to the Minister for the Army, F.M. Forde. Armstrong took his friend in to see the Director of Military Intelligence, Colonel Roberts, who in turn escorted Jinkins to the office of the Chief of the General Staff, General Sturdee, who talked one-to-one with Jinkins about the dramatic escape. Before returning Jinkins to Roberts' care, Sturdee said there was someone waiting to meet the young lieutenant. He then ushered in Sir Guy Royle, the First Naval Member, who was overwhelmed to meet Jinkins and told him he'd done a marvellous job.

I said, 'Sir Guy, it's not what I've done – it's what I want to do. I want to arrange for the pick-up of the prisoners of war at Ambon, and that's what I'm here for. I want to know that we're going to try to pick up those fellows, and it'll take a day or two to plan, but I'll be available'. He excused himself from Sturdee and asked me to accompany him. He then introduced me to a chap named Wright [Commander H.C. Wright, the Director of Naval Plans] and one of two brothers named Bachelor. Sir Guy said, 'This young man has come back to Australia to help work out a plan to relieve all the prisoners of war in Ambon'. He asked them to handle the planning, and keep him informed as to its progress. He then said, 'This young fellow is going home now, but he'll be back in my office at nine o'clock tomorrow morning'. The two men said they knew what to do and then disappeared. We went back to Sturdee's office.

After another brief chat with Sturdee, Gary Armstrong took Jinkins around to the Minister's office. After a very pleasant fifteen minutes over a hefty Scotch the minister asked Armstrong to organise some transport home for Jinkins. Forde shook his hand warmly and said he would see him the following day.

I was provided with a lift and motored out to Hawthorn in a staff car where I thanked the driver very much. By this time it was about half past twelve or one o'clock. Nobody was home, so I went into the outside toilet, and hanging on an appropriate nail was the key of the door. I went in and went through all my gear looking for a clean shirt and tie to wear. I then had a shower, a shave, and cleaned myself up, then got out my winter uniform. I had no idea when my mother would come back so I left a little note saying I'd arrived home, I'd be back a little after five, and I'd be glad to see her. I then hopped on a tram straight in to Flinders Street, got out, and went into Snows and bought myself a cap to go with my uniform. I was back in the Barracks about two; I truly wasn't interested at that stage in anything but the plan to get back to Ambon.

I finished up talking generally with Roberts about the battle and about what had happened on Ambon, and spent about an hour and a half with him. At about half past three he said, 'Well lad, it's about time you went home. From here on in you don't do anything more for the army or navy – you just work to the plan that's been teed up for you and that's all. Just report to me once a day.' So I went home that night, got home about half past five and mum was there, putting on tea.

And this part is really spooky – she had been recently told by a lady spiritualist that I would be home within days, and had been expecting me! She'd taken one of my ties to this lady, who without being told said it belonged to her son. When my mother confirmed this, the spiritualist said 'There's no need to worry about him, he's quite well and you'll see him very soon'. And of course mum took this as being right. I couldn't believe it, but mum wasn't at all disturbed when she got the note. She already knew I was on my way home!

The plan Commander Wright organised with Bill Jinkins called for the use of two destroyers which would sail into Ambon Bay at night. One would patrol the bay and engage any hostile target. The other would come to at the toilet area of the camp at the reef edge in deep water, 30 metres from shore. Jinkins would be in command of two raiding parties comprising 23 men responsible for overcoming each road guardhouse. They would then storm the camp and with the help of the prisoners overcome the guard company. Jinkins would contact the CO and organise the evacuation of all willing POWs. Landing nets would allow the prisoners to clamber aboard after swimming out to the nearest rescue ship. At some stage the two destroyers would change places.

Bill Jinkins believed the operation would be a morale-boosting success and would lead to the safe rescue of around 800 men. The defences around Ambon Bay were relatively light and he felt sure a surprise raid would catch the Japanese unawares. As the destroyers beat a hasty retreat from Ambon, RAAF fighters would strafe the island's defences to aid their safe departure.

Jinkins' superiors carefully examined the implications and dangers of mounting a rescue mission, finally deciding the raid was worth the risk. The Dutch destroyer *Tromp* was ordered to Fremantle to prepare for the mission, while the Australian destroyer *Arunta* returned to Sydney under similar orders. Jinkins and his men would join the *Arunta* at Townsville prior to a full-scale rehearsal of the operation.

Then came the bitter blow. Jinkins was notified that the project had been scrubbed by American Vice-Admiral Leary, commander of the South-West Pacific forces. Ambon Bay was too narrow a passage to allow the destroyers a comfortable access and retreat, Leary decided, although Jinkins had previously pointed out that 30 man-of-war ships could anchor there at dispersal. The Americans feared the ships might be spotted before entering the bay, then bottled up and captured by the Japanese. This capture of two ships and the men on board would be a catastrophic blow to the Allied thrust and, according to Jinkins, would have undermined the renown ascribed to General Douglas MacArthur at that time. The unexpected bestowal of an MBE did little to assuage Jinkins' disappointment.

His hopes dashed by this last-minute cancellation, Jinkins was still determined to be of some use in fighting the Japanese in the Ambon region, and was soon taken under the wing of Brigadier Hopkins, the Director of Military Operations and Plans. In September 1943 a group of 26 men known as Plover Force left Darwin to set up intelligence bases on the Kai, Tanimba and Aru Islands. There they would establish communications with Australia and conduct acts of sabotage and harassment against the Japanese. Included in Jinkins' party were Harry Coe and Alec Chew, together with six others who had earlier evaded capture on Ambon. They were the first pre-planned 'stay behind' parties in areas occupied by the Japanese.

Jinkins' party sailed aboard the MV *Southern Cross*, while another smaller vessel, the 12-metre lugger *Chinampa*, left under the command of CWO 'Chick' Henderson, who had welcomed the escapers into Darwin Harbour sixteen months earlier. There was a brief interruption to their passage when the *Southern Cross* sustained bearing damage in one engine and was forced to proceed at just two knots until repairs could be effected. The *Chinampa* meanwhile pressed on to Saumlaki. Sadly for the scheme, and for Henderson, disaster lay ahead. He berthed without incident at Saumlaki and that evening, accompanied by two of his sailors, he made his way up to the Controller's house. He was not to know that a Japanese occupying force had landed at Saumlaki the previous day and several officers had commandeered the house. In the dark Henderson assumed the guard outside the house to be a local policeman and walked straight to the front door, which opened to reveal a group of Japanese officers celebrating their occupation of the island. It would be hard to say which group received the greater surprise, but within moments the Japanese had begun drawing their pistols.

Completely unarmed, Henderson and the two sailors bolted back to their ship, somehow managing to make it to the jetty and cast off before fleeing at full throttle to the temporary safety of the middle of the harbour.

Henderson knew that Jinkins would not be too far away in the larger vessel, so they waited, filled with apprehension. Eventually they saw the *Southern Cross* approaching, but for some unknown reason Henderson swung around and headed back towards the jetty, where a force of Japanese gunners had assembled. They quickly opened fire as the *Chinampa* came in to the jetty and Henderson was mortally wounded. The vessel was quickly thrust into full speed reverse and went into a half turn, after which it was full speed ahead. The *Southern Cross*, also coming under mortar and machine-gun fire, hauled in alongside the crippled lugger. Chick Henderson was transferred to the *Southern Cross*, but died a little later in Bill Jinkins' arms. The two ships finally cleared the area and the following day Henderson's body was wrapped in an Australian flag and he was buried at sea with what Jinkins respectfully says were 'full naval honours'.

Jinkins' raiding party then made two difficult attempts to land on Jamdena, near Saumlaki, but the lack of a boat capable of landing through heavy surf made this all but impossible. Frustrated at their lack of success, they were recalled to Darwin.

Still determined to press ahead with his plans to return to Ambon. Jinkins suggested another raiding party be formed, but once again his scheme was aborted at higher levels of command. He later learnt that a dark-skinned Dutch naval officer had been landed on Ambon from a British submarine to make contact with a resistance group as well as the prisoners at Tan Tui and communicate his findings back to Australia. But the man vanished without a trace. As it was feared he may have been captured and revealed his instructions, the decision was reluctantly taken to cancel any further clandestine operations on the island. The men of Gull Force would now have to sit and wait a further three years for the general surrender, knowing that only death or liberation would finally set them free.

This cancellation was the virtual end for Bill Jinkins' bid to return to Ambon and rescue the survivors of Gull Force. Acutely disappointed, he nonetheless threw himself into the war effort with a vengeance, and was appointed Chief Instructor of Z Special Unit on Fraser Island, there continuing his role as a special operative. In this time he travelled on 'about' eight USN submarines and on 'one or two' patrols.

Following the escape by Jinkins' party, those left behind at Tan Tui camp managed to hide the shortfall in numbers for some time, thereby ensuring the escapers had a good head start. When the Japanese finally saw through this subterfuge they warned that those caught in the act of escaping, or assisting in an escape, would be summarily executed. They further warned that if any more escapes took place and the prisoners were not recaptured, a comparative number of POWs bearing equivalent rank would face execution in their place. A new four-metre barbed wire fence was erected around the camp perimeter, and further machine-gun posts constructed.

In June 1942 events changed for the worse when the Imperial Japanese Army handed over control of the Tan Tui camp to their naval forces, and the administration fell to the despised Captain Naburo Ando. According to Lionel Wigmore in *The Japanese Thrust* (Australian War Memorial, 1957):

Recreation of any form, conversation with Ambonese, instructional classes, keeping of diaries, were all forbidden, and nightly inspections took place. Men were beaten with canes or struck with swords, and surprise searches were instigated. In July the Japanese intercepted letters passed between the Dutch prisoners and their wives in an internment camp beyond Ambon. Thirty-four Dutch prisoners including nine officers, two doctors and the padre, their hands tied, were assembled on a rise overlooking the camp in full view of the prisoners. There with pickets, lengths of piping and pickhandles they were flogged by a platoon of young marines.

The marines erupted into an orgy of unspeakable savagery, wielding their weapons with impunity, battering their defenceless victims senseless. Incredibly, Ando acted as a timekeeper to this carnage, blowing a three-minute 'time out' every so often to allow his men a chance to catch their breath. When any marine paused to rest, he would laughingly egg the others on.

Soon after, the Japanese marines became the full-time guard company at Tan Tui, beginning an era of terror for the prisoners, who were continually whipped and beaten without any pretext of provocation. Rations were growing steadily worse, and the prisoners took on the haggard, gaunt look of the starved.

In October Lieutenant Colonel Scott was told that 263 Australian and 233 Dutch prisoners were being sent to what Ando euphemistically described as a 'convalescent camp' on Hainan, east of what is now called Vietnam. When the group left later that month they were escorted by Scott, who relinquished command of the remaining 528 Australians to the senior surviving Australian officer, Major George Westley. Scott's group took six weeks to reach Hainan, which was later described by one Australian POW as 'a godforsaken hole'. By the time of the Japanese capitulation three years later, 82 of Scott's men on Hainan had perished, many of maltreatment, neglect and starvation in the latter months of the war.

On Ambon, Westley took on responsibility for the remaining Australians, fourteen American and seven Dutch prisoners held in the Australian compound. With 500 fewer mouths to feed, conditions improved at Tan Tui for a while. Food became reasonably plentiful and nutritious, accommodation was adequate and the water supply was relatively clean, although it was still boiled as a precaution. The prisoners were even permitted more opportunities for recreation and exercise.

Before too long, however, creature comforts began to disappear. The Japanese became increasingly tense and morose, and conditions once again degenerated into a living nightmare. In July 1942 the Japanese commandeered eight of the prisoners' huts for storing ammunition. But worse was to come in November, when they established a massive munitions dump within the camp, siting 200 000 pounds of high explosives and armour-piercing shells within a few paces of the camp hospital and the Australian officers' quarters. It was just a stone's throw from the Dutch compound, which still held 250 women and children.

A formal protest was made to Ando through his despised interpreter Masakiyo Ikeuchi, and a request made that a Red Cross be painted on the roof of the hospital. Both pleas were dismissed by Ando, and three months later the worst fears of the prisoners were realised.

On 15 February 1943, just half an hour before noon, the dump was targeted by an American Liberator bomber. One of its string of incendiary bombs landed in a munitions hut, setting it ablaze. Within moments a frantic evacuation had begun from the hospital, as injured women and children were hurriedly turned out of their beds and told to flee for their lives. This still left nearly 50 patients who could only be removed on stretchers. Working with desperate haste, the hospital staff began evacuating these people, but time had run out. With devastating fury the bomb dump exploded.

According to Lionel Wigmore:

The explosion blew flat most of the camp and more than half was destroyed by fire. Nine Australians were killed, including five officers, and about 75 wounded. Westley was then ordered to put a large Red Cross on the roof of one of the few remaining buildings. After some Japanese aircraft had flown over the camp, the Red Cross was taken down. Thereafter requests to the Japanese that the hospital be marked with a Red Cross brought threats of execution. Westley deduced that the area had been photographed for propaganda purposes.

After the bombing the attitude of the Japanese towards the prisoners appreciably hardened. They would not regard the Australian casualties as serious and refused to help. The only Australian medical officer, Captain [P.M.] Davidson, had been killed in the air raid, and the care of the sick and wounded was left to a Dutch medical officer, Captain J.H.W. Ehlhart, and the Australian dental officer, Captain [G.C.] Marshall.

Following the bombing, in which 27 women and children were killed, conditions at the camp deteriorated even further and the guards grew increasingly belligerent and oppressive. In November 1943 Ando moved on, and his position was taken by the naval captain Wadami Shirozu. He had little interest in the administration of the prison camp, and only visited it on two occasions before the liberation of the island. In what proved to be a cruel blow for the surviving prisoners he delegated responsibility for the day-to-day running of the camp to the commanders of the guards, who were more than agreeable to let former interpreter Masakiyo Ikeuchi assume control over all administrative and punitive matters. Ikeuchi made all the decisions, rational or not, and did not seem answerable to any higher authority. The starving prisoners found themselves subject to the hostile vagaries and maniacal temper of a man who regarded extreme torment as a perfectly justifiable exercise.

Food ration issues dwindled alarmingly and disease began to take hold in the emaciated frames of the men. Despite this, the Japanese guards forced them to work on difficult and onerous military tasks, digging air-raid shelters and tank traps. Beaten without compunction, starved and diseased, the men began to die under the duress of the heavy workload. One of the principal causes of death was what one Australian later described at the trial of the Japanese officers as 'the long carry':

> The 'long carry' was a name which the prisoners gave to the task of carrying cement and bombs between two villages, approximately eight miles apart, and the route was over a very torturous track. The prisoners were required to carry, firstly, 90-pound bags of cement over this track, and when the first task was completed, and it took them about three weeks, they had to carry a large number of 150-pound bombs over the same route, one bomb between two men. They were kept at it from 6.30 a.m. until 5.30 p.m., seven days a week. The prisoners on this work were driven on like slaves by the Japanese guards, and the ground over which they had to move was so rough that sometimes they could only manage it on all fours.
>
> After a week of this back-breaking work none of the men was fit to continue, but there was no respite, and they were made to carry on until they dropped. Many prisoners collapsed unconscious.
>
> Each day the Japanese requisitioned at least fifteen men more than it was possible to supply. The Japanese then called out all the sick, and selected the other fifteen from those they considered capable of doing the job. Many of them could only walk with the aid of sticks, yet they were forced to take these heavy weights over the 'long carry' courses.

In August 1944 the Ambon town area, having been twice strafed by low-flying aircraft, suffered a heavy bombardment inflicted by a group of twelve Liberator aircraft. Later, Major Westley recorded his growing concern that the Japanese had

> deliberately set out to kill off the prisoners by hard labour and short rations. Never at any time were medical supplies adequately available to treat the sick, and often the administration of the hospital was interfered with. With some exceptions the average Jap guard was not willingly a party to this policy. The blame lies squarely with the Jap Commandant, their officers and particularly Ikeuchi, the Camp Administrator. All protests regarding any matter whatsoever were ignored, and in many cases brought reprisal on the camp. They had to be made through the Camp Administrator, and never got any further. In many cases he even refused to accept them or listen. This applied to both verbal and written requests.

The scrounging of food became a priority for all prisoners, especially those on work parties, but even in this grim fight for survival the Japanese attitude hardened.

Towards the end of 1944 an Australian prisoner by the name of Tait was caught in the act of 'liberating' a pair of binoculars while on a working party. Back at camp the unfortunate man was beaten unconscious several times by guards armed with pick handles. Each time he lost consciousness water was thrown over him until he showed signs of life and he was set upon once again. The following day a furious Ikeuchi stormed into the hospital and cruelly assaulted Tait, raining sickening blows on his bloodied, emaciated body. His rage finally subdued, Ikeuchi ordered that Tait be taken out of his stretcher and placed on the concrete floor with a single blanket. Somehow Tait managed to survive, but died within six months of malnutrition and disease.

The following year two desperate Australians, F.N. Schaeffer and J.F. Elmore, decided their only chance of survival lay in escape and slipped away. It was a forlorn bid, as the men were barely capable of walking, and they were soon recaptured. Elmore was in a bad way and died of bacillary dysentery soon after his recapture, but Schaeffer suffered the final punishment of execution.

In April 1945 Ikeuchi called an entire working party on parade. It had been discovered that instances of pilfering had occurred where the men had been working and Ikeuchi threatened to execute the entire working party unless the culprits stepped forward. He promised that only light punishment would be exacted upon these men, and more importantly they would save the lives of the rest of the prisoners. Four brave men named Wadham, Soloman, Simpson and Morrison decided to save the lives of their mates and confessed to the pilfering. The four Australians had their hands tied behind their backs and were summarily executed.

On 11 July, an Australian named Boyce was caught stealing food, beaten and thrown into solitary confinement for four weeks, where he received only one pathetic meal a day and little or no attention for his infected tropical ulcers. Throughout most of his ordeal he had a rope noose placed around his neck and wrists and pulled up behind his back. Any attempt to straighten his arms would tighten the noose around his neck. By the end of his confinement Boyce's ulcers had putrified and the appalling stench meant that his guards only approached with the greatest reluctance. Miraculously, Boyce survived and despite his crippling wounds, managed to escape in a desperate search for food. He was quickly recaptured, and on 24 July was thrown into the back of a truck and taken away for execution. The guard charged with carrying out this onerous task later described how Boyce was made to kneel in front of the hole which had been quickly excavated as his grave.

> When I received the orders to kill the prisoner, I had the feeling as if my own body was being torn apart. However there was no escape . . . At the instant the platoon commander gave the 'Stab!' orders . . . Tanaka stabbed the prisoner first on the right chest. I followed by stabbing him on the left chest. These were repeated four times when the platoon commander ordered the 'Halt!'

Somehow, most of the men of Gull Force managed to survive, helplessly witnessing the deaths of their comrades from neglect, disease, execution and starvation. Despite these daily tribulations they managed to remain stoical and mutely defiant in their attitude, believing implicitly in an Allied victory and relying heavily on each other for comradeship and moral support. Reduced towards the end of their captivity to four ounces (113g) of rice per man daily, and crowded quite unnecessarily into just a handful of huts, they silently directed their rage at their captors. Men beaten, starved and treated like pariahs eked out a pain-ridden existence, waiting and praying for the day when the tables would be turned.

When the Allies finally set foot on Ambon on 10 September 1945, following the Japanese capitulation, liberating forces uncovered an unused store of rice which would have been sufficient to feed the entire population of the camp for at least eighteen months. It had been withheld, together with a vast number of letters intended for the prisoners, which had arrived two years earlier.

*

Meanwhile, on Hainan Island, another dramatic escape had taken place, this time under the leadership of Major Ian Macrae. On 25 October 1942, the 37-year-old Macrae was one of the 500 prisoners shipped to Hainan on an 11-day journey aboard the *Taiko Maru*. Most of the prisoners, under the command of Colonel Scott, were those deemed too ill to remain on Ambon.

On 5 November the 500 prisoners disembarked at Bakli Bay on the west coast of Hainan, and were marched three kilometres to a place one of their number later described as 'a godforsaken barren hole called Haicho'. Although the centre of the island was dominated by a thick forest of tall trees, their new camp sat in an area surrounded by desolation. 'The outlook was deplorable,' Colonel Scott later reported, 'a barren, sandy island with nothing but a little cactus here and there, a hot wind.' In *Gull Force* (Allen & Unwin, 1988), unit researcher Joan Beaumont described conditions at Haicho:

The camp itself was, if possible, even more depressing than the landscape. The compound covered about 10 acres (4 ha), and was surrounded by a low barbed-wire fence. Within this area there were a few small buildings, which served as storerooms and the Japanese guard house, and several huge wooden huts in which the prisoners were to be accommodated. Measuring about 200 feet by 30 feet (60m by 9m), these huts were in an appalling state of disrepair. Originally they had been occupied by Chinese labourers, and they seemed to have been constructed of scrap iron and timber, with no concern for protection from the weather. At floor level they had open louvres. Above these were ill-fitting wooden shutters which took the place of windows. The roofs, made of pieces of iron, were more notable for their holes than the cover they provided . . .

There was no privacy and conditions at first were very crowded, as all 263 Australians were housed in one hut. Within a month the pressure was relieved a little when another hut was vacated by Chinese labourers and was assigned to the Australians and the Dutch as a hospital. A third large hut provided sleeping quarters for the 267 Dutch prisoners who had also come from Ambon.

No one had believed the Japanese when they described Hainan as a place of 'convalescence', and within hours of arriving the prisoners were forced to unload heavy sacks of rice and supplies from the *Taiko Maru*. These sacks, weighing over 100 kilos, had to be carried on the men's backs and loaded on trucks throughout the day. If any man collapsed he was slapped around by the guards.

Surprisingly, the Japanese ensured that each of the new arrivals was inoculated against cholera prior to their landing on Hainan – something they did not do for the thousands of Chinese shipped there as slave labour. As the Australians were taken to the port each day they trudged past the Chinese labourers' rough huts. Outside, stacked like piles of wood, were the bodies of the Chinese – most of whom had died of cholera. The injections undoubtedly saved the lives of many Australians.

During their time on Hainan the prisoners were forced to build a viaduct over a creek bed and drive a roadway through the treacherous bog of a sticky clay pan. One of the most debilitating tasks was the seemingly endless shovelling of sandhills into the sea to reclaim land. Despite the work and a starvation diet, the men somehow managed to maintain a sense of the ridiculous – they figured if they kept shovelling sand into the sea they would eventually have a land bridge stretching all the way home to Australia!

Deficiency-related diseases began to decimate the prisoner population through 1943, and their daily rice ration was slashed from three cups of cooked rice daily to just under a cup. Colonel Scott reported in November 1942:

> The duplicity of the Japanese in sending all the sick men to such a dreadful spot, the total absence of facilities and drugs for the treatment of urgent cases, lack of proper food, bitter resentment and complaints from the men who faced a dreary future of hard manual labour under appalling conditions, all took toll mentally.

Outside the confines of the camp, livestock grazed and grain crops rustled tantalisingly in the gentle breeze. The island's infestation of water rats dwindled and disappeared as hungry men cooked and ate anything they could catch or scrounge. Local natives showed them which grasses could safely be eaten. However, in the last year of their captivity the men were literally dying of starvation and disease. It was generally believed that they were kept in a pitifully weak state to prevent their aiding an Allied landing or a Chinese uprising on the island. They also thought it was part of a Japanese plan to deliberately kill off every prisoner in their hands – a fear echoed by Ian Macrae:

> About six months before the Japanese surrender a party of six Dutch, led by the surgeon Von Metzke, escaped. Conditions were extremely bad. Because of the progress of the war (the Americans were fighting on Luzon) all outside work was stopped and we were confined inside the barbed wire of the camp. The daily food deliveries certainly indicated that the Japs were trying to starve us to death – there was plenty of food on Hainan. We had a pretty good

idea of the progress of the war by reading between the lines of Japanese news sheets – cleverly interpreted by decoding by a Dutch artillery officer and our Lieutenant Colin McCutcheon.

By now Macrae had heard of an escape attempt being organised by a small group of prisoners, and approached one of the two instigators, Staff Sergeant Ron Leech (2/12th Field Ambulance). Both Macrae and Colonel Scott knew it was more than possible the Japanese would massacre all the remaining prisoners rather than allow them to fall into Allied hands. Macrae asked to join the escape team; he felt he could link up with Chinese guerrilla forces on the island and, when the imminent invasion came, take a vanguard of soldiers directly to the camp site to save those who were left. Leech agreed, but only on the proviso that he remain in charge of the escape.

'Not that we had anything against him,' Leech recalls, 'but we were organised, we knew what we were doing, we didn't want anybody stepping in and taking over. We only took him if he guaranteed to drop rank when we got under [the wire] and . . . he stuck by it.'

The arrangement suited Macrae, and he carefully went over all the options with Scott. Macrae had broken out of the camp on numerous occasions and reached villages a kilometre or so distant in an effort to secure guides who would take them to Chinese guerrilla headquarters at an appropriate time. It was an extremely hazardous undertaking. In 1943 a group of Dutchmen were caught following an escape from Haicho, brought back to the camp and executed. Returning to camp by himself on 17 February Macrae was seized by camp guards, interrogated by the senior camp NCO, Hideo

Akiyoshi, and forced to stand outside the guard house for three days. During this time he was not permitted any food, although some was smuggled to him. He was released, albeit with reluctance, as the Japanese found themselves losing face over the incident. When work details left the camp each morning the senior officer or NCO would order his detail to march in unison past Macrae, turn their heads as one, and salute the well-respected officer. Following his release the perimeter fence was electrified. Macrae continues:

> There seemed no retaliation following the Dutch escape so a party of five Australians – Staff Sergeant Leech, and Privates Higgins, Lockwood, Campbell and Perrin (all 2/21st Bn) – got permission to escape. I persuaded Colonel Scott to let me join the party – a courageous action on his part as my bed was next to his, and it would have been very hard to convince the Japs that he didn't know anything about it.
>
> About two weeks after the Dutch escape we broke out. At the last moment, when any altercation would have disclosed the party all packed up and ready to go, a Dutchman thrust himself into the party. We had no alternative but to take him in with us.

The escape took place on the evening of 16 April, soon after the moon had set. It was a difficult and hazardous undertaking, crawling beneath a carefully selected section of the electrified fence and then gingerly through patches of cactus. However, things did not go entirely as planned, according to Ron Leech:

> Just as we got out, [and] for the first time since we'd been locked up, the Yanks came over and dropped phosphorus flares. Campbell and

I were outside the fence, and the other [escapers] were still inside. We were only about ten yards from the fence, and the Japs ran up to the fence and started shooting at the planes over our heads! I think the only reason they didn't see us was because of the blinding flare, and when the light went out it was pitch black.

Before we went we did give our word that under no circumstances would we come back, because the Dutch [in the 1943 escape] did bloody come back, and they cut their heads off.

The escapers quickly headed off towards the mountains, at times wading chest-deep through paddy fields which fortunately threw off their scent trail for tracker dogs. Eight hours on, still in darkness but with sunrise only an hour away, Macrae collapsed from the illness and exertion. He begged the others to leave him, but they picked him up and carried him to an area which appeared dry and reasonably safe. Leech recalls:

We got to a little mound and we lay down to go to sleep. In the morning somebody shook me and said 'Look where we are'. I look up and we've camped under a bloody Japanese fort! Would you believe it? They had the Indian guards on, and I am sure they would have had to [have seen us but] didn't give us up . . . they were Sikhs . . . captured by the Japanese . . . looking out over us.

The escape party remained there throughout a long hot day, several times imagining that nearby bushes were being beaten, at one stage throwing stones to shoo off a herd of goats let out to graze by the Japanese. The men ate their rice, which by now had soured in the sun, and sipped at their precious water supply. That evening they set off eastward as the moon set, again hiding in some bushes a couple of hours before dawn. Ian Macrae takes up the story:

Later Tom Lockwood and I went looking for water and food. We had left camp with some water in bottles and pannikins of cooked rice given by generous comrades. A pannikin of rice was worth gold at that stage of Japanese cruelty. We returned to find the others captured by about twelve picturesque characters – each with a dirty piece of cloth tied in a piratical bow on one side of his head. They were armed with muzzle-loaders and bows and arrows.

They took us to a village where we were marched between two rows of Chinamen each with a Luger pistol pointed at us. Whatever the reason for this demonstration we were soon reassured as the headman signified his welcome, and we were given an ex-Shanghai house boy as interpreter – the only English speaker in the village. Fortunately the village was Nationalist because I believe instructions from Chunking were to succour escaping POWs. I don't think the village was more than twelve miles from the prison camp, and the Chinese kept us confined in case the Japanese got news of our whereabouts.

The village was surrounded by a palisade consisting of two ringed walls made from stout logs driven into the ground. The escapers were told that their hosts were as wary and apprehensive of attacks by *derobos* (bandits) as by the Japanese. By way of explanation their hosts told them that some peasants had once been harshly treated during the Kuomintang regime, and they had subsequently formed these bandit groups, which became the nucleus of Communist groups in Hainan.

Macrae persisted in pressing the headman to take them to Chinese headquarters. After what seemed an interminable time a tall, distinguished-looking native gentleman arrived at the village and a travelling party was organised consisting of this leader, a dozen Chinese soldiers, ten native bearers, six Australians and a Dutchman. Macrae, by that time falling in and out of delirium with disease, continues the story:

Details of the journey are unclear. I forget how the soldiers were armed; they always carried a large basketwork pannier for steaming rice for the evening meal. I have never tasted better rice. I remember the leader using strong-arm tactics to make the bearers carry on when they wanted to go home. Early on our trek we stopped overnight at a village where we feasted on roast pork. Fred Perrin's audible appreciation was greeted with joy by our hosts. Pigs were only slaughtered on very special occasions, so this was a generous gesture.

We were at a village during a sort of harvest festival. Gambling seemed to be the main amusement. Very small children were playing some game that resulted in paper notes of very small amounts changing hands. At the same time their elders were very serious about their *fan tan* and more impressive-looking currency. On a board between two stumps overlooking the ripened rice were eight or nine intricately carved and painted idols – the old gods of China [who] governed the fortunes of men before Confucius, before Buddha. Fun and games were all around with no respect being paid to the gods; one had the impression they were brought out to join in the fun.

The scenes we saw must have been the same throughout rural China for thousands of years. Paddy fields of deep mud being

A German collection station with wounded Australian prisoners on the morning of 20 July 1916, following the battle of Fromelles. (AWM photo A01551)

The excavated tunnel at Holzminden POW camp through which 29 prisoners made a mass escape in July 1918. (AWM photo P03473.003)

An exposed section of the tunnel following the mass escape. (AWM photo P03473.006)

Sergeant Peter W. Lyon, 11th Battalion, AIF, was recaptured on the Dutch border 12 days after his escape from Holzminden. (AWM photo PO8451.001)

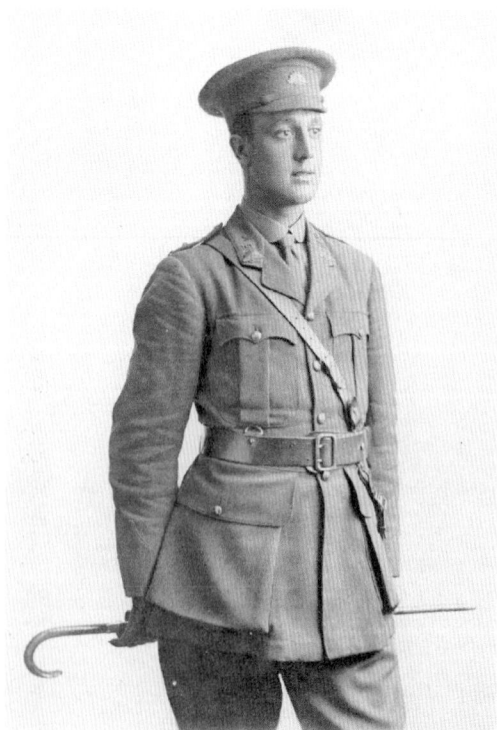

Capt. George G. Gardiner, 13th Battalion, AIF, who worked on the tunnel but was unhappily trapped in it the night of the mass escape. (AWM photo PO5382.004)

A signed studio portrait of Lt. Henry C. Fitzgerald, 19th Battalion (left) and Capt. John E. (Jack) Mott, 48th Batallion, who became the first Australian to escape from captivity in Germany.
(AWM photo A03034)

A group of Australian POWs at Soltau camp, 1918. Back row from left: Frank Carr (15th Bn), Don Fraser (13th Bn).
Front row from left: Arthur 'Sandy' McNab (13th Bn), Arthur Greasley (15th Bn) and Jack Faull (16th Bn).
(Photo: Don Fraser)

At age 17 Mert Thomas (left) poses in
Cairo with two friends from the 30th Bn
prior to leaving for the Front in 1915.
Jack Steggles (centre), Jimmy Kics (right).
(Photo: M. Gibbs collection)

His second war. Mert Thomas
of the 2/3rd Army Field
Workshop Unit prepares to
leave for the Middle East.
(Photo: M. Gibbs collection)

Nell and Mert Thomas celebrate their diamond wedding anniversary in
December 1982. (Photo: M. Gibbs collection)

The brutal code of Japanese Bushido led to the execution of Australian Sergeant L.G. Siffleet. Escapers knew they faced a similar fate if recaptured. (AWM photo 101099)

Above: Prior to leaving Darwin for Ambon; Lt. Colonel L.N. Roach (left) and Major I.F. Macrae.
(Photo: Bill Jinkins)

Left: William T.L. Jinkins, MBE.
(Photo: Bill Jinkins)

Tantui barracks on Ambon Island, the Australian HQ which became a POW camp holding hundreds of Australian and Dutch internees. (AWM photo 118253)

Bill Jinkins photographed at Darwin the morning after his incredible journey to freedom had ended. Thirty minutes later he was clean shaven and back 'on parade' once again. (Photo: Bill Jinkins)

Private Ron McPherson poses in his uniform as a new recruit to Gull Force. (Photo: Elsie McPherson)

Dispatch rider Ron McPherson. (Photo: Ben Amor)

Dispatch rider Ben Amor, Darwin. (Photo: Ben Amor)

Ron McPherson (left) and Ben Amor at a 2/21st reunion service. McPherson passed away in December 1992, soon after relating his amazing story for this book. (Photo: Ben Amor)

Bob Hooper prior to his capture.
(Photo: Bob Hooper)

Hooper's audacity finally paid off.
Looking highly uncomfortable, he is
photographed in England following his
successful escape. (Photo: Bob Hooper)

On the Esplanade at Tel Aviv, 1940. (L to R) Oscar Gibson, Jim Gilson,
Norm Campbell, Hooper, George Hendy and Fred Tippen. (Photo: Bob Hooper)

POW huts behind the inner fence of barbed wire at Campo PG 57, Gruppignano, c.1941. (AWM photo: P02793.007)

Campo PG 57, Gruppignano, Italy. The main entrance to the POW camp is shown with the watch tower and a Carabinieri guard on sentry duty. (AWM photo: P02793.002)

A pensive Nelson Short prior to his departure for Singapore. (Photo: Nelson Short)

An aerial reconnaissance photo of Sandakan camp taken before the second death march. (Photo: Nelson Short)

Bombardier J. Richard 'Dick' Braithwaite, 2/15 Australian Field Regiment (AIF) and Lance Bombardier William 'Bill' Boxham, also of the 2/15 AIF. They were two of only six survivors of the Sandakan-Ranau death marches. (AWM photos 041488 and 041486)

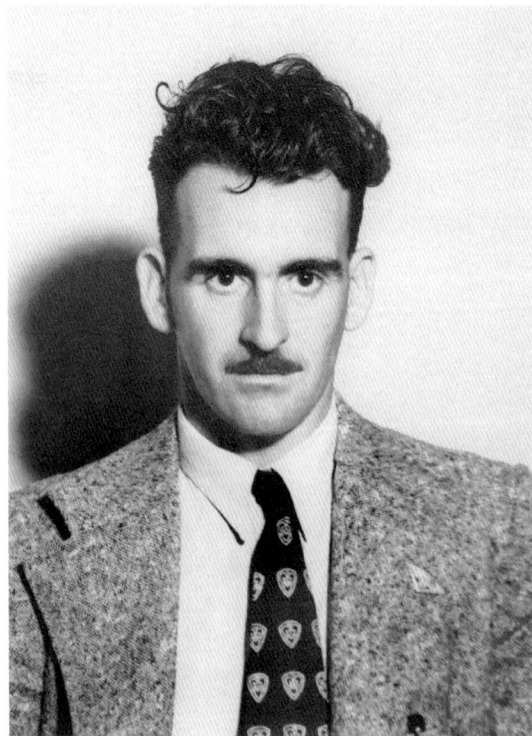

Another of the six survivors of the Sandakan massacre: Gunner Owen Campbell, 2/10th Field Regiment. (AWM photo: 041489)

With the departure of the second death march, Sandakan camp was put to the torch. The large tree which towers over the compound was the hiding place for the secret camp radio. (Photo: Nelson Short)

Three of the surviving escapers photographed at Labuan, 19 September 1945. From left: Nelson Short, Bill Sticpewich and Keith Botterill. (AWM photo OG3553)

Two POWs tending a small wood stove inside their Stalag VIIIB Lamsdorf barracks. (AWM photo P10548.001)

S/Ldr Keith 'Bluey' Truscott (left) and F/Sgt Keith Chisholm (centre) of No.452 (Spitfire) Squadron, RAAF, with the squadron's intelligence officer, 20 September 1941 (AWM photo SUK10019)

Only three of the 76 evaders in the Great Escape made successful home runs: Per Bergsland, Bob Van Der Stok and Jens Muller. In this photo Bergsland is on the left, Muller on the right, with fellow Norwegian Halidor Espelid in the centre. Espelid was one of the fifty airmen shot after being recaptured. (Photo: Jonathan Vance)

The 102-metre-long tunnel known as Harry began under a stove in Hut 104. On the evening of 24/25 March 1944, 76 airmen prisoners escaped through the tunnel before the Germans were alerted. (Drawing: Ley Kenyon)

Above left: Allan McSweyn.
(Photo: Allan McSweyn)
Right: The east bastion, Oflag IXA
Spangenberg. The castle's dry moat is
in the foreground. (C. Burgess collection)

Still determined to escape, McSweyn was transferred to Oflag XXIB Schubin,
where he attempted to recreate the highly-successful Warburg Wire Job.
Three RAF P/Os joined him in this Schubin photo: (L to R) Bill Wild,
Will Hetherington, McSweyn, and Timon Timmins. (Photo: Allan McSweyn)

ploughed by wooden ploughs drawn by water buffalo. Three generations of a family planting rice or harvesting it with sickles, then going back to a village at the close of the day, those of the youngest generation on the buffalo's back. The reaped rice loaded high onto an all-wooden squeaky cart drawn by a buffalo much bigger than the cart, slowly making its way to the village threshing floor. The village street at night, full of sleeping men in all sorts of uncomfortable postures – on the paths, on the little carts – anywhere on a warm night. Even on the less-fertile west coast of Hainan it seemed rice could be harvested twice a year.

Village hygiene was on an ad hoc basis. The houses were clean and cooking utensils bright and shiny, but the escapers were not permitted to drink any water until it had been boiled. As Macrae noted:

> Promiscuous defecation was the custom – on the paths en route to the paddy fields, and particularly round the village wells where women waited their turn to draw water in the mornings. Fortunately this did not create the fly menace it otherwise might have done, because the ultimate disposers were the pigs. It was disconcerting to be engaged in this necessary bit of personal hygiene and to be reminded by a pig grunting behind one that it had an interest in the result!

As they travelled into more mountainous terrain their circuitous route through successive villages became a test of the men's stamina. When Macrae suffered another attack of dysentery a pony was procured for him, and they made better progress. As the weary travellers climbed the spine of the mountain the scenery was little short of magnificent, but the weather became colder and it began to rain and hail.

After a two-week trek they reached Chinese headquarters, at a place called Holam. Here they were reunited with Von Metzke's Dutch escape party. The GOC for this Route Army in Hainan (under Chiang Kai-shek) was a General Wang, who greeted the men warmly. His headquarters was a collection of huts built of local materials, within which domestic life continued. Macrae and his group were finally able to tend to their illnesses.

Immediately after our arrival Von Metzke took me to the open shed where a team of skinny Chinese women were polishing rice by pounding it in stone mortars. This left a white pollard, containing Vitamin B, which the Chinese fed the pigs. We brought some tinfuls of this back and boiled it up, then drank that emulsion. Overnight the body discharged surplus liquid, and the swelling in my legs and feet disappeared. That so many died for want of Vitamin B, so readily available, is a main indictment of the Japanese. Our chaps would risk search and brutal punishment if they were found having looted little brown bottles of the stuff when unloading ships.

Beri-beri being brought under control, our main menace was malaria. The Chinese gave us (via Von Metzke) some quinine; never enough, except to suppress attacks that recurred every ten days. These recurring attacks dragged down our health, they made food – particularly rice – quite inedible. I got our interpreter Wong Ah Choy to bring us some block palm sugar, whereafter everyone started eating with no bad consequences. So health generally improved.

Sadly, it was all too late for one of the escape party, Private Miles Higgins, who died of cerebral malaria. There was little to do now but wait for word of the invasion, so the men participated in village life as irregular news of the Allied thrust caused mounting expectation and excitement for them and the guerrillas.

As Macrae's health improved he began to walk around outside the camp as much as possible to regain his strength. He was given some footwear manufactured from car tyres, then some sandshoes arrived, but these soon disintegrated and he took to walking around in bare feet.

> Partly to test myself out I accepted an invitation from Wang to go fishing. Quite a large party set off at the usual pace of the Chinese soldier – about four miles an hour maintained over any sort of country, steep or flat. After an interminable walk we reached the fishing spot . . . Two or three bombs made with gelignite packed into sections of bamboo were thrown into a large pool. The result was a lot of stunned fish which were cooked and eaten on the spot!

To their mounting chagrin, the men were even less informed about the true progress of the war than when they had been in captivity. Communication with the mainland was accomplished by means of a pedal wireless, but this proved erratic, leaving gaps in the received transmissions which were filled with the use of a little optimistic imagination.

As the men regained their strength Macrae asked Wang if he could supply them with weapons. Failing that, he asked if they could be taken across to the mainland. Both requests were politely but firmly refused.

It was only our poor condition that justified our time in this paradise, and the thought of what might happen to our POW comrades if an Allied landing did not get to them quickly was very worrying. The lack of a definite objective if we did get out made the case harder to present.

There was little evidence of offensive action against the Japanese, although I believe some went on. The Chinese kept about two Jap divisions in Hainan, which helped our cause to that extent. I believe the bandits worried the Japs more than the Kuomintang force on Hainan. Once we were invited to see a captured Jap being tortured to death. After what the Japanese had done to them – burnt hutfuls of old people, women and children – Chinese feelings were understandable. However my stomach was never strong enough for that sort of entertainment.

Came the day when the General kissed me and told me a hole had been blown in Japan seven miles deep and ten miles round, and the war was over. That night the feast was terrific! Next morning we were told the news was premature and Japan had not surrendered. This was followed by another announced surrender and feast, a further correction, and a third and final feast after confirmation of the Armistice, by which time the spirit was coming up hot from the still – potency plus!

General Wang despatched a message to the commander of a large Japanese fort informing him that a force of Chinese soldiers would be coming to commandeer the fort. After a march of a day and a half Wang and Macrae's men arrived to find the fort not only vacant, but tidy. Soon the Chinese had fowls and pigs running everywhere.

The island was inundated with leaflets dropped by American bombers, asking the Chinese to deliver any escaped prisoners they were sheltering. An American liberating force, commanded by Office of Strategic Services' (OSS) Major Jack Singlaub, of the U.S. Intelligence Service, had already identified the main prison camp as one which required an American presence as soon as it was considered safe to send his men in.

Meanwhile Colonel Scott and those still held at Haicho noticed a sudden shift in the attitude of their captors. From 17 August their food rations improved in volume and nutrition, and a Japanese medical officer actually paid a visit. Japanese officers began to tender apologies for the inadequacy of the rations, and offers were made to place sick prisoners in a nearby Japanese hospital. More life-saving drugs than the prisoners had seen for years were brought into the camp, and every man was issued with cigarettes.

In a complete about-face the Japanese paymaster informed the Australian Quartermaster, Captain P.P. Miskin, that all officers would immediately be paid the monies credited to them. Miskin conferred with Colonel Scott, then tersely informed the paymaster that the men would not accept the pay. With controlled fury he told the chastened man that the funds so suddenly available could have been used to save the lives of many dozens of men throughout their years of internment.

On 25 August a Japanese fatigue party scrambled onto the roof of the camp hospital and, to the astonishment of the prisoners watching from the compound, painted 'P.W.' in large white letters. Liberation was obviously at hand and that evening the senior officers were officially informed of the Japanese capitulation.

The following day an American bomber swept over the camp, dropping leaflets telling of the surrender and stating that a force of American troops would be arriving by parachute the next day. There was indescribable joy throughout the compound as the prisoners realised the nightmare was almost at an end.

They were all out there on 27 August, watching with muted exhilaration as an aircraft roared overhead dropping medical supplies. Then Major Singlaub parachuted down with his party of volunteer helpers – six Americans, one Chinese, and an Hawaiian Japanese to act as interpreter. After what Macrae later described as 'a dicey interval' the Americans persuaded the Japanese they would have to do as they were told. Colonel Scott conferred with the Americans and was told that his men would be transported to Samah, where the Americans had set up their regional headquarters, and from there they would be evacuated home via Hong Kong.

Meanwhile, Major Singlaub had become aware of Macrae's group and requested they stay put until help arrived. On 11 September he drove up to their fort with his team in a captured Japanese staff car. They had brought along quantities of tinned ham and fruit, but were taken aback by the lavish spread the Chinese laid out by way of welcome.

Scott and several Australian, Dutch and Indian ex-prisoners were transported to Hong Kong by ship, where they were joined on 18 September by the remaining men of Gull Force for the journey home. On 3 October the aircraft carrier HMS *Vindex* sailed into Sydney Harbour. Within two days the men had travelled south by train down to their homes and loved ones in Victoria.

It had been three long, wearisome years for the men, but the return was tinged with sadness. They knew many other families, who had waited and prayed in hope for all those years, would know only grief as the fate of their loved ones was finally revealed. And there was considerable mourning. Of the 263 men of Gull Force sent to Hainan, only 183 lived to return home.

PATIENCE, PERSISTENCE AND GUTS

These days Ian Macrae looks back on his wartime experiences with feelings of loss and a deep regret for the men who died needlessly on Ambon and Hainan:

> I did my best to forget as soon as it was over. I don't know how many others were affected like this, but I still have no great urge to go back over the time. I think the behaviour of the men generally was as good as you could possibly expect in the circumstances . . . I think back on some of those magnificent characters and their unselfishness – strong men helping weak men – but [overall] I'd much rather it hadn't happened.

In the aftermath of Ambon and Hainan some long-overdue retribution took place. Admiral Hatakiyama was killed in battle, but two of those who had caused the greatest torment to the prisoners at Ambon, Captain Naburo Ando and his sadistic interpreter Masakiyo Ikeuchi, were captured and told they would be brought to trial before an Australian military court. Ando managed to elude proper justice by swallowing cyanide-laced coffee, but an unrepentant Ikeuchi stood trial alongside many of his fellow Japanese officers and guards from Ambon, charged with numerous war crimes. He was found guilty and was later executed by firing squad. Two of the worst perpetrators of war crimes on Hainan, Shigeo Aoyama and Terutami Kano, were found guilty and hanged.

The statistics of surviving Australians bear grim testimony to the brutality they had endured. Of the 528 who remained on Ambon island following the division of their forces in 1942, only 123 were still alive – a 78 per cent death rate, which far exceeded that of the notorious Burma–Thailand railway.

203

Gull Force had been decimated in captivity. Four hundred and five men had perished as POWs on Ambon and Hainan, and another two died on the way home.

Fifty years on, the surviving members of Gull Force maintain strong links with Ambon. They rightly feel that many of their number would not have survived their ordeal without the selfless help, support and courage of the Ambonese. In 1967 Major Bill Jinkins arranged the first 2/21st Battalion pilgrimage to the island, where a moving ceremony was conducted at the Commonwealth War Graves Cemetery, on the site of Tan Tui camp. Jinkins arranged annual pilgrimages up until 1972, when he handed over the organising role to Lieutenant Colonel Rod Gabriel, who is now chairman of the Ambon Committee of the Gull Force Association. Early in 1992 Gabriel undertook his twentieth pilgrimage back to Ambon with a group of 38 survivors and sons for the 50-year commemoration service. All services are now conducted at the Cross of Remembrance.

Politically, relations are often strained between Australia and Indonesia, but the often-unheralded work of Gull Force goes on. Under the banner of international friendship and over many years the men of Gull Force have established a medical aid project involving the transfer of personnel and medical equipment donated to the Ambonese, a scholarship scheme, and a trust fund for an orphan girl whose family was killed during a monsoon. Books and equipment are donated to the University of Pattimura, there is aid to a technical school, and in a somewhat whimsical event harking back (in reverse) to the seaborne escapes of many Australians, there is an annual Darwin to Ambon yacht race.

Rhyll Rivett, the daughter of ex-POW author Rohan Rivett, accompanied Rod Gabriel's Gull Force group on a recent pilgrimage to Ambon, and she was struck by the care and attention given the War Cemetery on this tiny Indonesian island:

On entering the Australian War Cemetery at Tan Tui, the site of the Australian and Dutch POW camp, one is struck by a sense of heavenly peace and beauty. The manicured terraced lawns and neat variegated hedges combined with arbors of cascading luxuriant creepers and exotic flowering trees stand in ironic contrast to the row after row of war graves with their bronze plaques inscribed with simple poignant messages. Standing in front of an 18-year-old's grave one wonders about the whole meaning of life, and how such beauty can emanate from such unspeakable cruelty, suffering and total human waste.

5

IN THE FOOTSTEPS OF THE DEAD

IT WAS A DAY OF CONTRASTS. Outside the Kirribilli Ex-Service Club, on Sydney's northern foreshore, some clouds billowed majestically in a deep blue sky over picturesque Lavender Bay. It was 1 August, 1992, and the cold grip of winter was beginning to lose its bite. Inside, at a memorial service attended by nearly 400 people, the long dark shadows of cruelty and suffering reached out over 47 years to touch those present, emanating from what was once an almost impenetrable jungle area in the north-eastern tip of British North Borneo (now Sabah), and from a day of infamy those assembled commemorated with long-held feelings of sadness and tragic loss.

At the service the officiating chaplain, the Rev. John Brendan Rogers, told of the horrors of Sandakan – of the 2550 young men whose lives had been taken from them in one of the most barbaric episodes of the Second World War.

Keith Botterill, gaunt and frail, sat pensively alongside his wife Ruth as a succession of speakers paid tribute to the young men whose relatives and friends had come together for the service.

Occasionally he bowed his head, still haunted by the memories of Sandakan; of seeing once able-bodied soldiers, many of them friends, starved, bayoneted, shot or beaten to death. Nelson Short, quietly composed, hung on every word. He had gone on the second death march between Sandakan and Ranau, a helpless witness as one by one these starving, disease-ridden and beaten men, exhausted beyond human comprehension, simply lay down beside the jungle track, said their goodbyes, passed on messages intended for their families back home, and were shot dead by a rear guard of dispassionate Japanese guards. He too endures lingering ailments which can be traced back to that time.

They are two of just six men who managed to escape from their captors and live to tell their stories. Owen Campbell, the third still living at the time of writing in 1993, was too ill to make the trip down from Queensland. Had they not escaped they too would be remembered today as part of the massacre that was Sandakan. Just six men – the sole survivors of 1800 Australian and 750 British prisoners of war who were the victims of a plot by the Japanese Army to kill every prisoner they held, rather than allow them to be freed by invading Allied forces.

By 1 August 1945 only 33 men survived out of those who had endured the death marches from Sandakan to Ranau. But on that terrible day their gallantry and survival against ferocious odds meant little more to the Japanese than an annoying interruption to their scheme of total annihilation and these pathetic men were ruthlessly shot dead. On that same day 47 years later, Keith Botterill and Nelson Short relived once again the horrors of the death marches from Sandakan.

The extent of the ill-treatment of prisoners of war inflicted by the Japanese is abundantly clear in the following statistics: in the

European theatres of war 235 473 British (including Australian) and American prisoners of war were captured by the Germans and Italians. Of this number 9348, or about 4 per cent of the total, died in captivity. In the Pacific theatres of war 22 176 Australian servicemen were taken prisoner, of whom 7829, or just over 35 per cent, died in captivity.

When interviewed for this book in 1993, Nelson Short was living a sedate life of retirement in Sydney's inner west with his wife Colleen. By this time three of his escaping colleagues, Dick Braithwaite, Bill Moxham and Bill Sticpewich, had already passed away.

Nelson Short was born in Enfield, New South Wales. At the age of 22 he enlisted, and joined the 2/18th Battalion as a cook. A few months later he was in tropical Singapore, having been married the day before his unit sailed. On 15 February 1942 he became a reluctant prisoner of the Japanese following the fall of the island fortress.

> I was taken near the botanical gardens in Holland Road. We had been getting a pretty good caning, with bombs and such going off everywhere around us. That afternoon some big trucks came along filled with British troops and big white sheets hanging over the back. They were all shouting 'Come on, it's over. It's all over!' That's how the war ended as I remember it. It wasn't the Australians who capitulated – it was the British.
>
> The next day we were lined up and Captain O'Brien, the officer in charge, told us to take the bolts out of our rifles, and shove all our rifles and helmets in a heap. The next thing I can remember is seeing the Japanese coming over the hill and then Captain O'Brien

walked over to them with his hand up in a sign of peace. One Jap spoke English, and he asked all Bren carrier drivers to step forward; our Bren carriers had given them hell, and they didn't like it. My poor old mate Mick Simmons stepped out and they took him away. They took all of them away, all the men who drove the Bren carriers, and they made them get into the Bren carriers. Then they threw petrol over them and set them alight, burned them alive, inciner-ated them. That's the start of the Japanese for me. Bloody animals!

The Japanese, now flush with captured manpower, decided to utilise the thousands of able-bodied prisoners in work designed to aid their war effort and which was in clear violation of the Geneva Convention. Large parties of prisoners were taken out of Changi and sent to various camps and territories under the administration of the Imperial Japanese Army. One such group, containing 1496 Australians and known as B Force, was crammed into the holds of the 1500-tonne *Ubi Maru* on 9 July and shipped to Sandakan in North Borneo, where they were to be used in the construction of two large airfields on the north-east coast.

They arrived nine days later, spent the night in a Catholic school, and were then marched out to an area known as Eight Mile Camp, situated at the Agricultural Station. Eventually it was to be called Number 1 camp. A second camp later housed 771 British officers and men. Eight months later a further 20 Australian officers and 480 men of E Force arrived at Sandakan.

E Force had an interrupted journey on the way to Sandakan, their dilapidated steamer *de Klerk* pulling in to Kuching in Sarawak to disgorge 500 British POWs and a group of Australian senior officers. While there, they were forced to work on the wharves.

Later, their officers left behind at Kuching, E Force was shipped to Berhala Island, just off Sandakan harbour, arriving on 15 April. They were placed in some temporary accommodation and put to work clearing the area.

The huts at Berhala were overcrowded. Despite this the men felt their situation was quite tolerable. Food was plentiful, they were permitted to swim at the beach and play such sports as boxing and baseball. Captain Roderick J.D. Richardson was placed in charge of the men, with Captain Ray Steele (2/15th Field Regiment) as his second in command. Escape plans were soon under way, according to Richardson:

> Our guards were a few Japs and a dozen native police, 'boys' who were supposed to have changed sides. However, almost immediately I was contacted by their leader, Corporal Koram, who said they were still loyal and would help in any way possible. Through him we were able to establish contact with the underground on the mainland.

Captain Steele began making preparations for an escape by canoe, together with Lieutenants Rex Blow and Miles Gillon. He had met the two men as part of a working detail at Bukit Timah on Singapore Island.

> I very soon found out that Rex Blow and Miles Gillon, who were both in the camp but from a different unit [2/10th Field Regiment], had the same idea. We started to talk about getting away and very soon it became known among the other fellows that there was an escape being planned. They started to call us the Escape Club, or the Dit Club, dit being morse for E and E being for Escape.

When the men heard that they were being shipped to Borneo they decided to wait and make their escape from there, as it was closer to home. Once on Berhala Island, they introduced Lieutenant Charles Wagner from the 2/18th Battalion into the Dit Club and began looking at possible avenues of escape. Through Koram they discovered that Filipino and American guerrilla forces were still active on one of the closer Sulu Islands named Tawitawi, and they decided to make for the island by boat. Then word of another escape party comprising Privates Rex Butler, Jock McLaren and Jim Kennedy reached Steele's ear. They were approached and it was agreed to unite the teams in a single escape.

Then came an unexpected complication. At Sandakan on 8 May three prisoners escaped from the Japanese while on a working party. Two of the escapees, Signalmen Howard Harvey and Daniel McKenzie, were recaptured and executed for their efforts. The third man, Walter Wallace, had gone into hiding. Koram knew the fugitive's whereabouts and told Steele he would arrange to transport him over to Berhala. Knowing that Wallace would not last long at Sandakan, Steele agreed.

> We had no alternative but to take him with us because if he'd been left there he would have died or been discovered. There was no point in taking him into the camp because he wasn't on the rolls. He was a fellow that had had a fairly mixed life; he was a permanent coastal soldier for some time, he was a prison warder, and you know what Australians think about policemen and prison warders. He was a blustering type of fellow. But let's face it, he was an Australian, he was a volunteer soldier, he was with us, and he needed help. And we took him.

Koram transported Wallace over to Berhala. He was concealed just outside the camp, where food could be smuggled to him. A compass would come in very handy for the escape, and Wagner knew where he could get one, as Nelson Short explains:

Things weren't too bad at Berhala. I was running a little concert party there, and was always entertaining the chaps. A mate of mine was there with me, a thin little bloke named 'Turk' Hewitt who had an army water bottle and a compass. Back at Selarang he had cut the bottle in half, hiding his compass wrapped in cloth in the bottom section, and then filled the top half with water. It was very clever. I knew that my officer Charlie Wagner was planning to escape, so I asked if I could go as well, but he told me they would actually be escaping later from the mainland. He got to know Turk Hewitt, and Turk gave Charlie the compass, thinking he might be able to go with them, but they never took poor old Turk or me.

On 4 July the Japanese announced that the POWs would be transported to Sandakan the following day. That evening, as Nelson Short conducted a singalong elsewhere in the camp, the eight men made an uneventful exit. Steele continues:

Right on the water's edge there were the usual native toilets. The only way to get out was to wait till as near dark as possible, wander out to the toilets, drop through the floor onto the mud under-neath – and what else was there! It was all a bit hazardous. It wasn't quite dark and there were guards on the gate 40 or 50 yards away. We had already taken our gear out during the day and planted it close to where Wallace was; we only had a tiny pack each. All we had to do was drop into the mangroves and run like hell.

Three of the escapers left the island almost immediately in a stolen canoe, but this episode almost ended in calamity. McLaren, Butler and Kennedy had fashioned some rough paddles in the camp and waited anxiously as the two stronger swimmers, Blow and Wagner, swam out and hauled up the mooring anchor on a suitable vessel. Unfortunately the owners, a small colony of lepers, heard the noise, confronted the three men waiting on the beach and began to scream for help. Under a bombardment of threats the two swimmers brought the canoe ashore and the three relieved men jumped in and paddled furiously out to sea. After ten days of almost continuous paddling they finally put to shore on Tawitawi and were eagerly welcomed by friendly guerrilla forces.

The remainder of the escape group remained hidden on Berhala Island for 22 days, staying one step ahead of Japanese searchers. Koram kept them supplied with food. The five men were finally picked up on 26 June by an 8-metre sailing boat, and they too received a tremendous reception once they reached Tawitawi:

They all descended on to the beach. They were all yelling and waving and going on. And of course they wanted to carry us ashore and hang garlands around our necks. That night there was a big fiesta, and everybody got very full. We certainly had one hell of a time.

I personally felt that a weight had been taken from my shoulders. We were prisoners for only sixteen months, but sixteen months was like sixteen years to us fellows. And all of a sudden we hit this beaut place with not a care in the world, and everybody dancing and singing and eating and drinking. It was tremendous; it was just as though we had new life.

Once they'd settled down, the eight Australians were introduced to Lieutenant Colonel Suarez, commander of the 125th Infantry Regiment in the Philippines. Later, they joined in the guerrilla activities on the island. In one attack on a group of pro-Japanese Moros they found themselves surrounded in an ambush. Rex Butler was killed and Miles Gillon wounded in the legs and left arm. They assisted Gillon back to their base camp, but had to leave Butler's body behind. The Moros hacked off Butler's head and took it to the Japanese to claim a reward.

In October the seven surviving escapers received instructions to proceed to Mindanao. Here they once again teamed up with the local guerrillas, but soon suffered another cruel blow when Charlie Wagner was shot dead by a sniper. Finally, in March 1944, Steele, Kennedy and Wallace were picked up by an American submarine and transported to Darwin. Blow, Gillon and McLaren, who chose to stay behind, all survived the war, returning home on 22 April 1945.

Having endured fierce beatings following the mass escape, the remainder of E Force were shipped to Sandakan as planned. On landing they were marched through the jungle along a small-gauge railway line until they reached an area which was being cleared for the aerodrome. They continued on until they arrived at what had become known as Number 3 camp, prepared especially for them.

During the first year at Sandakan only about 24 POWs died. Food was adequate and conditions reasonably tenable, although accommodation was poor and overcrowded, while the water pumped into the camp was muddy and polluted. The only real problem lay in the attitude of the Formosan guards, who were particularly brutal. Continually subjected to beatings with fists or pick handles and unable to retaliate, the prisoners bore these bashings with grim stoicism.

Some escape attempts took place, and collective punishment was imposed on the other prisoners. This entailed the withholding of rations for a week.

The Commandant at Sandakan was tall, well-educated Lieutenant Susumi Hoshijima, who rode around the camp on a magnificent white horse and was already known to many of the men who had come from Berhala. On 2 September Hoshijima called all the prisoners on parade, and as they arrived they were surprised to see the camp surrounded by a large number of guards carrying machine-guns and rifles with bayonets.

Hoshijima mounted a small platform where, through an interpreter, he declared that each prisoner had to sign a document stating that he would not escape and would obey all orders given them by members of the Imperial Japanese Army. Any prisoners subsequently caught in an escape attempt would be shot. The senior Allied officer at Sandakan, Lieutenant Colonel Alf Walsh, was instructed to read the document out loud and then sign it. Walsh threw the document to the ground and in a loud voice proclaimed 'I for one will not sign!' He was dragged away on Hoshijima's orders, taken outside the camp and had his hands tied behind him. Hoshijima then called up a firing squad. The prisoners began to call out that they would sign the paper. They knew it was illegal and they could not be bound to obey its terms. A couple of small alterations were requested, which Hoshijima permitted, and the document was signed.

By the time E Force arrived at Sandakan their B Force colleagues had virtually completed a 3-kilometre road leading to the proposed aerodrome and were engaged in clearing an area for the runway. Most of the work on the white, sandy soil was being done with picks and shovels. Basically a small hill was being excavated, and the spoil was used to fill in a swamp on the site of the runway.

At first officers from B Force kept watch over the working conditions of prisoners from the ranks and kept confrontational problems between the men and their guards to a minimum. This situation changed late in September when Lieutenant Hoshijima decided that the officers should also be employed in manual labour. Despite outraged protests Hoshijima got his way.

A group of young Formosans was added to the guard population in March 1943. Known as the *Keichi* (small guards), they were more brutal than the guard company they joined. They came from the lowest ranks in the Imperial Japanese Army and took craven pleasure in beating defenceless men, particularly those of higher rank than themselves.

The 'cage treatment' was introduced into the camp by Hoshijima and three of these contrivances were soon in use. They were of heavy bamboo construction, each measuring about 2 metres long, by 1.5 metres wide and high, which meant that the occupants were unable to stand erect. The walls of bamboo bars were set about seven centimetres apart, with a small door at one end. Prisoners were locked in these cages for the most trivial offences, with no protection from the sun, rain, or the night cold. As many as seven men at a time were held in each cage, so only a few could lie down at any one time. Three prisoners caught stealing food from a store were thrown into one of the cages for an indefinite period. After three months, all had died. Private Keith Botterill (2/19th Battalion) from Katoomba, west of Sydney, was one who managed to survive a term in the cage:

I was confined in the cage at Sandakan for 40 days and 40 nights, during which time I was bashed every day. I was not allowed to have a wash or a shave all the time I was imprisoned, and was seven days without food. We didn't get any water until the third day – and then they stood over us and forced us to drink and drink until we were sick. There was a Formosan guard called Kitamura, a horrible-looking, hairless creature like an animal. He would deliberately spill half our food on the ground in front of us. Or he'd give it to the dogs. When we were being starved he'd walk up and down outside the cage eating a big fish or a pineapple and he'd throw stones in at us.

When my 40 days were up I had scabies all over my hand. I had no clothes at all except a lap-lap. On another occasion I was locked up in the cage for twelve days for breaking away from the aerodrome to get tapioca roots.

Each morning, those in the cage were taken out and given what the Japanese called PT. This consisted of a severe bashing. Men had to be carried back into the cage crying. Some collapsed, but a bucket of water was thrown over them to bring them to again. Some of the prisoners who were bashed were in a very weak condition and sick. The sick prisoners were actually beaten more than the others because the Japanese hated them and considered them a nuisance.

Sometimes the men were made to stand to attention while the [guards] brought up their knee into their testicles. If they collapsed water was thrown over them; then the bashing would continue.

217

In a brave act of defiance a South Australian, Captain Lionel C. Matthews (8th Division Signals), directed the construction of a secret radio. He had also managed to make contact with an underground movement comprising loyal Asiatics and a few influential allies in Sandakan – one of whom was an Australian doctor by the name of James Taylor, who worked out of internment as Principal Medical Officer at Sandakan Hospital. Taylor was asked if certain drugs could be smuggled into the camp, to which he agreed. With this clandestine operation under way, Matthews also requested some valves with which to make his radio, and soon the prisoners (and Taylor) were able to receive legitimate news of the war's progress.

The radio was hidden in the hollow trunk of a tree, where it was eventually discovered by a Japanese search party on 22 July 1943. That in itself was catastrophic, but worse was to come. The searchers also uncovered a diary hidden with the radio, in which was listed the names of all those who had helped in its assembly and operation. Taylor and several civilians, Matthews and some other officers – a total of 65 men – were seized. After a lengthy period of beatings and torture by the *Kempei Tai* (the Japanese equivalent to the German Gestapo) they were transferred to Kuching and thrown into gaol. Dr Taylor survived the war and spoke of the tragic end of Captain Matthews (executed on 2 March 1944), who was posthumously awarded the George Cross for bravery.

I had never met Captain Matthews until we lay side by side in the hands of the *Kempei Tai*. Tall and thin and bearded, his appearance was – there is no other word for it but Christ-like. He knew he was going to he killed, yet even when he was racked with pain from the fearful beatings and tortures, his constant thought was for others. No man ever wore the uniform of an Australian officer more honourably. We were taken to Kuching and tried, after the Japanese fashion. Matthews was sentenced to death, and I to fifteen years gaol.

I remember him, on the morning he was to die, calmly dividing his food with his fellow prisoners, and he called back to them as he was taken out to be shot: 'Keep your chins up, boys. What the Japs do to me doesn't matter – they can't win!' He faced a Japanese firing squad with eight of my loyal Asiatic helpers – they were buried in a common grave – and I believe that he tore the handkerchief from his eyes and went to his death unflinchingly. I should call Captain Matthews the hero of Sandakan camp. I have never met a man so unselfish and so unafraid.

After the discovery of the radio almost all of the Australian and several British officers were sent to Kuching and Labuan. The Japanese realised that this move would deprive the remaining men of a good deal of leadership in the event of an Allied landing. But the slow attrition rate was still not enough for Hoshijima. In the two years the prisoners had been at Sandakan only 67 had died, and he began to perceive the remaining 2400 as a very real threat in the event of such an invasion. He resolved to take the drastic action of severely cutting the prisoners' rice ration, working them all the harder, and using any power within his means to break their will.

The prisoners now found themselves working to a brutal work schedule. The guards' behaviour grew worse, and they hit out at the weakening men without mercy. Rations were cut even further, then further again, but still the POWs toiled on, digging up tree roots, moving huge rocks and shifting dirt while suffering the ravages of malaria and beri-beri. Tropical ulcers ate the flesh down to the bone. Soon they had to exist on just a handful of weevil-riddled, poor-quality rice per day. Some tried eating *kang kong*, a green vegetable, but the result was a painful colic. Despite their hunger, whenever the men got their rice they'd give some to mates too ill to work. By October 1944 an average of ten men were dying every day.

The Allies were now occupying the island of Morotai, just 1000 kilometres east of Sandakan. When aerial reconnaissance established that work on the aerodrome was in its final stages, they undertook bombing forays beginning on 14 October. The prisoners saw the raids as triumphant morale-boosters and marvelled at their first sight of the famed 'split arse' P38 Lightnings which zoomed virtually unimpeded over the camp. Nelson Short was one of those employed on building the aerodrome.

We were just white coolies to the Japs. We had no boots to work in; I worked all the time on the drome in bare feet. I had tropical ulcers on my feet, and the sinews were just hanging out of my toes. Our ulcers were being treated with spirits of salt. Do you know what spirits of salts is? It'll eat through steel, it will go through tin. For the bad parts we'd line up and they had a long piece of wire with a knob on the end and they'd dip it in the spirits of salts and oh, put it on. The men would scream and go mad with the pain, but at least it was something.

And, for trivial things like talking with each other we got punishments like the one we called 'The Wings', standing with arms outstretched holding bars up and made to look into the sun for hours. I've had solar burns behind both eyes, and had to get contact lenses implanted into both eyes. The men were dying like flies, and the whole place stank. At first we started to burn them but there were just too many, so we had to take them out and bury them.

It was wonderful to see those Lockheed Lightnings swoop out of the clouds – like Speed Gordon coming to the rescue! It told us we were really winning the war.

But there was a sad side to the bombing. The Japanese allowed us to put a big POW sign in black and white on the highest point, but the planes continued to bomb and strafe the camp. So the Japanese made us take up the POW sign and give them an open go. Bombs left craters right in the camp, and there was one just outside that went right under a hut and killed twenty or 30 blokes. I can't understand it. When we had the POW sign there anyone could see it, and they just continued to strafe and bomb. The Japanese opened up on us as well. They were putting rifle fire into the camp. They were having a go too. They wanted to get rid of as many as they could!

Despite the Allied attacks work continued on the airfield until January 1945, but it never became operational.

That same month the Japanese decided to evacuate the camp and march all the surviving POWs to Ranau, an isolated camp at the foot of Mount Kinabalu, 250 kilometres to the west of Sandakan. This was to be accomplished by evacuating the men in two great marches.

By now Hoshijima's cruelty was unstoppable. He cut all rations to the prisoners, which meant they were reduced to drawing on their own dwindling reserve stocks. The quartermaster begged Hoshijima to allow the men to buy food from the locals, using their POW funds and promissory notes which he said would be honoured by the Allies, but the Commandant was unmoved, even though rice intended for the prisoners was still pouring into Hoshijima's Q-store at the rate of a quarter of a kilo per man per day.

The first evacuation march to Ranau began on 28 January 1945. A total of 470 men were marched out of Sandakan camp over the next nine days, a party of about 50 men leaving each day accompanied by twenty or 30 guards. Two of the six men who would ultimately survive the horrors of the marches were in this first evacuation – Keith Botterill and Lance-Bombardier Bill Moxham (2/15th Field Regiment) from Toongabbie near Sydney. After the war Moxham recorded his feelings on leaving the camp:

> You wouldn't have called us fit men, but we were fitter than those who stayed behind in the camp, in most cases. We had no idea where we were going. On the second day out when we'd eaten half our ration, we were told it had to last us eight days! We got a pint of watery rice twice a day, and what greens we could scrounge, such as fern tips. We had shirts and shorts and our battered hats, and about one man in six had a pair of army boots. As well as your own gear, you had to carry anything a Jap guard felt like hanging on you.
>
> We did eleven miles the first day. The Jap rubber boots were dragged off our feet as soon as we hit the mud, and most of us were barefoot by the second day. We were easy meat for the leeches; we pulled [them] off all day. At night, if we were lucky, we'd strike a bamboo hut at a staging camp. Otherwise we'd sleep in the open, under what shelter of leaves we could get. It rained nearly every night in the jungle.

Keith Botterill was in Number Three party, which lost its first man on the sixth day out – a sergeant suffering from beri-beri who sat down and simply refused to go any further. Botterill and three others begged the man to try to keep going and a passing AIF officer told them to get him on his feet. The poor fellow implored them to leave him, saying he couldn't go another step and didn't want to live. Eventually they were pushed on by other guards, and a little later they heard a single rifle shot. Botterill recalls having to leave one or two men behind every second or third day:

> Each morning those who were too sick to move would tell our Australian officer in charge that they could not move out with the party and the Japanese sergeant or officer would count us and move off. We would get along the road about a quarter of a mile and then hear shots. The Japanese officer would tell our officers that they had to shoot the men who were left behind. Men dropped out from the march as they became too weak to carry on and were immediately shot.
>
> After we crossed the Muanad River, 50 miles from Sandakan, we went through another long stretch of swamp mud in the second 50 miles. I think that was the worst part of the track – if anything could be worse than the mountains we had to climb before we reached Ranau – which is about 150 miles. When we were a week out of Ranau we crossed a large mountain at Boto and while we were making the crossing two Australians fell out. They were suffering from beri-beri, malaria and dysentery and became too sick to travel on. A Japanese private shot the corporal and a Japanese sergeant shot [the other man]. Altogether we lost five men on that hill.

Two Australians were also bayoneted to death for refusing to move on when only 30 kilometres from Ranau. On 17 May Captain Takeo Takakuwa took over as camp Commandant of Sandakan, but life became even more intolerable under his rule. Prisoners died needlessly as their rice rations dwindled and medical supplies they had brought across from Singapore were withheld, as were Red Cross parcels. By the end of May only 900 men were still alive at Sandakan, and nearly half this number were seriously ill.

Bombardier Dick Braithwaite (2/15th Field Regiment), from Newcastle in New South Wales, had been a process engraver in civilian life. He now utilised this skill to fashion small nameplates for the simple graves of those who died.

We thought the war must end in victory soon, and we tried to live for that. But men died every day; they died faster than I could engrave plates for their graves, and I got weaker and slower at the engraving.

About three-quarters of a cup of sloppy rice, and at midday we got some tapioca root . . . *ubi kayu*. It sours the stomach. We used to eat ashes to try and get right. We ate almost anything we could find. Snakes – the camp was overrun with them at first, but when we left you couldn't find one – and frogs, and grasshoppers grilled – they tasted to us like prawns. Some ate rats. I could never come at rats myself, but I've eaten slugs . . . I suppose most of us lost weight mentally as well as physically. Some men went mad. What kept me sane, I think, was a set of chessmen I carved out of wood with a pocket knife. One by one, the chaps I used to play chess with died. And others I tried to teach couldn't concentrate sufficiently to learn.

Following increased Allied bombings Captain Takakuwa received orders from the commander of the 37th Japanese Army, Lieutenant General Masao Baba, to evacuate the camp. Ten days later these plans were hastened along following an Allied naval bombardment and air raid.

Takakuwa believed that only one person in five would survive the gruelling trek, but on the morning of 29 May the prisoners were given an hour in which to pack up any belongings. Of the 824 surviving prisoners, only 566 were fit enough to muster. The Japanese began blowing up their nearby ammunition dumps and burning down the compound huts. Those in the hospital were carried out of the building and placed row by row in the vegetable gardens in Compound 2. Several died in the process. Captain W.H. (Bill) Sticpewich (8th Division AASC) was one of those assembled for the march. He recalls that rumours were rife: 'I had been told on several occasions by several Jap guards that we would all be killed. "The words *Marti marti* all Australian English soldiers *marti marti bagous*"... This meant that all Australian and English soldiers were to be killed and that this was a good thing!'

Fortunately this was not the case. The prisoners were separated into ten details of 50 and one of 66. Once the hospital had been fully evacuated it too fell to the torch. Soon, only the Japanese huts were left standing.

The guards were anxious to get as many prisoners on the move as possible and many gravely ill men from the hospital were included in the 566 who were to leave the camp. Before he left, Nelson Short paid a final visit to one of his friends in the hospital group and was urged to stay behind. His mate argued that it was only a matter of time before they were turned over to the Allies and given proper medical care. What else could the Japanese do with nearly 300 men incapable of even walking? Short was not convinced, and decided to take his chances on the march.

At 5 p.m. Takakuwa's deputy, Captain Genzo Watanabe, addressed the prisoners through the camp interpreter San Osawa. The men would begin leaving the camp in staggered groups in an hour's time. The first eight groups comprised entirely Australians; nine and ten were a mixture of Australian and British troops, while the last was wholly British. Twelve Japanese guards were assigned to each group.

They were told that light rations would be issued to each prisoner once they were under way. It was later discovered that a vast store of rice remained behind in the camp site; it would not fit in the packs each man was forced to carry, which were already crammed with food and equipment for the guards. They were further informed that medical treatment would not be available. Five of the camp pigs were to be killed and cooked, and the meat carried on the march by the prisoners.

It was nearly 8 p.m. and darkness had fallen before the first group moved out of the camp. The remaining huts had now been set ablaze and the flames provided an eerie backdrop to the straggling exodus. Many prisoners hobbled along with the aid of crude walking sticks, but all marched with a glimmer of hope in their hearts. It was this hope of imminent liberation that kept despair at bay. Nelson Short reflected on this false optimism:

> The men thought the war was over and we were going to Sandakan; that was the strong rumour. When we came down to the bitumen road the men said if we turn left we'll be going home, we'll be going to Sandakan. If we turn right we don't know where we're going. So when we got there we turned right – straight into the jungle!

As they turned away from Sandakan some men began to ask their guards where they were headed, and many of the Japanese were quite amused to learn that the prisoners had anticipated being handed over in surrender. They were going to a place called Ranau, the prisoners were informed. Some men, who knew the location of Ranau, cried out in horror. It was nearly 240 kilometres away, through mud, swamps and thick jungle.

As the silent marchers reached the 15-mile peg they were issued with their rice, which turned out to be less than two kilograms per man, and told it would have to last each of them several days. The leader of each group was handed a sheet of paper and told to complete a nominal roll of the prisoners. Bill Sticpewich was placed in charge of the second group and counted himself fortunate as one of the fittest men on the march. He had been with the technical party working for the Japanese quartermaster and had been treated a little better than most. He knew as he led his group on the march that many would never make it to Ranau.

The whole of the track was mud over our knees, mountainous with numerous rivers and creeks to be crossed. We managed about six and a half miles per day. The first group would stop marching about three o'clock and then others would come in anything up to half past four or five o'clock. Thirteen miles was our biggest march in one day. When we moved out in the morning there would be some men who simply could not move, who would be crippled by exposure and who were in bad shape before they started.

The Japs staged this march to break the powers of resistance, and ultimately kill all men who might give trouble to them when the

Allies invaded Borneo. Even cripples with sticks and crutches were driven till they dropped, or were shot, or even beaten to death.

As men fell out of the march, too ill to continue, the four guards bringing up the rear shot or clubbed them to death. Their emaciated corpses were then tossed into the jungle. Others tried to escape, but were easily hunted down and killed.

Back at the camp, the Japanese guards barely waited until the last of the marchers had left before they began systematically killing off the 300 unfortunates who had been too ill to leave. Seventy-three men were belted to their feet, forced to move away to a site near the Tangkual Crossing and machine-gunned to death. Others were simply left to die, riddled with disease, starved, and without any form of shelter. A further group of 22 men were forcibly evacuated to the nearby airfield, where they were massacred. A Chinese lad employed in the Japanese cookhouse testified at a later military hearing of crucifixions.

Wild-eyed, frantic men were forced to eat weeds in a desperate but ultimately futile battle against starvation, while others dragged their disease-riddled, ulcerated bodies to the edges of filthy drains to obtain a drink of fetid water. Just weeks before the end of the war the last surviving prisoners were beheaded by a Japanese officer. All were certainly dead by 15 August.

Those on the march were consumed with their own fight for survival, but as the march continued their numbers began to diminish. Nelson Short still remembers the march with a mixture of revulsion and helplessness.

They marched us through the night and in mud up to our waists,
up to our necks. My only clothing was a pair of shorts a mate made

from an old kitbag and a little mat I used to sleep on. It was raining and I slipped and rolled back down the mountain and hit a rock. My mat cushioned the fall and saved me. Above was a Jap watching to see if I was able to proceed, otherwise he would have finished me off. I can still hear the Japs screaming at us with 'Lekas, lekas!' – 'Go quick, go quick!' – belting us with sticks and butting us with rifles.

We'd be marching all night till about three o'clock in the morning . . . then when they wanted a rest, we rested. When the time came to go on again, after three or four hours' rest, the men couldn't get to their feet – they became paralysed in the legs. The ones that couldn't get up, they were all put together. And if blokes couldn't go on we shook hands with them and said, you know, hope everything's all right. But they knew what was going to happen. There was nothing you could do; you just had to keep going yourself – more or less survival of the fittest. We went on for a distance and all we heard was the rattle of a Tommy gun, and that's what they did with them – and that's at every resting place. Blokes fell over, couldn't go on, and they just machine-gunned them. There was nothing you could do.

The prisoners' despondency grew as they began to notice human skeletons beside the track and the remains of insect-infested bodies; horrifying signs of the fate which had befallen many of those on the first march. When the camp interpreter, Osawa, fell ill and it became obvious he was dying he was shot by a Japanese medical orderly acting on specific instructions. On 1 June the weary marchers reached the swamps and began a torturous wade through glutinous grey mud infested with small crabs. The guards screamed at any man who faltered, urging them on with blows from their rifle butts. Dick

Braithwaite realised his only chance for survival was to escape. He knew he was using up his last reserves of energy, and his attempt would have to come soon. By about the sixth day he was so weak his mates had to support him during the *tenko* (rollcall). He fell back towards the rear of the long column, but was helpless to prevent the bouts of malaria which sapped his remaining strength. The Japanese rearguard continued to kill those who could not keep up. It was time to make a break, but the thick mud threatened to forestall his plan.

As it sucked down your feet and gripped you to the knees you seemed to be leaving the last of your strength behind you. I felt that I was getting to the stage where I could not carry on. I knew now that I'd never make the distance to Ranau. If I didn't get away I'd soon be dead. I was blacking out in the mornings and it was agony to start. One of my ears was smashed and the hearing was gone in it [this was to become a permanent disability], my mouth was cut and my body ached with bruises. That was from a couple of days before when I was trying to get up a greasy hill with a Jap guard bellowing at me behind. Suddenly he smacked me across the back with his rifle and, when I fell down, beat me with the butt and kicked me. I rolled over as he was rubbing the butt of his gun in the dirt to gouge at my eyes. He searched me for any rice I had – but [my] quota had been eaten the night before. He left me then to die or be finished off. Somehow I managed to struggle in with the last party.

I was going along, some miles past the Muanad Crossing, when I heard, in the distance, the firing of machine-guns. And I told myself I knew what that meant. 'It's to the north; there's been an Allied landing on the coast!' Those shots decided me then that I'd go at the first opportunity, and make for the coast.

Braithwaite and the other men were sadly mistaken. The machine-gun fire signalled the massacre of 73 men back at Tangkual Crossing. On 6 June the men were given another small ration of rice and told it would have to last them for ten days.

The next morning the desperately fatigued men were camped under a tree near the Sapipayou River. Braithwaite told his friend Gunner Wal Blatch that he was going to escape, but Blatch was sceptical. No one in their condition could survive the rigours of the jungle. Better to die in the jungle than at the hands of the Japanese, Braithwaite reasoned, and finally Blatch agreed to escape with him. But the more Braithwaite thought it over, the more he realised he would become a liability to his friend. Before he fell into an exhausted sleep he decided that he would escape at the first opportunity – alone.

Earlier that day an Allied Beaufighter reconnaissance aircraft had flown over the area, and members of the crew saw the straggling column of figures moving along the track. Believing they were about to be strafed, many of the prisoners and guards dived for cover. This diversion provided the perfect opportunity for Gunner Owen Campbell (2/10th Field Regiment) from Toowong near Brisbane and four others to make good their escape.

> I said to my mates: 'Now's our chance!' We grabbed what we could from the Jap haversacks – some rice, six tins of salmon, some dried fish. Then five of us shot through into the jungle. We slid down this dirt bank . . . into the bracken and rubbish, and we just lay doggo until all the Jap parties went past.

Almost a month later, on 3 July, two natives named Lap and Galanting were making their way by prau up the Muanad River when they heard a call coming from the nearby jungle. The two men paddled over to the river bank and Galanting cautiously approached a naked and delirious heavily-bearded white man sitting in a small clearing, who swooned and slumped forward as the native approached him. Galanting helped the man to his feet, and with Lap's help lugged him into the prau. The two men quickly paddled upstream to where their people had set up a temporary camp, having been driven from their *kampong* (village) by looting Japanese.

The villagers had rescued Gunner Campbell in the nick of time. The sole survivor of the five escapers, he would certainly have died if Lap and Galanting had not chanced upon him. It had been a close thing, as Campbell recalls:

Five of us made a break from the track [those accompanying Campbell were Corporals Emmett and Webber, and Privates Austin and Skinner]. We had the food we'd taken from the Japs' packs, some fishing lines, and a compass which one of us had hung on to since Singapore. We only did three miles in the first two days through that thick maze of jungle. I got an attack of malaria. We camped one day while I dosed myself with a few quinine tablets I'd got from a Jap in exchange for my watch. We pushed on and one man [Private Skinner] got dysentery. After we'd camped three days we split the tucker, and the other three went on to try and reach the coast . . . I stayed behind with my mate. He tried to persuade me to go on after the others.

On the third day I went down to the river to try to catch some fish and get water, and when I came back I found that my mate had cut his throat. He had killed himself so that I would be able to go on. I scraped a hole and buried him, and pushed on by myself.

Suffering from the debilitating effects of beri-beri Campbell headed in a north-easterly direction, following signs left by the others, existing on fresh water and any beetles or grubs he could find along his way. On the second day he caught and ate a few small fresh-water crabs. He soon came across Emmett and Webber, who were attempting to catch some fish while Private Austin, now suffering badly from malaria and dysentery, rested beneath a thin blanket. Distressed to hear of Skinner's death, Emmett and Webber decided it was time to try to obtain help from the natives. Having made this decision, they settled down to wait. Soon after they heard Malay voices coming from the direction of the river and ran down as quickly as they could; Emmett and Webber out in front, while the weaker Campbell brought up the rear. His frailty was to save his life.

The two who were ahead of me hailed the [prau] and it came in towards the bank. When it was about twenty yards from the bank a Jap came out from under the roofing. He threw up an automatic rifle and fired four shots, hitting [Webber] in the chest and [Emmett] through the head. They fell dead into the river. I was far enough behind them to go to ground. The [prau] went on.

There was nothing I could do but go back to [Austin]. I stayed with him for three days. We lived on fish I caught and a fungus that grows on jungle trees. Then he died. I buried him as best I could, and pushed on down the river. To cross the river I got a log and was halfway across when a Jap appeared on the bank and fired at me, hitting me on the wrist. I swam underwater to some mangroves and the Jap fired into the mangroves, but I got away.

Around 25 June Campbell became delirious, wandering semi-naked through the jungle. On one occasion he was asleep under a tree when a wild pig began to snuffle at his knees, thinking he was dead. Campbell grabbed a stick and thrust it into the animal's eye. He later followed the pig's trail down to the river and kept a watchful eye on the passing boats, many of which carried Japanese soldiers. Eventually he noticed a small canoe carrying a pair of natives and decided it was time to make a move. His cries for help sounded more like a series of grunts, but just as he was about to give up the prau turned towards him and one of the natives stepped out onto the river bank. The excitement was too much, and Campbell fainted.

Too weak to know what was happening, Owen Campbell was bathed in the *kampong* and dressed in a pair of trousers, then given some boiled water to drink. Over the next two days he was given a simple broth to eat, and was then permitted a small amount of rice supplemented with slivers of fish and fruits. If anyone approached the temporary camp he was taken into the jungle and hidden until the danger had passed. Slowly he regained a little strength and, with someone holding him upright, even managed to bathe in the river.

Thirteen days later a guerrilla leader named Orang Tua Kolong came into the camp and was told about the nearly dead Australian. Kolong was shocked by the appearance of the thin, hairy man covered in scabies standing before him, but he presented the Australian with a letter which affirmed that he was in the employ of the Australian Services Reconnaissance Division, and as such could be trusted. Australian forces had landed east of Borneo and several clandestine reconnaissance units had begun penetrating the interior. Kolong arranged to take Campbell upstream and they left by night in one of four praus. The native paddlers finally reached the mouth of the Bongaya River early on the morning of 20 July, where they located the SRD unit. Owen Campbell was overwhelmed with joy.

When I met Lieutenant [Jock] Hollingsworth of SRD I really wept for joy as he put his arms around me. I'll never forget it; it was a fantastic feeling to see him, you know. He picked me up and carried me into this hut they had built, and said to the fellows to get a hot meal ready. They made a rendezvous for a flying boat to pick me up off the coast and it flew me out. I don't know how I survived those ten days of delirium in the jungle, when I used to think my dead mates were back with me, and I talked to them, and they seemed to talk to me.

On 26 July the flying boat transported Campbell to the USS *Pocomoke*, an aircraft carrier at anchor off Tawitawi Island. Here he was gently taken aboard and treated until he was considered fit enough to be sent on to Morotai and then returned to Australia.

Owen Campbell's group of five men had escaped on 7 June. The following morning, the remaining prisoners were beaten to their feet, but two men near Dick Braithwaite were unable to stand, try as they might. Braithwaite was filled with a helpless rage as he reluctantly moved on.

I knew I'd never see those two again. Later on I heard two shots – and I knew what that meant. I was full of a cold hate as I went along the track, and it seemed to sharpen my resolution to escape.

I watched for a chance and it came when we had to cross a small river full of logs and bracken, with a steep bank.

When I got up the bank I saw the Jap ahead was 100 yards in front, and rounding a bend in the track. The Jap behind me was still out of sight, crossing the river. I went straight into the jungle on the left-hand side. I pushed in about fifteen feet and struck a long-fallen tree. I couldn't get around it. I lay down beside the log. Big ants crawled over me, but didn't bite me. The Jap went by. I wanted to cough – I had a racking cough from chronic malaria. I stifled the cough until I could restrain it no longer.

The cough jerked me up into a sitting position. A Jap who was going by stopped and peered into the jungle and, as he unslung his rifle, he seemed to be looking straight at me. I froze, and the Jap went on. I lay there until about four o'clock and the last of the parties had gone through. Then I got up and started, wearily, back down the track. Keeping close to the side of the track, I saw a solitary Jap who carried no rifle coming up along the track towards me. A branch lay handy and I picked it up and waited.

I don't think he ever knew what hit him. I seemed to go berserk then. I hit him and hit him and smashed him as he lay dead. I was crying, and saying as I did it, 'That's for Cec! That's for Reg! That's for murdering my mates!' I dragged him into the jungle. I searched his pack for food, but he had none. I got on to the river we had crossed and followed, north to the coast, wading in shallow water. I found some slug-like shellfish, and ate them raw.

Over the next three days Braithwaite fought his way towards the coast, eating whatever he could find to sustain him. Survival was simply a race against time and the insidious dangers of the jungle.

I had had no food for five days, but I'd gone past feeling hungry; it didn't seem to worry me anymore. I was only skin and bones and weak as a kitten, but my brain was extraordinarily clear; and my senses sharp. I remember the incessant drip, drip, drip of the jungle sounded so loud, and at times nearly drove me crazy.

I was still trying to make my way down to the coast, travelling by the sun. I'd followed up elephant tracks and pig tracks and they led nowhere. Then I got into a morass – a moss swamp – and as I went further in it was like a cavern, an eerie twilight. As my bare feet sunk through the moss, snakes slithered about and once a big scorpion dropped from a branch down my back. I remember putting my head down as I rested beside a tree and thinking 'Now I've had it!' and what a horrible place it was in there to die.

Somehow he managed to keep going, but after breaking through a patch of thorny scrub he found he had circled back again to the Lubok River. Braithwaite set about making a small raft, on which to float downstream. Gathering dead wood and vines was slow work and as he had not completed the task by nightfall he settled against the trunk of a tree for the night. As he drifted off to a fitful sleep, animals howled in the distance and birds shrieked overhead, while all around were the unnerving sounds of small animals and insects scurrying through the leaves and bushes. His sleep was interrupted by a deep cough-like noise, and he was instantly alert.

I knew what that sound was – a crocodile. On the bank where I was, I'd have to stay awake and be on guard. I was sitting there when suddenly I felt a pain shoot through my foot like an electric shock. There are jungle ants that live and move just under the surface of the ground. They seem to sense anything that moves above, and come up after it. I scrambled to the other side of the small river bank clearing but they followed me – they came up in millions. I was walking on a moving carpet of ants! I scrambled into a tree, and they followed me up it. Once I heard Japanese voices on the river and I thought I would call out and give myself up to the Japs, but I stayed with the ants.

I thought the dawn would never come, but it did, and I heard a prahau [prau] on the river. In it was a solitary old man, a native. I called out to him in Malay, 'Mara sini!' ('Come here').

The old man was Abing bin Luma, out checking his fish traps. Although he could not converse with Braithwaite, he moved his small boat over to the bank and helped the Australian to board before paddling downstream to his *kampong*, known as Sapi. Braithwaite was too weak to climb the ladder into Abing's hut, but with the assistance of the elderly man's son-in-law Amit he was soon pushed upwards and into the comfortable atap hut.

At the rear of the hut Abing had created a false atap-palm wall, behind which they hid a store of rice from the marauding Japanese soldiers. They gently assisted Braithwaite into this small area, and then brought him some food and water. As he ate, they looked at his emaciated body and shook their heads in sorrow. As soon as his small meal was over Braithwaite could no longer keep his eyes open, and passed out.

When he woke he heard several voices behind the false wall in the hut, chattering away in Malay. When the occupants realised the Australian was awake he was escorted onto a large enclosed verandah where he was greeted by the senior men of the *kampong*. They were squatted in a circle, and he was beckoned to sit on a cushion in their centre. A feast of fruit, fried bananas, small cakes and coffee was placed before him. As he ate, a discussion took place on the best way to help him reach safe hands.

Abdul Rasid, a Filipino who spoke good English, translated the discussion. As it transpired, there was a good reason for wanting their guest to reach Allied hands as soon as possible. The village had recently been strafed by Allied aircraft and they wanted Braithwaite to pass a message that they were a friendly village without any Japanese presence. He agreed to do what he could.

Braithwaite asked if he could be given a prau, but his request was rejected. There were too many Japanese patrols and camps along the river, on top of which he was too weak to make the arduous journey by himself. But there was no end of volunteers willing to paddle him downstream past the enemy patrols and on to the coast.

They left that night, Braithwaite lying in the bottom of one of the two slender praus, covered with banana leaves. There was little sound as the men paddled along, and he was soon fast asleep, waking only as the praus broke out of the river and into the sea. At 10 p.m. the paddlers finally rested. The following morning they journeyed on to Liberan Island, where the local villagers said they would take him to the Allies the next day. Braithwaite could hardly contain his excitement; an American naval force could be seen sitting calmly at sea in the distance.

The following morning Dick Braithwaite was up early, scanning the horizon, but the force had moved on during the night. It was a crushing blow, but the villagers reassured him that the Americans would soon return. Happily, their words came true as an American PT boat hove into view the next day, and a prau containing the excited Australian, holding aloft a white flag, was quickly despatched to intercept the craft.

> The Yanks crowded to the rail as we came alongside. They thought I was a Jap that the natives had captured! We got up alongside, and I see this giant hanging over the side. He said 'Good Christ – it's an Aussie!' And he said 'What would you like, Aussie?' I said, 'A pint of beer!' He said 'Not a so-and-so doubt about you Aussies'. Then they hit me with seven-pound cans of bully beef, you know, and all sorts of stuff.

The Americans told Braithwaite they had to complete their patrol and would pick him up a little later. While he waited impatiently he presented the cans of bully beef and other supplies to the delighted villagers. When PT Boat *112* finally returned, the crew handed down a few cartons of cigarettes which he also passed to the natives. At last he was able to clamber aboard and meet the boat's skipper, Lieutenant James, USN. One of the first questions Braithwaite asked was the date, and he was surprised when told it was the 15 June, making it cause for double celebration. It was his twenty-eighth birthday!

Dick Braithwaite was taken to Tawitawi Island, which had recently been occupied by Australian forces. Here he was hospitalised in a ward containing twenty other patients and given proper medical treatment. He gave what information he could on the location of his fellow prisoners. His recuperation was slow; he had a badly poisoned leg as a result of the ant bites, and was given hourly injections to the liver, as well as a mountain of vitamins. A week after his arrival he was visited by an Australian colonel who said they were going in to Sandakan to look for the rest of his friends.

At this Dick Braithwaite choked and broke down completely, turning to face the wall and crying helplessly. Finally he was able to speak, and his voice trembled with quiet grief as he whispered, 'You'll be too late . . . you'll be too late.'

When the survivors of the second death march finally straggled into Ranau on 26 June, only 142 Australians and 61 Englishmen were still alive. Nearly two-thirds of the number who had begun the march were missing or dead. On arrival they were given a sombre greeting by just six of their mates – the only survivors of the 470 who had departed Sandakan on the first march.

For the new arrivals it was hard to comprehend; the men in the first march had been much fitter, and suffering far less from the debilitating effects of starvation. Their march had been completed in the much shorter period of 21 days, and only twenty prisoners had died on the way.

However, there had been no rest for those from the first march when they reached Ranau. On arrival, Major Yoshio Watanabe immediately assigned them to work details carrying rice bags 40 kilometres back along the track to a staging camp at Pagina-tang. Each bag weighed almost 20 kilograms and was filled with rice intended for the Japanese guards and their prisoners en route from Sandakan. Many of the men were incapable of walking any further, but Watanabe was none too concerned about this. His orders were to eliminate any prisoner unable to work. Any stubbornness or refusal to work just made his task easier.

Keith Botterill was one of those who'd reached Ranau in the first march. On arrival the POWs felt their lot would improve markedly.

There was an abundance of food growing in the lush, elevated valleys of the 4000-metre high Mount Kinabalu, while green paddy fields choked with rice stretched as far as the eye could see. Their illusions were quickly shattered – the Japanese intention was to do away with all the prisoners, and they were denied access to any rations. The men lived wholly on what they could steal, scrounge or catch. Botterill tells of men crunching up beetles, or eating snails and grubs in a pathetic quest for sustenance and vitamins.

Gunners Albert Cleary and Wally Crease managed to escape in late March but were captured and betrayed to the Japanese by natives who handed them over for a bounty. Both men were tied to a post and savagely beaten, then subjected to two days of excruciating torture. As they lay face down in the dirt, logs were placed beneath their legs and behind their knees. The guards then took turns jumping on the ends. They would also tease the men by slowly placing the points of their bayonets between the men's eyes and shouting abuse.

Crease had endured enough and on his release he decided to make a run for it. The guards chased him into the scrub and rifle shots were heard back in camp. Cleary was stripped and chained to the post. He was starved and left in the open throughout each day and freezing night. As the guards passed they would laugh and kick out at the poor man, and quite often urinate on him. The one thing they would not do was touch his filthy body, fearing dysentery. After twelve days, when they realised he was about to die, the Japanese finally allowed Cleary to be unchained.

Keith Botterill was one of those who carefully untied the man's bonds and carried him down to the creek where they gently washed his wasted body. He was then carried back into their hut where, surrounded by his mates, he died.

According to Botterill the uppermost thought in their minds at this time was self-survival, and he was one of those who reluctantly carried the crushing bags of rice for the Japanese. He knew he was just delaying the inevitable.

We'd get through the flats of Ranau and start up the mountains, and then men would start to get sick and sit down. The Japanese would shoot them and divide the rice up among the fit men. The killing would start about five miles out of Ranau, and the second day there'd be more killing of a morning. We'd arrive at Paginatang on the third afternoon, rest up there, and head back on the fourth day. There'd be more killing on the way back, and on the fifth day, within sight of the compound, they'd still be killing us.

No effort whatsoever was made to bury the men. They would just pull them five to fifteen yards off the track and bayonet them or shoot them, depending on the condition of the men. If they were unconscious it would be a bayonet. If they were conscious, and it was what we thought was a good, kind guard, they'd shoot them. And there was nothing we could do.

On the last rice-carrying trip we refused to carry the rice, and this Captain Nagai, the Japanese commander, came out and he said, 'If you don't carry the rice I will march you all back to Sandakan'. Well we knew that 95 per cent of the men could never get back to Sandakan. So twenty of us decided to carry the rice for them, and only five returned on that trip – we lost fifteen. So that was the last rice-carrying trip.

By contrast, the Japanese were well fed and in good condition, apart from a few who were receiving treatment for malaria. Keith

Botterill managed to survive as his mates 'died like flies' around him. He remembers with sadness that the dirt-floored hut the prisoners shared at Ranau had been quite crowded when they first moved in.

But as time went by the person next to you would die during the night, and his place would give more space. You'd wake up of a morning and you'd look to your right to see if the chap next to you was still alive. If he was dead you'd just roll him over a little bit and see if he had any belongings that would suit you; if not you'd just leave him there. You'd turn to the other side and check your neighbour; see if he was dead or alive.

There'd be a burial party every morning, approximately nine o'clock, which consisted of two men to each body. We used to wrap their wrists and ankles together and put a bamboo pole through them and carry them like a dead tiger. We had no padre. And no clothes on the bodies, just straight into 6-inch-deep graves. The soil was too hard to dig any deeper. We'd lay the body in and the only mark of respect they got, we'd spit on the body, then cover them up. That was the soldier's way.

Towards the end of April only 150 prisoners of war remained alive. By 25 June this number had dropped to just five Australians and one Englishman. As they talked about making a desperate, suicidal attempt to escape, the survivors of the second march began filtering into Ranau.

If the exhausted survivors of the second death march expected any respite after their exertions they were sorely disappointed. Within days they too were involved in burdensome tasks and the dying continued. Those who put their final energies into ill-fated escape attempts were executed upon recapture. For many, this was preferable to dying a slow death under the Japanese yoke. In his self-published 1988 book *Sandakan: The Last March,* historian Don Wall paints a grim picture of the conditions prevailing at Ranau:

There had been no provision made for the men at all in the Ranau Camp. The Japs had three huts built under jungle cover in the creek bed in preparation for an Allied invasion. The men were confined in an area about 50 square yards, which was above the Jap quarters. They had no shelter other than jungle scrub, no cooking facilities, no sanitary arrangements, no medical treatment or supplies available. They were forced to walk half a mile to draw water for all purposes and the Japs limited the number of buckets of water the men were allowed to struggle back with. The PWs were only permitted to get water from below the Jap camp and the Japs would do their laundry, bathe and urinate in the creek before it reached the area where the men were permitted to fill their buckets.

By July discipline had broken down – it was a matter of every man for himself, there was nothing they could share. The strong issued the rations.

The Japs continued their beatings of the sick and starving men for not being able to remove their dead quickly enough, for getting a drink of water from the creek, for relieving themselves. The men were so weak it was impossible for them to lift the bodies of their mates and it would take five men to drag a body along by rattan tied about the arms to a hole which had taken four men three hours to dig. All the time they were trying to do these jobs they were persistently harassed and beaten by the guards. Botterill asked one man to help. The man said he was too weak and Botterill said 'Well you get on the front end and I'll push you along'. When they got to the gravesite the man sat down by a tree and died.

'Taking' was not regarded as 'stealing' – it meant survival; anything a prisoner got he would eat even if it was a spoonful of salt; it would be taken with water – he couldn't hoard it as there would be many starving eyes watching. If you left it in the place it would be gone. Even the Japs would question the prisoner if he was eating away from ration time; if moving his lips he would be asked to open his mouth. You were not supposed to survive – there was always the thought in the guards' minds the prisoners just might outlast them.

One Japanese-conscripted Formosan guard, unhappy with the camp staff after he'd been beaten for having a dirty rifle, gave Warrant Officer Bill Sticpewich the spur to begin planning a desperate escape. Sticpewich fell to talking with the guard, who became quite chatty and told the Australian of his bitterness at the disciplinary action he'd received. As he talked he revealed that he had actually seen the instructions to eliminate all the prisoners among Takakuwa's papers. The guard was doubly outraged, as he had also been informed that the Formosans would then be required to serve on work details. Takakuwa was no good, he said, and would die very soon. Sticpewich dismissed this as wishful thinking.

The following evening he was preparing a sparse meal in the cookhouse when the sad-faced guard came in, said goodbye, and left. Minutes later three rifle shots echoed across the camp, followed by a short period of silence, and then another shot. After leaving

Sticpewich the guard had killed Lieutenant Suzuki, then shot and wounded Takakuwa and a medical sergeant named Fujita before throwing a grenade, which failed to explode, into the midst of this carnage. Before anyone could retaliate the distressed Formosan had jammed the muzzle of his rifle into his mouth and killed himself.

Nelson Short was nearing the end of his tether. At one stage he and some others were given the task of chopping down bamboo with blunt parangs, then dragging it down to the creek.

At the end of the day, raining, this little bastard called Suzuki [shot that night by the Formosan] told me to go and get him a bucket of water. And so I went down, but on the way back up the bank was slimy, slippery and muddy, and I couldn't bring it back up. By the time I got back to him the bucket was almost empty, and he went mad – you could see the mad look in his eyes. Up with his rifle and he ran at me. I ducked, but he caught me across the top of my eye and it opened up. At that moment I thought 'That's enough for me!'

I told my mate Les Fitzgerald I was going that night, come what may, and he told me that Botterill and Moxham were going too, and I should mate up with them. It was okay with Moxham, although they had a magnifying glass, a billy, and some clothes they'd taken from the men who'd died, and I had nothing except what I had on – a pair of shorts a chap had made for me out of an old kitbag. Les was really crook with malaria and said he couldn't make it, so I asked Andy Anderson if he'd like to shoot through with us. He had a dirty great ulcer under his foot, but he said, 'Sure, I'll give it a go, although I don't know if I'll make it with my bad foot!'

That night, 7 July, Keith Botterill, Bill Moxham, Andy Anderson and Nelson Short finalised escape plans. Two medical officers, Captains Oakeshott and Picone (later shot dead), gave them some Japanese money, suggesting they could use it to bribe local natives. 'Little did I know,' says Short, 'that all the natives at that time brought you back for the bag of rice the Japs placed on your head as a bounty.'

The four men crawled out of the Ranau compound in a blinding monsoonal storm. Holding hands in the torrential downpour, and barely able to see where they were going, they sneaked down the Tambunan Road, so close to the Japanese tents they could make out the glow of the guards' cigarettes inside. They finally made their way to a hut containing Japanese rice stores, where Nelson Short checked the strength of the door.

There was a lock on it, but it was only done up with wire, so I got a stick and put it through the wire and just turned it, and it busted. But we didn't know whether it was going to be guarded or not. We carried away as much rice as we could. We put it in billy cans and bits of sack and carried it away with us.

We had to sneak right through Ranau Kampong to get clear, and we made three miles past Ranau the first night. Then before it started to break daylight we decided to go down to the river at the bottom of Kinabalu. So we made our way down and came to the river; fresh water, beautiful water. There was also a little bit of a cave. When the sun broke through we got some water and I told the others to scrape some bamboo as tinder with Moxham's jackknife, which I knew wouldn't make too much smoke when it burned. I then started a fire using the magnifying glass. We boiled up a feed of rice, and stayed there for a few days.

Moxham had a small map of the area, and the four men decided to make their way across to Jesselton (now Kota Kinabalu), 80 kilometres away, which would involve an exhausting trip back up the mountain. Later, they had to slip past a *Kempei Tai* hut full of Japanese, but they pressed on, marching through the night along the Jesselton track. Eventually they could go no further; the cold had penetrated through to their bones. They moved off the track, huddled together for warmth, and fell into an exhausted sleep.

Next morning the men had to press on before any Japanese patrols stumbled onto them. They descended into a large valley, and soon they came across an empty native hut. Short noticed some fruit peelings on the ground and collected them to supplement their rice breakfast, while the others settled into the hut. Then, without warning, they had an unwelcome visitor.

All of a sudden I hear, 'Heh! Kotchi koi!' ('Come here!'). I look up and here's a Jap and he's got a rifle over his shoulder. He sang out to me, 'Api!' ('I want a match'). I said to the others, 'I'm spotted. There's a Jap up there and he's got his rifle and all.' He didn't see them. I must have looked like an animal, but the Jap yelled out again that he wanted a match. I called out, 'Tieda uda api!' ('I haven't got a match'), and all the time I was slowly backing away. I finally made a dash over the top of the mountain and tumbled down and down the mountainside. I waited there for about ten minutes or so in the long grass. Suddenly I pulled myself up and realised I couldn't run out on my mates, so I went back to the hut. The Jap had gone.

So away we went down the side of this mountain through the long grass, and sure enough we came to another little hut. We decided to cook up here so I went and got some water and lit another fire. We were sitting there having some rice when we hear behind the hut, krump, krump, krump. Somebody was coming. All of a sudden a native with a basket of bananas on his back was standing in front of us.

Short greeted the surprised native in his own language and said they were friends. After a tense moment the native smiled. He turned out to be a Christian by the name of Barigah, and as he gave the Australians some of his bananas, he told Short there were constant Japanese patrols in the area. He said he had to leave, but would come back and help them. They could do little else but trust the man.

Not long after, an unarmed Japanese soldier unexpectedly blundered into the hut. Moxham still had his small jackknife and quickly told the others he would stab the man if there was any trouble. The soldier was surprised to find the men but regained his composure and began to bargain with them. It never seemed to cross his mind that they were escapees, and they kept his suspicions at bay by stating that their Japanese officer would soon be returning with medicine.

Providence then lent a hand in the shape of an Allied fighter aircraft out on a strafing patrol, shooting up any signs of Japanese habitation. The pilot had obviously noticed the spiral of smoke rising from the hut and zoomed in. The four Australians and their unwelcome visitor quickly moved outside and ran for their lives into the surrounding jungle – the Australians taking care that they headed in the opposite direction to that of the fleeing Japanese. Nelson Short tripped and fell in the long grass, once again opening up his injured eye.

Happily they soon ran into Barigah once again and followed him to an area where he cut some bamboo and made a crude *sulap*, or lean-to shelter. He begged them to stay hidden until he could return and when he finally did they were delighted to see he was bearing some food.

By this time Anderson was gravely ill with chronic dysentery. When Barigah informed them they would have to move again, as Japanese patrols were nearby, Anderson begged the others to leave him. They refused, and with Barigah's help moved on, Anderson crawling on his hands and knees. When they reached a safer location Barigah had built another *sulap* for them, but Anderson collapsed outside in the open, too sick even to crawl any further. Short checked on his friend throughout the night, but there was very little he could do. On 29 July Anderson died. Barigah organised a stretcher and a hoe and they carried the body a short distance away for burial.

Despite the unselfish help of the kindly Barigah and the villagers who would later bring them whatever food they could spare, Keith Botterill was beginning to doubt that any of the Australians could survive.

We were sick, we were filthy; we were almost down to the level of animals and we hated the sight of each other. But if we got an egg we'd cut it up into three even parts. We'd watch each other like cats all the time to see that we got equal shares of everything. I spent my twenty-first birthday living like that! I'd enlisted when I was seventeen.

Then Barigah brought in news we could hardly believe. He said there was an Australian SRD party of commandos only fifteen miles away. Moxham wrote a note and a native took it, and on the 13th of August the native came back with a message signed by Lieutenant Ripley of the commandos. It said the war was practically over; that was wonderful! So was the food he sent us, and medicines. Well we started out a few days later, to walk the fifteen miles to the SRD camp. My legs were so swollen up with beri-beri the natives had to lift up my feet over logs on the track. We started at night, the natives carried bamboo torches to light the way until the moon came up.

The Australians and Barigah moved on with caution and weary determination, knowing that safety was almost at hand, but not quite. Nelson Short recalls that it was a time of great tension for all.

On 22 August I turned to Moxham and said 'Did you hear that?' It was the sound of machine-gun fire echoing through the jungle. Moxham said that he had heard it as well. That was the last of our men – the Japs murdered them. Oakeshott and all the others. The Japs gave them a last cigarette I believe, and machine-gunned all of them before they even put them in their mouths. Others were shot in front of graves they'd been forced to dig for themselves. They say now that this happened on 1 August, and this is the date everyone thinks is the anniversary of their deaths, but I don't agree. I firmly believe they weren't killed until the day we heard all the shooting coming from the direction of the camp, and that was 22 August. By which time of course the war was over. Rotten bastards!

We marched all 24 August. And in the afternoon about four or five o'clock we heard this trampling; crash, bang, coming through. We said, 'Hello, what's this, is this Japs come to get us? They've taken us to the Japs or what?' But sure enough it was our blokes. We look up and there are these big six footers – Z Force. Boy oh boy!

The commandos had come out with stretchers to meet us. They carried Botterill and Moxham in; I managed to walk. I'll never forget how big and strong they looked – like giants – in their jungle greens hung with Tommy guns and equipment. God they looked wonderful, and they were wonderful. They put us to bed at their camp and brought us food and vitamin pills and cigarettes. They treated us like babies. We didn't weigh any more than kids. Botterill was six stone, and at least a stone of that was beri-beri swelling. Moxham was four stone ten, and I was the smallest of the three – only four and a half stone!

They were introduced to another Australian, Bill Sticpewich, who had also escaped from the Japanese.

After a short convalescence the four escapers were moved to a small airstrip carved out of the jungle. Four small Auster aircraft flew in and touched down. Someone produced a camera and the gaunt men had their photographs taken. But fate nearly lent a final cruel hand, as Short recalls:

Moxham, he was the first one, away he goes but doesn't even get airborne. Crash – straight into the trees. He had his head cut open, but he was otherwise okay, and went on another plane. I took off, just made it, and after a while we landed on the sands at Labuan Island. We were treated there in hospital, the 9th Divvy boys looking on. The doctors were going to give me a transfusion but changed their minds. They said I was too fit! Edwina Mountbatten called in to see us while we were there. After this treatment we were flown over to Morotai.

When I finally got back to Australia I was quarantined for four days in Darwin. From Darwin I was flown in a big Liberator bomber together with some other blokes who'd been prisoners of war. The aircraft had no seats – we just sat in the belly of it. So we're going across and getting towards Cloncurry when the engine caught fire!

Anyway, we made an emergency landing at Cloncurry. They fixed it up, and gave us some lemonade. We then took off again and landed at Archerfield airport.

In Brisbane, while waiting to go home, I decided to go to the pictures. It was a shilling in. The lady at the ticket window took one look at me and shook her head. 'You needn't pay,' she said. When I asked her why she just smiled and said 'You'd be a prisoner of war, right?' I looked at her in surprise, all four and a half stone of me, and said, 'How did you know?' Brother, what a silly question that was!

The men of Z Force had earlier rescued the last of the six men who managed to escape the clutches of the Japanese in North Borneo – Bill Sticpewich.

Having been warned of the impending massacre of the surviving POWs, he had begun planning his escape. Then on 27 July a Christian guard named Takahara, who sometimes managed to sneak supplies of quinine to the prisoners, also confirmed that the remaining POWs were to be killed. At this time just over 30 men were still alive at Ranau, of whom six were unconscious. The only man he could find capable of escaping with him was Private Algy Reither from Ballarat in Victoria. Sticpewich tells of their escape:

The next day it was impossible to bury the dead because there was no one fit enough to do it. I laid up for the day with the pretence of being too sick, in preparation for my escape. On the night of 28 July I cooked the meal and served it as usual. At nine-thirty Reither and I sneaked out of the camp. When we had moved into the new hut the guard on the camp had been doubled; their beat would be less than a quarter mile around where we had camped. The guard house was just above us and it had a good view of us as there were no sides to our hut.

We got up to the track however and laid low for the next day. We were still in the camp area and could see the general confusion in the camp at our escape. There was plenty of Jap guards' face-slapping by the Jap officers and we saw the search party go out looking for us and return about 5 pm that evening. At dusk we made our way out along the track toward Ranau. We went into the mountains and contacted friendly natives who helped us and fed us.

Although still recovering from being wounded by the Formosan guard, Captain Takakuwa promptly mounted a vast search of the area. He knew he could not allow any POW to survive and inform the Allies of the atrocities he and his men had perpetrated. Then on 1 August he set in motion the final, bloody massacre at Ranau. He called a meeting of his staff and said that it was time to carry out Suga's orders for the disposal of all remaining prisoners. Captain Genzo Watanabe, his second in command, would later testify at Takakuwa's trial as to the methods used:

Three days after Warrant Officer Sticpewich escaped at Ranau, sick prisoners were taken on stretchers up the hill to the cemetery. This was August 1, 1945. There were seventeen of these sick men. After they were killed there were about sixteen left in the camp and these were also taken out and shot on August 1. Eleven of these were taken about 100 metres along the road towards Tambunan and shot. Sergeant Major Tsuiji with a fresh lot of about fifteen or sixteen Formosan guards shot the second batch.

Following this, the camp at Ranau was abandoned. Meanwhile, Sticpewich and Reither had been taken in by Adihil bin Ambilid, a Christian native who hid the men and sought help from Australian paratroopers rumoured to be in the area. On one heart-stopping occasion a Japanese patrol entered the hut in which they were hiding but failed to notice the two men, who were concealed under some grass mats.

Escape had come too late for Algy Reither. He slowly succumbed to chronic dysentery and died on 8 August. Meanwhile Sticpewich prepared a letter which was delivered to the commanding officer of the SRD forces in the area, Lieutenant Ripley. Ripley despatched one of his sergeants with medical supplies for the two men, but Reither had passed away on the day he arrived. A local constable placed the desperately ill Sticpewich on a pony and he was escorted to the Allied commando camp, arriving on 10 August. He informed Ripley that the Japanese intended killing all the surviving POWs back at Ranau but, unbeknown to him, this massacre had already taken place. He also told them that another group of four escapers were on the loose somewhere in the jungle. Two weeks later the three survivors of this group – Nelson Short, Bill Moxham and Keith Botterill – were located and rescued.

Only twelve men managed to escape captivity in British North Borneo and reach home. Eight escaped from Berhala Island, but two were subsequently killed fighting alongside guerrilla forces in the southern Philippines. Dick Braithwaite and Owen Campbell escaped from the second march and reached safety, while Botterill, Short, Moxham and Sticpewich made successful breaks from the death camp at Ranau. There were no survivors among the British POWs at Sandakan.

IN THE FOOTSTEPS OF THE DEAD

During the trial of Takakuwa and his Camp Adjutant Genzo Watanabe, the prosecutor, Lieutenant Ray Balzer, spoke of the heinous crimes perpetrated against the defenceless POWs during the second death march. In part, he stated:

> The heroism of the victims will form an epic in the history of war and comradeship. The iniquities of the accused will also be long remembered. The evidence will show that each day the men who were too ill to continue or who were ordered to fall out handed over their rations and shook hands with their comrades, said goodbye, and were then taken away to be killed. Some were shot in the back, some were killed outright, others were wounded and left to die by the track. There is no evidence that they were buried and the bodies were apparently thrown into the jungle or left along the road.
>
> Of the 536 men who started from Sandakan only 183 arrived at Ranau on 25 June 1945. Of these, 142 were Australians. The accused were responsible for all these deaths and killings. Their orders to their subordinates were that all the sick should be killed and none left behind.
>
> Many foul inhuman crimes have come out of this war, but I submit that this is the worst of all. Over 500 Australians were included in the 824 prisoners in Sandakan camp on 29 May last. Excepting for a very small few they are all dead now and hundreds of homes in England and Australia are empty because of the iniquities, the murders and massacres committed at the instigation of Captain Takakuwa and Captain Watanabe, and undoubtedly this is the greatest mass murder of Australians which has ever been committed.

I submit that these cold-blooded murders and massacres will form one of the filthiest pages in the history of this war. Death by shooting is too good for the accused. The ignominy of their crimes deserves the greatest ignominy in punishment and I submit that death by hanging is the least punishment which these foul crimes merit.

Defiant to the end, Captains Susumi Hoshijima and Takeo Takakuwa of the Imperial Japanese Army were tried in an Australian Military Court and found guilty of war crimes relating to the deaths of the Australian and British prisoners of war. Takakuwa was hanged at Rabaul on 16 March 1946 and Hoshijima followed him to the gallows on 6 April, in company with Watanabe. The general commanding the 37 Japanese Army in Borneo, Masao Baba, was convicted of ordering the death marches and was also hanged in Rabaul on 7 August 1947.

At the conclusion of the remembrance service held at the Kirribilli Ex-Service Club in 1992 a plaque of dedication was unveiled on a wall of the club. The text reads in part:

This plaque was unveiled by Father John Brendan Rogers, O.F.M., Chaplain Sandakan and Kuching P.O.W. Camps, British North Borneo 1943–1945 on August 1, 1992. In Memory of 1800 Australian & 750 British members of the armed forces whilst prisoners of the Japanese at Sandakan during World War II. There were only six survivors. The 33 remaining survivors from the death marches were callously shot by the Japanese August 1, 1945. The losses would have been greater had not the Japanese removed all but 12 of the officers to Kuching in 1943. We will remember them.

Looking back over half a century, Nelson Short can never forget or forgive what the Japanese did to his mates and comrades in arms. As a result he came back to Australia angry and intolerant. He worked for a time as a lift driver at City Mutual, then held jobs in a timber mill and a textile factory. He subsequently worked through to his retirement with the Water Board. Suffering from angina and chronic ill-health, he applied to the Repatriation Commission for a TPI disability allowance, but this was refused. He took the Repatriation people to court and the decision was overturned. The newspapers hailed Nelson Short as 'a forgotten hero' and his wartime escape as 'a kind of miracle'.

The passing years may have mellowed his outlook on many things, but the wartime memories remain vivid.

How many times have I been asked why I was spared? Yes, it's a miracle, isn't it? How many times was I dead, I mean to say? When I started on that march and I was swollen up with beri-beri, and the sinews were hanging out of two toes with ulcers, that old chap told me to stop behind, but I went. Within four or five days the beri-beri had left me; within about six days the ulcers had all cleared up on my feet, but the other men got worse. I can't explain that – I cured up. I healed, and the other men got worse. I never ever thought I'd die, never entertained the thought of dying, but always entertained the thought of escaping – always.

How do I feel about the Japanese these days? I hate every Japanese and the young ones and every one of them that ever was. If it happened tomorrow they'd do the same things; it's born in them. These rotten animals chopped heads off all over Singapore and stuck them on spikes in the streets – men and women, and for nothing.

Down at the wharves someone might pinch a bit of tobacco leaf and get caught; they'd make everyone else stand around and, swish, cut off his head. You could hear the hiss of the blood, and then the head would turn white, the blood all gone. They're animals. I watched one Jap cutting off a head and joking and laughing. As he laughed he turned his sword around and touched the back of the blade on the poor bloke's neck. It was a big joke for him. Then he turned it around and, chong, off came the head.

Colleen, my wife, she's been my salvation. I came back in a terrible state of anxiety, a bit of a madman I guess. But when I met Colleen a few years back she pulled me out of everything, by understanding and being compatible in every way. She pulled me through. These days we travel all over the place, and have been right around Australia.

I had a lot of years of hell, but it's better to talk rather than bottle it up inside you. I've been back to Borneo three times since the war, the first in 1981, and I got pretty sick. It's hard going somewhere when in your mind you've got this awful picture of the brutality that went on there. But I also remember with gratitude the small kindnesses of those native people. They risked terrible reprisals from the Japanese, but smuggled us food when we were starving, aided us when we fell, and sheltered us when we fled. And that's one thing worth remembering.

Nelson Short was lost to a heart attack at the age of 78 while on a flight to Broome on 14 October 1993, and Keith Botterill passed away from emphysema on 25 January 1997, aged 72. The last of the six Sandakan escapers, Owen Campbell, died in an Adelaide hospital on 5 July 2003. He was 87 years old.

IN THE FOOTSTEPS OF THE DEAD

From walking in the footsteps of the dead,
Treading the selfsame earth, the grass, the mud,
The upland stone, the roots that ridge the track,
Taking the only path, their path, between
The jungle and the jungle – that green cage
Which does not hold the teeming life within
From reaching out with tendril, frond and thorn
As though to stay what it would soon devour . . .

From walking in the footsteps of the dead,
Feeling their presence in a rotted boot,
A blaze upon a tree that marks a grave,
A bullet scar still unhealed in the bark,
A scrap of webbing and an earth-stained badge,
A falling bamboo hut, a giant tree
They rested at; this log, this creek,
This climb that runs the sweat into your eyes –
Though you aren't laden, fevered, driven, starved
. . . You tell yourself you know how they went by.

– Colin Simpson

6

AIRMEN ON THE RUN

It was a stock German phrase, one heard by many a serviceman taken prisoner, and it would mark for them the beginning of a strange new life; one filled with locked doors, barred windows, guards and guard dogs, and barbed wire fences. Just six words, but for those to whom they were directed it signalled the end of freedom and the beginning of an uncertain future: *'Für Sie, ist der Krieg vorbei!'* ('For you, the war is over!'). Over the six-year course of the European war, 1475 Australian airmen would find themselves burdened with the unwanted tag of *Kriegsgefangener* – a prisoner of war.

Early on in the war, captured Allied officers were sent to their own purpose-built prison camps, called Oflags (*Offizierlager*), while enlisted personnel were held in camps known as Stalags, short for *Mannschaft-Stammlager* – 'for men other than officers'. These Stalags were originally set up as base camps for outside working parties, but captured airmen soon created a whole new problem for the Germans. Wholly comprised of officers and NCOs, they could legally only be held in non-working camps, which meant that a special camp had to be constructed so that all captive air force personnel could be kept in one place. This special camp became known as Stalag Luft I, but as the war continued to engulf Europe, the number of airmen taken prisoner meant that more camps were required. From early 1942 on, the sprawling, purpose-built Stalag Luft III at Sagan in Lower Silesia became the central camp for air force prisoners, including most of the Australians captured. Two years later the mass tunnel escape of seventy-six airmen, an audacious but ultimately tragic undertaking which came to be known as 'The Great Escape', led to the cold-blooded murder of fifty recaptured escapers.

Before this tragedy, escape was not only regarded as an officer's duty, but something to which many prisoners of all nationalities, ranks and services dedicated many of their waking hours. Fortunately, the German hierarchy in most camps – particularly those at air force camps controlled by the Luftwaffe – generally obeyed the rules of the Geneva Convention, which dictated that any prisoner involved in an escape attempt could only serve a short period of imprisonment in solitary confinement before being released back into the main camp.

Altogether, forty-one Australian airmen managed to escape from German prisoner of war camps, although only five eventually made it back to England through neutral territory.

A number of RAAF prisoners changed identities with enlisted men from working camps, where escape was markedly easier. Nineteen Australians were able to evade their captors using this ruse, principally from camps located at Lamsdorf (Stalag VIIIB) and Mühlberg (Stalag IVB). Official records also reveal that of the eleven air force prisoners who finally made it back to England or the Allied lines from the Lamsdorf camp, three were Australians. One of the most persistent was Flight Lieutenant Keith Bruce Chisholm from Balgowlah, New South Wales.

Keith Chisholm was both courageous and patriotic in serving his country at war, much like his father, Kenneth, a member of the original 17th Battalion, AIF, who had fought and been wounded at Gallipoli in August 1915. Following pilot training in Canada, Chisholm was assigned to fly Supermarine Spitfires with No. 452 (RAF) Squadron, one of three such squadrons mostly comprised of Australians. Within weeks of the squadron's formation it had accounted for 22 enemy aircraft – the highest number scored by any squadron in Fighter Command at that time. This was hardly surprising, considering that two of Fighter Command's most aggressive and successful pilots, Brendan ('Paddy') Finucane and Keith ('Bluey') Truscott, were well trained and ready to strap on a Spitfire in defence of Britain. Over his ninety missions, Chisholm managed to shoot down six enemy aircraft, for which he would later be awarded the Distinguished Flying Medal. But then his luck ran out.

On 12 October 1941, in an uncharacteristic moment of inattention while chasing an enemy aircraft, he was caught by surprise in a hail of bullets from an attacking Messerschmitt. When the crippled Spitfire began belching smoke and spiralling down, Chisholm was forced to bail out over the Channel, in the area of the Pas de Calais. A German search patrol plucked him from the icy waters a mile offshore and hauled him into their boat. While his squadron colleagues back at RAF Kenley anxiously waited to hear if he had survived the crash, Chisholm became a prisoner of the Luftwaffe. Following mandatory interrogation by Luftwaffe personnel he was sent to the German prison camp designated Stalag VIIIB at Lamsdorf, Silesia, located between Breslau and Oppeln. He would spend the next eight months at Lamsdorf in a state of frustration, always on the lookout for any opportunity to escape. During this time he was promoted to the rank of pilot officer.

Chisholm knew that one of several working parties sent outside the camp could present him with a perfect opportunity to escape, but airmen were strictly excluded from joining these parties. Nevertheless, in June 1942 Chisholm and Flight Sergeant Archie Stuart, also from 452 Squadron, managed to trade identities with two willing Australian soldiers and following cursory identity checks were marched out of the camp on a work detail to nearby rail lines. One moonless night, while locked into an old flour mill for the evening, they were able to rip up a number of floorboards and make good their escape, along with another dozen or so men who decided it was a good idea. In the ensuing chaos, Chisholm and Stuart became separated, and while Stuart was later recaptured, spending the rest of the war in captivity, Chisholm fled in company with a Canadian and an Englishmen. They were still dressed in their uniforms, which necessitated travelling by night. By day they stayed hidden from enemy patrols, and with the use of a rough map cautiously made their way along secondary roads towards Czechoslovakia, where they hoped to link up with some helpful patriots.

After eleven days' hard slogging, the three escapees finally made it to the large Morovian capital of Brno, where they furtively knocked on the cottage door of the city mayor, who was known to be sympathetic to escapers and might be able to arrange their passage out of the country. Once they had identified themselves they were hurriedly ushered in, and to their joy were presented with a welcome hot meal. Just as they had finished eating the cottage door burst open and they were confronted by a number of armed German policemen.

They later learned to their dismay that a German-appointed town mayor now occupied the house, and he had secretly called the police while his 'guests' were enjoying their meal. Following two weeks of relentless interrogation and severe beatings in a Gestapo prison, Chisholm was finally sent back to Lamsdorf, spending several days in the camp hospital as he recovered from injuries he had suffered at the hands of the Gestapo.

More determined than ever to escape, he fell into conversation with another hospital patient, the legendary legless fighter pilot, Wing Commander Douglas Bader. Bader was also keen to escape, despite his obvious handicap of two prosthetic limbs, and they agreed their best chance was to join another work party and try to steal an aircraft, which they would fly back to England.

Joining forces with another two RAF airmen, air gunner Flight Lieutenant John Palmer and Sergeant Pilot Geoffrey Hickman, the four men were able to change identities with soldiers who were scheduled to carry out manual labour at a smaller working camp, fortuitously located near Gleiwitz (Gliwice) airfield, right by the German–Polish border. If their luck held, Chisholm and Bader hoped to locate an untended Me 109 and fly it across the channel, obviously trying to avoid being shot down by one of their own fighters. The switch subterfuge worked: following cursory identity checks all four men were escorted under guard out of Lamsdorf.

Unfortunately, the plan quickly unravelled due to Bader's reputation and high profile with German authorities – especially the Luftwaffe. A surprise medical examination of the patient known as Douglas Bader revealed that the handicapped airman now possessed two perfectly good legs. The British soldier who had volunteered to take Bader's place for the escape was unable to explain this little anomaly and frantic security checks subsequently found that both Bader and Palmer had somehow absconded from the camp. Armed patrols were immediately alerted and despatched to scour the surrounding countryside.

One obvious place to check was the Gleiwitz work party. Overseen by a German Feldwebel (sergeant) and a small group of armed guards, the work party was ordered to form up, and once they were assembled the Feldwebel ordered them all to drop their trousers. It was quite clear to those in the know they were looking for someone sporting a pair of tin legs. At this, Bader knew the game was up, so he stepped forward and identified himself, much to the German's surprise and satisfaction. That was not the end of it, however, as the officer then referred to a list, looked up, and asked Lieutenant John Palmer to step forward. Knowing he had to give the other men a chance to escape, Palmer sighed, stepped forward, and was also taken into custody. No other names were read out.

Chisholm and Hickman were relieved when the German party finally moved off with Bader and Palmer, which meant they were not looking for anyone else. As part of their escape plan, the two airmen had already teamed up with Nick Carter, a Polish Jew who had been captured in Greece and was pretending to be a British soldier. Carter was able to converse in Polish, German and English – very important attributes when attempting to cross hostile enemy territory. Following the arrest of Bader and Palmer they had also recruited for their escape an American pilot from the Canadian Air Force, Charles McDonald.

Once the fuss had died down at Gleiwitz, the four men were able to break away from the camp, eventually making it all the way to Poland. Here, hungry and exhausted, they met up with members of the Polish Resistance near Oświęcim in November 1942. With the colder weather and deep snow making any overland travel both difficult and dangerous, they elected to stay in Warsaw and help the Resistance smuggle Allied soldiers across the Polish border. It was hazardous work, with violent death everywhere – some thirty to forty people were being executed by the Germans every day – but Chisholm felt he was finally doing something useful after so many months of dull routine and monotony stuck in a German prison camp. Having accepted his offer of assistance, the powerful Polish underground movement placed him with a counterespionage cell, where he was appointed officer-in-charge of all escaped British POWs who had reached the city. His principal task was to ensure they had proper food, clothing and shelter. During this time, Chisholm was secretly boarding in the home of Halina Kozubowska, a woman who had been a lawyer before the war but joined the Polish resistance movement in Warsaw in 1939.

Chisholm had soon learned sufficient Polish to get by in most certain situations. Several times he was stopped in the streets and asked for his papers. Aware this was bound to happen, he was always well dressed and groomed, posing as a representative of the large Polish firm Spotanski and Company, dressed in a Homburg hat, beaverskin coat, and even spats. His papers had been expertly forged, so he was always cleared to proceed.

Despite this, the risks involved in his clandestine work became all too obvious when Nick Carter's identity was somehow exposed. He was arrested, interrogated and then taken to a park, where he was summarily executed by a German firing squad. Soon after, another of Chisholm's companions, Geoffrey Hickman, was also seized by the Gestapo, interrogated and executed. The third escapee,

McDonald, had seen enough and following his request in March 1943 was quickly smuggled out of the country.

Twelve months later, having spent sixteen perilous months in Warsaw, Chisholm also felt it was time to move on. He had teamed up with a German-speaking Dutch naval officer, Lieutenant Fritz Kruimink, a recent arrival in Warsaw after escaping from the notorious castle prison, Oflag IVC, Colditz. One evening the two men were strolling through the Powisle district of Warsaw and discussing their plans as they approached the Kierbedź Bridge. Without warning, a German sentry appeared out of the shadows and demanded to see their papers. The sentry seemed satisfied with Chisholm's papers but grew suspicious of the Dutchman and began ordering him away at gunpoint. Chisholm quietly followed the two men, and then he seized his chance. Recalling his days as a Rugby player at high school, he dived at the legs of the sentry in a perfectly executed tackle. The surprised German yelled out before hitting his head and toppling over the riverbank, breaking through the thin ice still crusting the Vistula, and disappeared in the freezing waters. The two men then fled for their lives.

With an increased sense of urgency for Chisholm's safety following this incident, the Polish underground supplied him with a fresh set of false papers and some money, then he and Kruimink caught the first in a series of military trains on 23 March 1944, intending to make their way to Brussels via Germany and Holland. Chisholm was now travelling as a civilian Belgian in the German army, helped immeasurably on the journey by the fact that his Dutch companion spoke perfect German.

With Kruimink doing most of the talking for them, the two men later boarded another train and to their relief were able to pass through a Gestapo control post on the German–Polish border, finally arriving in bomb-damaged Berlin at 7 a.m. without incident. They had several hours to wait until they could catch their onward train into Holland, which they spent lurking in cafes and movie theatres. Chisholm later recalled that it had been a pleasant sort of day until 700 Allied bombers flew overhead and 'pounded the hell out of the place'. Eventually they boarded the train on the next leg of their journey.

Although they had earlier been informed they would not need special frontier passes to cross into Belgium, their journey nearly came to an abrupt end in the south-eastern Dutch city of Venlo, just two miles from the Belgian–Dutch border, when their lack of the necessary passes was challenged by rail guards and they were escorted off the train. The forged papers were seized for further examination while Chisholm and Kruimink were escorted to Gestapo headquarters in Aachen for questioning. They found they had been misinformed about the need for border passes, but Kruimink convincingly protested their innocence in fluent German. Finally the authorities relented, handing back their papers, along with the correct border passes, and they were allowed to proceed.

There were still many obstacles to face. Before reaching Brussels they had to survive three Gestapo inspections and two military inspections at the border, but were passed through each time. On reaching the Belgian capital their next task was to arrange passage to Paris. The two men finally reached the French capital on 10 May. Once they had successfully made contact with the French Underground, the escapers decided to join the French Forces of the Interior (FFI) and assist them in their covert operations. Chisholm began by transmitting secret information to London's War Rooms, an underground bunker-like command centre situated beneath the Whitehall district in Westminster. It was here that vital intelligence was gathered from every theatre of the war, and a daily report prepared for Prime Minister Winston Churchill, who in turn could also communicate via a special telephone line directly to the US President, Franklin Roosevelt. Chisholm also became a bodyguard and chauffeur to the leader of the Underground, Colonel Henri Rol-Tanguy, and was overjoyed when he heard about the Normandy landings early in June. He was still in Paris when the city was finally liberated, with the German garrison surrendering the French capital on 25 August 1944.

Keith Chisolm arrived back in Australia on 14 February 1945, where he was duly awarded the Military Cross for his 'ingenuity and outstanding courage and determination' and his 'dogged persistence and careful planning' in making a successful escape from Germany. He would also receive Poland's Gold Cross for his many and dangerous activities while serving with the Polish resistance movement.

On 3 July 1942, Sydney-born Warrant Officer William Gerald ('Kleet') Reed was the rear gunner on an all-Australian crew aboard a Wellington Mark IV operated by No. 460 (RAAF) Squadron. They were heading back to RAF Binbrook, Lincolnshire, from their assigned target of Bremen in northern Germany at around 8000 feet when they flew directly into a savage flak barrage near the city of Vechta in Lower Saxony, near the Dutch border. The port engine received a direct hit and immediately exploded into flames. As the stricken Wellington began spiralling downwards, the pilot, Flight Sergeant Arthur Johnston, yelled that he had lost control and ordered everyone to bail out. Four of the crew managed to evacuate in time, but the second pilot, Sergeant Darryl Downing, only managed to get out when it was far too late and his parachute did not have time to open. Arthur Johnston was still at the controls when the Wellington bomber slammed into the ground, erupting in a massive fireball. Meanwhile, wireless operator Bill Taylor's parachute had deployed after he leapt out, but sadly he drifted into some high tension wires and was electrocuted.

On landing, Bill Reed was in considerable pain and realised that he had dislocated his shoulder. Over the next four hours as he aimlessly walked from the crash site he tried but failed to shove it back into place. In desperation he knocked on the door of a farm-house and asked the surprised occupant for help. The man said he would summon a doctor, but instead rang the local police station, and soon after an armed policeman arrived along with a curious town bürgermeister. Once they had checked Reed's story – which meant taking them back to the crash site and locating his parachute – they escorted him to a nearby airfield where an air force doctor adminis-tered a general anaesthetic and fixed his shoulder. The next stop was the bürgermeister's office, where he was surprised to find fellow crew members, observer Max Wyllie and wireless operator/gunner David Radke, seated under guard. Both men had been injured after bailing out – Wyllie suffering from a badly strained back and Radke was limping with a sprained ankle. They told Reed that the other three crewmembers were dead – they'd been shown some of the men's personal effects retrieved from the scene of the crash.

The three men were then handed over to the Luftwaffe, and driven under guard to a reception centre for captured aircrew outside Frankfurt. Administered by the Luftwaffe, Dulag Luft (short for

Durchgangslager der Luftwaffe, or transit camp of the air force) was where skilled officers tried to learn all they could from newly captured and therefore psychologically vulnerable airmen before sending them to a permanent POW camp. This included asking them to fill out information on bogus Red Cross forms. But Reed – like all airmen – had been forewarned about these tactics and refused to give any details apart from the standard name, rank and service number. Bullying and physical tactics were rarely used during these interrogations, and torture was never employed. After five days, all three crewmembers were sent off to Stalag VIIIB, located near the small south-western Polish town of Lamsdorf (now called Lambinowice), around 25 kilometres from the border with the Czech Republic in what used to be known as Upper Silesia.

Bill Reed's escape attempt exploits began soon after his arrival at the camp. On 20 September 1942, he was caught in a futile attempt to cut through the camp's wire fence along with two other prisoners. A guard opened fire and a bullet went through Reed's food bag before they surrendered. Two months later, along with the other prisoners at Lamsdorf, Reed's hands were tied in front of him with a stout cord. Later, the cord was replaced by a set of steel manacles with just twelve inches of play between them. The prisoners were informed the manacles had to remain on for eighteen hours each day, apparently in reprisal for the tying of the hands of German troops captured by Allied forces at Dieppe before they were loaded onto barges for transportation to POW camps in England. It only took a few minutes for the prisoners to find they could easily slip the manacles off their wrists, and this bit of foolishness ended soon after.

Meanwhile, Reed had befriended a young German-speaking Viennese named Egon Blumenthal, who was passing himself off as an Australian sergeant named Hayes. By arrangement in early April 1943, Reed changed identities with an English sergeant, Harry Bagshaw, of the Royal Engineers, while Blumenthal swapped places with a New Zealand soldier named Sutton. They planned to be sent on a work party going to a stone quarry, and everything went well. Once they'd reached the quarry on 17 April, the two men managed to slip away unseen. Three days later they reached the Polish seaport of Stettin and were able to sneak onto a Swedish ship. Hiding in a lifeboat, they became trapped when a Swedish sailor unknowingly lashed down its cover, sealing them inside. Unfortunately they were found by one of the crew during checks before the ship sailed. Though sympathetic to their plight, the sailor feared reprisals against the crew and reported them to a German patrol. They were handed over to the Gestapo on 24 April.

After several days of interrogation, during which his identity was confirmed, Reed was sent to a German prison on 2 May, from where he was taken under guard and returned to Stalag VIIIB. On arrival back at the camp he was shocked to learn that fellow crewman Sergeant Wyllie, who had escaped Lamsdorf around the same time, had been shot dead after being recaptured near Krakow.

Max Wyllie's time in captivity had been somewhat eventful, but in April 1943, he also managed to change identities with a willing NCO and escaped from a work party at Tarnowitz along with fellow POW Joseph Terry. On 22 April they were recaptured near Krakow on a railway line between Trzebinia and Kressendorf by German Special Service security patrolman Alfred Gebauer and a Polish railway policeman, Stanislaw Krakowski. As soon as they had admitted to being escaped Allied POWs, Gebauer unholstered his pistol and callously shot Maxwell Wyllie twice in the chest at close range. Wyllie was just twenty-seven years old and was initially buried in Kressendorf Cemetery, Poland. In 1945 a war grave investigation unit found his burial location and his remains were reinterred in the British Military Cemetery in Krakow Cemetery. He was Mentioned in Despatches in June 1944. It has never been established whether Gebauer was ever charged or even punished over the brutal murder of an unarmed, surrendered Allied escaper.

Sergeant Reed's third escape bid once again relied on departing Stalag VIIIB on a working party after an exchange of identities, this time with a Jacob Minsky. The work involved railroad maintenance, so he traded his Red Cross food and cigarettes with Polish and Czech workers for clothes and money, and made his third escape attempt on 27 July 1943. This entailed slipping away from the work detail and subsequently travelling by train through Berlin and Frankfurt until he once again reached Stettin on 1 August. Luck was not with him and he was picked up by the Gestapo four days later while looking for a Swedish ship. Further ill fortune came his way when one of the Gestapo officers interrogating Reed recognised him from his previous escape attempt. After spending seventeen days in solitary confinement for his escape attempt he was sent back to Lamsdorf.

Once the freezing weather of winter had abated, and the spring of 1944 brought a new escaping season to the fore, Bill Reed was ready to try again. Since his previous failed attempt he had formed another friendship, this time with Sapper Henry Toch, a German speaker from the Royal Engineers, and the two men decided to attempt an escape together. Toch had been captured near Kalamata, Greece, on 29 April 1941 and spent six weeks in a POW camp in Corinth before being transferred to Stalag 503 (Grube Erika) in June. A month later, was on the move again, this time to Stalag VIIIB. On 10 May the two men were able to become part of an outside working party to the Hohenzollern Grube mine outside Beuthen, Poland. He felt some of his previous attempts had not worked well due to being recognised, so when he changed identities with Private Elykim Wald he had grown a moustache, close-cropped his hair, and removed his false teeth. As before, they joined the work party before it was marched out of the camp and taken under guard to Annahof station for the day-long train ride to Hohenzollern Grube.

Much to their annoyance, just as they were on the verge of making their escape, another two prisoners took their chance, broke free and ran off. As Reed and Toch watched, the guards raised their rifles and shot the two men dead. Although a subsequent thorough search uncovered his escape kit and delayed any immediate plans, he and Toch were able to maintain their subterfuge and remain on the mine work detail. Undeterred, he began carefully assembling fresh supplies.

Their next opportunity to escape came on 11 July. This time they managed to take off from the mine without the guards noticing and once sufficiently clear they changed into civilian clothing they had smuggled out of Lamsdorf and headed towards Beuthen. Using forged papers, they paid for tickets and took a train heading for Katowice, which was in the opposite direction from their intended route. It was all part of a plan to throw any pursuit off the scent. At Katowice they caught another train that travelled back through Beuthen and continued straight on to Breslau. Once there, they caught a series of slow trains to Frankfurt, then once again to the familiar territory of Stettin seaport. After taking a tram to Gotzlow, within the city of Stettin, they waited for darkness to fall and then carefully climbed aboard a Swedish ship. Once Toch had been concealed in the engine room, Reed decided to press his luck and wake one of the Swedish seamen, an engineer. This time his luck held; the man was sympathetic to their plight, and he hid both men under a false bottom in the engine room, where they evaded the standard search by German soldiers.

At seven o'clock the following morning, 15 July, they were greatly encouraged when they heard the engines start, and once the ship had been cleared after a second security search at Swinemünde the engineer invited them to join him in his cabin. The following day the ship docked at Sölvesborg, Sweden, and once they had thanked their benefactor the two beaming escapers caught a taxi to the Swedish Consulate in the coastal city of Malmö.

Arrangements were finally in place to fly Reed out of Stockholm on the evening of 9 August, bound for an RAF airfield at Leuchars, on the east coast of Scotland. The aircraft used was a civilian-registered Mosquito aircraft involved in covertly transporting ball bearings from Sweden to the United Kingdom. These aircraft were also used to return RAF aircrew who had escaped to or made crash-landings in Sweden during operations over Europe. Three days later Toch was similarly flown across to Leuchars.

After receiving proper treatment in hospital for the shoulder he had dislocated two years earlier, Bill Reed was able to return home to Australia at the end of March 1945, where he was awarded the Distinguished Conduct Medal (DCM) for his escape attempts and eventual success. This medal recognises gallantry displayed in the field by Other Ranks, which includes NCOs and Warrant Officers, and is regarded as second only to the Victoria Cross, the highest award for gallantry. Reed would later apply for training as a fighter pilot but this was refused and he was eventually demobbed.

Tragically, on 20 January 1954, Bill Reed was killed in a motor-cycle accident.

In May 1942 a mass tunnel escape took place from Stalag IIIE, Kirchhain, located 60 kilometres north of Dresden in the eastern Germany state of Saxony. Although the camp was only about 150 square metres, housing some 200 NCO POWs, there was one guard for every two prisoners. The men, from the British, Canadian, Australian and New Zealand air forces, together with some from the Fleet Air Arm, had been transferred to Stalag IIIE when the camps at Lamsdorf and Sagan became overcrowded.

It was a classic tunnel escape: a wide shaft was dug down to a depth of two metres below No. 2 barrack, and the tunnel, shored with bed boards, was driven out some 70 metres. On the evening of 11 May the end of the tunnel was breached and fifty-two men managed to make their escape before dawn. When the guards finally realised the extent of the escape, a massive search was organised within a 160-kilometre radius of the camp. Details of the escape were broadcast; the Hitler Youth and Home Guard combined with troops and aircraft to run the men down. Some were recaptured quickly, and all were rounded up within ten days. One barefoot Canadian, his hands held high in surrender, was shot dead by an overanxious policeman when he pointed to his feet, innocently requesting permission to put on his boots.

By coincidence, the same number of POWs escaped from a similar tunnel the following year at *Arbeitskommando* 865, a working camp attached to Stalag IXC (Molsdorf), situated near the town of Bad Sulza in Thuringia. Flight Sergeant Jack Garland (reluctantly accepting the nickname 'Judy') was the sole Australian involved in this particular escape.

Garland, from 97 (RAF) Squadron, was a Lancaster mid-upper gunner whose aircraft was shot down during a raid on Kassel on the night of 27–28 August 1942. He and Flight Engineer Fred Ambrose, another Australian serving in the RAF, were the only survivors from their crew. After receiving attention in a reserve hospital at Duisburg for a broken femur and shrapnel wounds sustained in getting out of the doomed aircraft, Garland was transferred to the hospital at Dulag Luft, a German interrogation centre for downed airmen. After being unsuccessfully interrogated in his bed he was transferred to Ober-massfeld military hospital, near Bad Sulza. When the airman was sufficiently recovered he was sent to the nearby *Arbeitskommando* 865.

This camp was situated on a flat area of ground two kilometres east of the village of Molsdorf. Designed to hold 300–400 prisoners, the camp consisted of a large group of huts surrounded by a three-metre-high double apron barbed-wire fence. A sentry box stood at the main southern gates and two sentry towers, complete with machine-guns and searchlights, were situated at diagonal corners of the camp. Guards patrolled the perimeter with Alsatian dogs, while others sporadically roamed the compound. Molsdorf was basically a transit camp populated by prisoners going to and from hospital, or from one workplace to another, and as such the guards' discipline and watchfulness was not of the highest calibre.

Garland soon discovered that a tunnel was being dug by a group of British engineers in the camp who had been captured at Dunkirk and St Valery. After making some furtive enquiries he was invited to join their effort and escape through the tunnel in exchange for a little work on the project. His escape partner was to be a large lump of a man named Jack Lawrence, a sailor who hailed from Bristol.

The tunnel took about six weeks to construct, with a planned exit about halfway up the side of a stormwater canal to the west of the camp, about two metres above water level. There was very little in the way of security in the camp and on the night of the escape all those who were going gradually made their way to Garland's room. It was a tense time for everyone as they sat and nervously waited for the designated hour. Finally, the bunk which hid the shaft was moved to one side and the hole exposed; a couple of engineers lowered themselves into the tunnel and started work on the final breach into the stormwater canal. A strict watch was kept on the area outside the hut, although not too many guards would venture outside their barracks at night except those in the towers and others detailed to patrol the outside of the camp.

It was growing hot and uncomfortable in the room when the first group was told they could start making their way into the shaft. Being the senior NCO in the camp who was going to venture through the tunnel, the soldiers had asked Garland to lead everyone else out. He later said he realised this had been a bit of a con job.

I think the English fellows had worked it out beforehand that if there was to be any sort of trouble on exiting the camp the Australian could carry the can!

The idea was for us to go out in parties of twelve. It was pitch black in the tunnel, and there was no moon as we emerged into the fresh air. We more or less fell into the canal, waiting till all of our group were in the canal before moving off, but we had only gone a few metres when one of the tower guards swung his searchlight down the canal, bathing us in the harsh light. It was as well we had been hugging the sides of the rough-hewn ditch, as we all merged into the edge and he was unable to see us. Luckily nothing happened, the light moved on, and we scrambled to the far end of the camp. We peeped over the rim of the canal and could see the patrolling guard disappearing towards the *Vorlager* [garrison area], so we quickly ran the forty or so metres to the cover of the woods where our hearts resumed their normal rhythm.

With only the stars to guide them, Garland and Lawrence made their way south-west towards the railhead at Eisenach, blundering at one time into an ice-cold stream, unseen in the darkness. Shortly after they observed a series of flickering lights approaching and froze in their tracks, but to their relief it turned out to be nothing more than a swarm of fireflies.

As dawn was breaking on that morning, 25 March 1943, the two men clambered into a ditch running behind a small village and covered themselves with straw to await the cover of darkness. Farmers came to work nearby, and they spent several uncomfortable hours watching them at work in the fields. At four o'clock in the afternoon a youth aged about eleven, apparently on his way home from school, came tramping up the ditch and trod on Garland's concealed leg. The lad screamed in fright and the farm workers came running over to see what the trouble was. Garland and Lawrence reluctantly emerged from beneath the straw and were soon in the custody of an overweight policeman brandishing an outsized revolver.

The watchful policeman marched them off to the local village and with no suitably secure place to leave them, innocently decided to lock his prisoners in the cellar of a *Gasthaus* for the night. This was quite some mistake on his part. In the morning, when he came to pick them up, he was greeted by an unexpected situation. His two prisoners had liberally sampled the contents of several of the bottles in the cellar, and were in a very happy state of mind. Nevertheless, the enraged policeman had orders to march his manacled, intoxicated charges back to the camp, all the time shouting to the field workers that he had captured some particularly dangerous enemy airmen. Many of these workers were Serbian prisoners, and as the prisoners passed they respectfully came to attention, saluted and cheered. This did not impress the policeman, who'd had about enough drama for the day. He waved his revolver and fired a couple of bullets over their heads, meanwhile shouting abuse that didn't seem to concern the Serbs one little bit.

In all, fifty-two men managed to escape from the camp, and though most were quickly recaptured, one managed to elude the patrols and reached eventual freedom in Switzerland. As a consequence, the camp Kommandant and some of his guards were removed, presumably to do penance on the Eastern Front. Jack Garland was sentenced to three months' road labour for his part in the escape, in direct contravention of the Geneva Convention rules regarding recaptured prisoners, specifically airmen. But he still managed to find some humour in the situation:

Ten days after the escape I was taken to a small village to do our hard labour. An old *Feldwebel* was in charge and he set us to digging up a section of the road. We would just lift the picks and let them drop to the roadway. The *Feldwebel* did his crumpet and after screaming 'Nein, nein, nein!' lifted a pick and demonstrated the correct method of road digging. He managed in five minutes the same amount of work that had taken us all of the morning!

On the evening of 10 August 1942, Sydney-born Flying Officer Robert Gemmell-Smith from Sydney was operating on what he hoped would be the final bombing sortie to end his first tour of duty with 108 Squadron, RAF. He was serving as the rear gunner aboard Vickers Wellington Mark IC DV667 as they headed across Egypt towards a Luftwaffe base located at El Adem, Libya, 13 miles south of Tobruk. As they approached the target area their aircraft came under attack from a Messerschmitt Bf 109 fighter, which the three gunners were able to shoot down. However the Wellington's two engines received direct hits, catching fire, and the crew was ordered to bail out.

Gemmell-Smith, wounded in the ankle, managed to jump out at around 1000 feet, right over the end of the targeted runway and almost straight into a waiting squad of Italian troops. They managed to round up four members of the crew as they parachuted down, blatantly stealing many of their personal effects, including their flying boots. After a period of mild interrogation in Tobruk, the men were taken to Derna, where they had to sleep on bare concrete floors and exist on a meagre diet of watery macaroni. In his wartime diary, Gemmell-Smith wrote that their next stop was a cluster of barbed-wire compounds in the Benghazi staging camp, where there was no shelter or blankets, and they were forced to sleep out in the open, on bare sand teeming with lice and fleas.

'We are starving at present,' he wrote at the time in his diary, 'as our daily food issue is a tin of Italian bully beef (about half the size of a 50-cigarette tin) and a loaf of bread (about the size of a luncheon roll) with a water bottle full of water every two days, and no cigarettes.'

Their only excitement during this time was on 22 September, when they witnessed with great enthusiasm a group of RAF Liberators bombing the nearby port and a newly arrived convoy of ships. As the prisoners cheered the crews on, an ammunition ship and a petrol tanker were hit and exploded.

On 14 October, the prisoners were marched out of the staging camp under heavy guard and marched through Benghazi town and onto a German cargo ship. In all, 2000 men, including 1500 Indians, were then herded into the ship's stifling holds, where they endured a nightmare four-day trip to Brindisi, on Italy's east coast. The morning after their arrival they were taken ashore and bundled into a series of lorries bound for the sprawling POW staging camp at Bari, a little over 100 kilometres further up the coast. Arriving at Bari late in the day they were marched through town and out to the camp. However they were not permitted into the camp until the following day, as they had not been disinfected. Instead, they were placed into a large ditch outside the camp, surrounded by barbed wire. No food or blankets were handed out, and they had to spend yet another a freezing cold night.

'It's a wonder half of us did not die,' wrote Gemmell-Smith. 'The next morning we were taken into the camp and had our heads clipped, but they left my nice ginger beard and moustache. Queer people these Italians, as that seems to be their idea of disinfestation.' Once they had undergone this process, the new prisoners were allocated fifty to a tent, made out of Italian ground sheets. They had to sleep on piles of straw covered by a thin blanket. 'It seemed like heaven after Benghazi and the German cargo boat,' Gemmell-Smith commented.

Conditions at Bari were appalling. The men were suffering from the cold and damp, and were becoming malnourished. Their Italian guards lacked discipline and seemed callously indifferent to the condition of the prisoners in their care. All too soon Gemmell-Smith joined the sorry ranks of those suffering from jaundice and scabies and was taken to the camp hospital. Many of the prisoners he joined there were Sikh troops, and to their surprise he was able to converse with them in their native tongue. Before enlisting in the air force he had lived for many years in Fiji, following in the footsteps of his father and grandfather, who was at one time general manager of the Colonial Sugar Refining Company, and he spoke the Indian language of the CSR workers from a very early age. This did not go unnoticed by the medical staff, who often called on his skills as an interpreter, and when he was due to be discharged from the hospital they pleaded with the authorities to allow him to stay on, but this was denied.

On 30 November a group of prisoners including Gemmell-Smith were loaded onto cattle trucks and driven north to Porto San Giorgio and on to a more permanent POW camp, PG 59, in Servigliano in central Italy. By this time the men were so physically weak from deprivation, disease and hunger that they had to be physically assisted into their new quarters. Much to their delight, they finally received the welcome and life-giving benefit of Red Cross parcels, and Gemmell-Smith was soon kitted out with a greatcoat, an angora shirt, a set of woollen underclothes, a pair of socks and army boots. Even more welcome than the warm clothing were the Red Cross food parcels and fifty English cigarettes the men now received each week. 'If it had not been for the food parcels,' he wrote in his diary, '90 per cent of the boys would have died of starvation and malnutrition.'

Otherwise, their daily Italian food ration comprised of a cup of coffee substitute (generally made from burnt wheat or barley), 150 grams of bread and 28 grams of cheese for lunch (except on Thursday and Sundays when they each received the same weight of horse meat). For their evening meal they received a pint of rice or macaroni 'soup' containing a number of dandelion leaves, with a few scraps of potatoes and onions thrown in. 'You can imagine how long we would have lived on that,' he reflected.

As his health improved and he slowly regained weight, Gemmell-Smith began to look at ways of escaping from his Italian captors and getting back to England. Together with three fellow prisoners he had come to know and trust, it was decided to attempt driving a tunnel out of the camp, and started looking for a clever place to begin. During random searches of their hut, they noticed that while the guards tapped all the floor slabs, listening for any hollow sounds that would indicate a tunnel entrance, their commanding officer always stood on the same concrete slab. It was an obvious place to begin, so in June 1943 they lifted the slab and scooped out the loose dirt with their hands, emptying the spoil into their greatcoats, which they then took outside and tipped down the camp's bore-hole latrines. The slab was then carefully repositioned and a little dirt used to fill any gaps.

Once the entrance chamber had been dug, the four men began work on digging the horizontal section of the tunnel, taking turns working at the tunnel face each night from 9 p.m. until 4 a.m. The tunnel survived several hut searches, and on the evening of 4 September, four months after they had started, the escapers carefully dug upwards and fresh air flooded the 120-metre tunnel beyond the barbed-wire fence. They did not want to waste any time, and decided to break out the following evening at midnight. They were not to know that Benito Mussolini had been recently over-thrown and only a day had passed since Italy's new leader Marshal Badoglio had signed a separate armistice with the Allies.

The following evening they were ready to go. 'Each with a Red Cross parcel and the clothes we stood up in,' Gemmell-Smith recorded. 'We enlarged the hole and crawled to freedom.' As dawn broke they were about twelve kilometres south of the camp. Not wanting to risk being seen during daylight they took refuge in a copse of blackberry bushes and managed to grab some sleep. They followed this pattern over the next few days as they headed south towards the Apennines, until they saw in the distance Gran Sasso d'Italia mountain, which they would use as their navigational aiming point.

Their aim was to keep heading southward down the peninsula and, hopefully with the assistance of friendly locals, find a way of getting through the known enemy front lines. Then they would chance their luck in finding some means of making their way back to England. They would be greatly assisted in this in July 1943 when Benito Mussolini was deposed, arrested by partisans along with his mistress Clara Petacci, and both were executed by a firing squad. Their bodies were hung upside-down in Milan to confirm their deaths to the Italian public. Two months later Badoglio approved a conditional surrender, and the Allies landed in southern Italy to begin beating the Germans back up to the Italian mainland.

By the end of the week the escapers' meagre food supply had run out and they agreed it was time to take a risk and seek the help of a local peasant family. Gemmell-Smith now spoke a useful amount of Italian, so he knocked on the door of a small house while his two companions remained hidden. The woman who opened the door was suspicious at first, but once she realised he was an escaped Allied prisoner she smiled and beckoned him in, telling him to his surprise that Italy had capitulated and they were now 'amigos'. With her permission he called his friends over and that night they celebrated with pasta and wine before being offered beds in the vestry of a nearby church. With heightened spirits they pressed on, until Gemmell-Smith's hand became badly infected and he sought the help of a doctor in the village of Monte San Martino. He would spend the next three months hidden in the village, cared for by the doctor and a local priest, while his fellow travellers pressed on. Unfortunately their luck ran out and they were recaptured, later sent to another POW camp, this time in Germany.

On 9 December 1943, Gemmell-Smith set off again, but winter was setting in with a vengeance. By New Year's Eve he realised he could go no further and sought help in the village of Villa Carucci, nestled in the province of Macerata. Once again his luck held and he was given a good meal and wine, after which he slept in the vestry of the local church. Over the next four months he could not proceed anywhere due to the incessant snow and icy conditions, but local sympathisers kept him safe and ensured he did not go hungry. He then began to hear of increased Fascist activity in the area, and that people were becoming wary of helping escaped prisoners. There were reports of the houses of sympathisers being burnt down and their possessions confiscated. In April he decided it was unfair to stay where he was and it was time to move on, but being forewarned knew he had to be careful who he spoke to or sought assistance from.

Over the next few weeks he defiantly headed south, sleeping where he could find shelter, mostly in barns and caves, and often being forced to steal vegetables from farms, not knowing any more who he could trust. Every so often he would sneak into a chicken coop and wring the neck of a hen, which he would later roast over a small open fire. Occasionally he struck it lucky when a local invited him in for a meal and a good night's sleep. On three occasions he barely managed to escape capture, once even to the extent of racing away as machine-gun bullets whizzed past him. Another time he even had to evade some pursuing German troops by diving into a shallow stream and lying prone in some reeds with his nose just clear of the water until night fell and he felt it was safe to re-emerge, suffering from mild hypothermia.

By now he was in a sorry and exhausted state. 'I was walking around barefooted, as my boots had worn out, and also without a shirt, underclothes or socks. One day two very attractive Italian girls saw me in this state, and asked me the reason, so I informed them and they told me they would try and get some boots and clothes for me. They told me to meet them at a certain spot three nights later.' He did not know whether he could trust the girls, so he managed to contact some local Patriots and explained his situation and concern. Patriots such as these, both man and women, could be found right across Italy during the war, developing offensive operations, committing acts of sabotage, and seeking out military information to pass on to England, greatly contributing to the liberation of their country. They told Gemmell-Smith to meet the girls as arranged and leave it up to them; they would be watching to see what happened. At the appointed time, Gemmell-Smith made his way to the agreed rendezvous place. Fifteen minutes later the two girls appeared, not only empty-handed, but accompanied by two uniformed, armed Germans. As they waved their guns at Gemmell-Smith he put his hands up, but moments later a group of heavily armed Patriots had surrounded the startled girls and the Germans, who wisely laid down their weapons. Now they were the prisoners.

'The Patriots marched me away with the Germans, leaving a few with the girls,' Gemmell-Smith recalled. 'After we had gone about a hundred metres I heard two shots, and the leader of the Patriots said to me, 'They will not betray any more ex-POWs.' The two Germans were taken away . . . I was again free to wander the hills and scrounge and steal food wherever I could.'

On 5 June 1944 he was overjoyed to hear from one of the peasants he encountered, who owned a radio set, that Rome had fallen. Over the following days the good news got even better when he learned that Allied forces had landed at Normandy and were rapidly sweeping through France and closing in on Paris. As well, news came through on 12 June that the Adriatic city of Pescara to their south had fallen and British troops were moving rapidly northwards towards them. Several days later, having passed through the village of Amandola in the province of Fermo, he was strolling down a narrow track on the side of a mountain when he suddenly ran into a young German officer. Once they had both recovered from the surprise encounter, the German seemed to sense that despite his ragged appearance Gemmell-Smith was an Allied serviceman on the run. He carefully took out his pistol, laid it on the flat of his hand, and offered it to the surprised escaper. 'I surrender to you,' he said in perfect English. The German was neatly dressed and well groomed, while Gemmell-Smith was unshaven and dressed like a tramp, but he quickly took the proffered weapon, wondering what he should do next. Gemmell-Smith explained that he was trying to reach the British lines, and could not accomplish this while accompanying a prisoner. He suggested they forget meeting, to which the German agreed, handed back the man's pistol, and with a nod of farewell both men continued on their journeys.

On 26 June, Gemmell-Smith managed to flag down an Italian driving a Jeep from a British Supply Company. Once the driver learned who had stopped him, he told him to jump in and drove to Allied headquarters, located temporarily at the Hotel di Grandi in Chieti. 'I walked into the entrance and was met by a British major,' he recalled. 'He took one look at my dishevelled state and started to laugh, then he said: "You need not say anything; I know who you are, and what you want." He took me in and let me have a wash, then set me down to a very large dinner.'

Bob Gemmell-Smith would subsequently spend two weeks in hospital being treated for a leg infection and the effects of malnutrition. Once he had recovered he was taken to Naples for a debriefing and eventually returned home to his family in Australia and a wedding to his relieved fiancée, Eileen Purves, on 22 August 1945.

7

DEFIANT ODYSSEY

PILOT OFFICER ALLAN McSWEYN WAS forced to bale out of his blazing Wellington IC on the evening of 29–30 June 1941, following a successful bombing run over Bremen in northern Germany. The 22-year-old pilot from No. 115 Squadron, operating out of Marham airfield in Norfolk, was on his 24th operation. For the following two years the young Australian from Rockdale, a southern suburb of Sydney just a short distance from Mascot Airport, was to lead the Germans a merry chase in and out of captivity.

The morning after Prime Minister Robert Menzies' radio announcement that Australia was at war with Germany, 21-year-old Allan McSweyn enlisted in the RAAF. Because he already held a pilot's licence, with the magnificent total of forty-eight hours' flying time to his credit, he was selected in a group of 40 volunteers from all parts of Australia to join No. 1 Course of the Empire Air Training School.

His initial training was taken at Somers, Victoria, and Narromine in New South Wales before leaving Australia in 1940 for further training at the RCAF station at Uplands in Ottawa. There he flew Yale and Harvard aircraft.

The theory at that stage of course was that we were going to be fighter pilots, and the biggest worry we had was that the war was going to be over before we had a chance to get into it! We had started to hear about the Battle of Britain and the supposedly magnificent victories of the RAF.

Most of the 40 managed to pass the course in Canada; thirteen (of whom I was one) being commissioned. We arrived in England just before Christmas 1940, reporting in at Uxbridge, just outside of London. Our course was split in two, with half going onto bombers and the rest onto fighters. I was one of the bomber contingent sent to Lossiemouth in Scotland, where I trained on Wellington IA aircraft preparatory to joining an operational squadron. I was then posted to 115 Squadron at Marham in East Anglia, flying Wellington IC aircraft. My own crew was assembled, and we went on raids to such targets as Brest, St Nazaire, Bremen and Hamburg before our luck finally ran out.

Not too many RAF Bomber Command crews had returned safely having completed as many as 23 operations over enemy territory. But now it seemed to Allan McSweyn and his crew that fate had caught up with them, and on operation number 24 their thinly drawn lucky streak had stretched beyond breaking point.

The flight to Germany was incident-free, but on their final course into Bremen their aircraft was picked out (or 'coned' as they knew it) by searchlights as they passed south of Oldenburg. Flak began whipping upwards, exploding all around the bomber. The port engine sustained minor damage and began overheating, forcing McSweyn to shut it down and drop his bombs on one engine. He turned for home, struggling to maintain altitude above the flak.

Once again their aircraft was caught in the brilliance of the search-lights and a fresh barrage floated up to intercept them. After some anxious minutes the flak suddenly ceased. The crew realised this was bad news, and became instantly alert. Such accurate flak would only stop if night fighters had arrived to take over the task of seeking out the homeward-bound bombers. McSweyn's crew scanned the skies, but as a burst of cannon fire hammered across the fuselage, demolishing part of the instrument panel, they knew they were in serious trouble.

While the rear gunner blazed away at the enemy fighter, McSweyn took what evasive action he could muster on his single engine. There was a brief exultant moment as the rear gunner cried out that he had shot down the fighter, but their cheers quickly faded as a burst from another aircraft slammed into their crippled bomber.

The starboard wing erupted into flames and McSweyn gave the order to bale out. The wireless operator and navigator made their way to the forward escape hatch, where the navigator let the forward gunner out of his turret, and all three baled out. Casting an anxious glance to the rear of the fuselage, McSweyn could not see his second pilot or rear gunner. The intercom was dead, but the rear turret was empty. With relief he noted that the rear escape hatch was open.

As the Wellington began to spiral earthwards McSweyn opened the bottom escape hatch with considerable difficulty and squeezed out, legs first. He hoped there was sufficient altitude for the parachute to open as he felt his flying boots being torn off in the fierce slipstream. He swung his legs further down, then dropped into a frightening maelstrom of noise, wind and fire. As quickly as it had come, the shrieking gave way to a curious silence. Shortly after he made a gentle landing in a paddock, finding himself surrounded by a herd of disinterested cows.

The odds were still heavily stacked against Allan McSweyn. In the two days following the loss of his aircraft he had moved in a generally south-easterly direction, but he was ill-prepared for a prolonged journey across enemy territory. The basic plan was to head for the Dutch or Belgian borders and link up with some local patriots, but the pain in his feet was agonising. Without some kind of assistance, and still dressed in his RAF uniform, it was only a matter of time before he fell into German hands. As chance would have it he virtually stumbled out of a wheat field onto a Luftwaffe airfield and into an opportunity for a truly audacious escape.

Concealing himself once again, the young Australian surveyed the scene. A bevy of fighter aircraft stood placidly on the airfield and a reckless but appealing scheme began to gnaw at him. Would he be able to steal a Messerschmitt fighter and fly it back to England? He pondered his ability to carry out the dramatic scheme as he crouched concealed in the field throughout that summer day.

Around 6 p.m. he noticed a twin-engined Me 110 sitting just 100 metres from his hiding place being refuelled and rearmed, and generally made ready for night flying. McSweyn was relatively sure he could manage the unfamiliar aircraft, given a few moments of grace in which to establish its start-up and throttle procedures. Every so often he caught sight of armed roving patrols, and prudently decided to wait until dark before he made his desperate attempt.

Darkness fell over the German airfield and McSweyn crept out of his hiding place and made his way towards the nearby aircraft.

As he approached the dark bulk of the fighter he saw that the cockpit canopy was open. With pounding heart he gently kicked the wooden chocks from beneath the wheels, clambered over the wing and settled into the cramped cockpit. He quickly ran his eyes over the instruments, and noticed to his dismay that the cockpit and panel layouts were totally dissimilar to anything he'd flown before. He tried to recall the short intelligence rundown he'd received on enemy aircraft during briefings held at the OTU, but to no avail. He might as well have been trying to hijack a train.

The minutes passed as he ran his hands over the instruments, until he felt he at least had the hang of the basic controls. By now he was perspiring freely, but he felt capable of taking off and flying the aircraft back to England in one piece – assuming he wasn't shot down by someone from his own side! That he could worry about later. The important thing was to start up and take off. Making a shrewd guess as to the starting procedure he turned on the petrol, set the throttles, gave a short prayer and pressed the starter button.

The port engine growled and began to turn over, but McSweyn was unable to get it to fire no matter what he tried. He stopped and took another searching look around the cockpit. No good. Despair coursed through him. Should he clamber out and make a break for it? His worst fears were realised when he saw one of the ground staff walk over to the aircraft and peer up at the cockpit. The man did not seem concerned at the pilot's presence, so McSweyn pressed the starter button once again. To his astonishment the mechanic walked casually beneath the port engine, fiddled around under the cowling for a few moments, then called out something. McSweyn realised the mechanic probably wanted him to have another go, so he took a deep breath and pressed the starter button.

This was obviously far from what the German had been expecting, as he was nearly decapitated by the whirling propeller. Not surprisingly the mechanic shouted and dashed over to the cockpit to see what the hell the pilot was up to. He nearly fell off the wing when he found himself facing a grubby, bestubbled, and certainly perplexed Australian. The man finally found his voice and began screaming for help. A few moments later a handful of guards came running over to the mechanic's aid and Allan McSweyn found himself looking down the barrels of some rather unsteady German rifles. He surrendered, climbed out of the aircraft and was hauled off to the guardroom.

Because of his daring effort, McSweyn became something of an instant celebrity among the Germans. When he met some of the Luftwaffe pilots it was almost as if he was back in his own mess in England. They treated him with near-respect, and once the station's intelligence officer had interviewed him arrangements were made to get some medical attention for his feet. He was even presented with a pair of soft leather shoes. Eventually McSweyn was picked up by some less friendly Luftwaffe guards for transportation to Dulag Luft, and so began his life as a *Kriegsgefangener* – a prisoner of war. But for Pilot Officer Allan McSweyn the war was very definitely not over.

Dulag Luft was the Luftwaffe's interrogation centre at Oberursel and McSweyn spent three days sidestepping the questioning of the young but wily chief interrogator, Sonderfuhrer Eberhardt – who had introduced himself as 'the camp interpreter'. The German kept probing away in his seemingly harmless conversations with the Australian airman, using subtlety rather than the bullying tactics adopted by the SS and Gestapo.

Eberhardt was clever at his game, picking up small morsels of information given quite unintentionally by newly captured and disoriented aircrew, and the knowledge he accrued was staggering. Once he knew the prisoner's squadron he would surprise his subject by talking quite freely about such things as the barman at the squadron's pub, the Station Commander's nickname, or even give the names of the local good-time girls. This would catch the young airman completely off guard and Eberhardt would skilfully reel in additional snippets of information.

McSweyn, however, would not play Eberhardt's game, and refused to fill out any details on what he believed to be a spurious Red Cross form beyond his name, rank and service number. These forms had already come to the attention of British Intelligence agencies, and aircrew were briefed to ignore any threats of reprisals if they were not completed. McSweyn handed back the partially-completed form to Eberhardt.

'You haven't filled it all out,' he remarked in his perfect English. 'You must do so, Pilot Officer McSweyn, or we cannot report your arrival to the Red Cross, nor can we notify your parents that you are safe. You will not be entitled to receive Red Cross parcels, or to send or receive mail.'

McSweyn then told Eberhardt exactly where he could file the form, but the German's expression indicated that he was inured to such rejection. As he left the room he said they would talk some more the following day. This they did, and the day after, but McSweyn refused to answer any questions or join in idle conversation. Eberhardt finally gave up – he wouldn't get anything out of this one.

I must say I was feeling very pleased with myself, and at the end of the three days I was told they were putting me over into the compound with the other prisoners. The interrogation period was over, and so I was escorted by Eberhardt and a couple of guards into the main compound. This was great, except that just as I got to the gates of the main compound three of my crew saw me coming, rushed up to the gates, and said 'Skipper! We thought you'd bought it!'

Eberhardt just stood there, with a smug smile on his face. 'So, Pilot Officer, this is your crew; this confirms you were the pilot of your flight, and you were with 115 Squadron!' All my good work for nothing!

McSweyn later learned that their rear gunner Jimmy Gill had baled out safely enough, although wounded in the shoulder, but had landed in a tree and was suspended high above the ground. Being dazed, he had slapped the release button on his harness and fallen nearly ten metres to the ground. He broke his back on impact and was in a bad way when the rest of the crew found him. Without any hesitation they attracted the attention of a nearby German search party and Gill was soon on his way to hospital, where, despite prompt attention, he later died of his injuries. Little wonder that Eberhardt knew what aircraft type they'd flown in, and the squadron to which they were attached.

After six days at the Dulag Luft transit camp the men were told they would soon be transferred to a more permanent air force camp.

The fortress prison camp at Spangenburg, 25 kilometres south of Kassel in Central Germany, was actually divided into two camps; the lower Elbersdorf (*unterlager*) camp of Oflag IXA/H held over 200 British army officers confined in a floodlit and heavily guarded space only 75 metres square, surrounded by barbed wire three metres wide and thick. Being an air force officer, Allan McSweyn was sent to the more imposing, albeit run-down, upper Schloss (*Oberlager*) camp, Oflag IXA, on top of a steep, almost-conical promontory just outside, and overlooking, the village.

The castle was typical of those dating back to the twelfth century, with high walls and bastions, round turrets and a steep-sloping roof. It was surrounded by an 8-metre-deep dry moat, with a daunting outer wall lined with large smooth stones, into which the Germans had thoughtfully placed six wild boars. The sole entrance to the castle was by a well-guarded wooden drawbridge. Although the castle was perched on almost solid rock a tunnel had been patiently chipped out and excavated from a central storeroom. The diggers' task was made doubly difficult by the fact that the vertical shaft had to be deep enough to allow the horizontal tunnel to be driven out below the level of the moat. Almost a year's work had gone into the tunnel when the Germans discovered it. At the same time they located the prisoners' cache of forged documents and the secret camp radio. A few days earlier a supposedly British NCO, who was already under suspicion for being overly inquisitive, had been transferred from the camp.

Nevertheless, by the time McSweyn arrived at Spangenburg, three prisoners had managed to escape, albeit briefly, and there was continual escape activity going on. Having received proper treatment on his feet he now felt it was high time he put them to good use by fleeing his captors. He soon became friendly with a number of prisoners, particularly Warren Sandman, a young New Zealand pilot officer; Squadron Leader Neil Svenson, also from the RNZAF; Nat Maranz, who had flown with the RAF's Eagle Squadron, and an English pilot officer 'Andy' Andrews. After surveying the camp they'd decided that the drawbridge provided the only feasible means of exit. The difficulty was that the Germans knew this too.

The guards' vigilance certainly paid dividends at Spangenburg, thwarting many fine ruses, including those in which prisoners tried to leave dressed as guards, and others in which they concealed themselves at the bottom of laundry baskets and garbage carts.

Svenson and Andrews came up with a brilliant and innovative scheme, and brought in the other three to assist. Their plan required the manufacture of a long rope and a sturdy grappling hook. One of them would toss the hook from a window, hoping it would secure itself against the side of the wooden drawbridge. They would then crawl hands and heels down the rope, ease their way onto the drawbridge and make a run for it. The plan called for a stormy night, with thunder and lightning to drown out the sounds of the escape and driving rain to keep the sentries under shelter. In every other respect they were terrible conditions in which to flee across country.

When a suitable night finally came along, the escapers were ready. With utmost stealth they made their way to an unoccupied room with a camp-made rope and grappling hook. At an opportune moment, Svenson hurled the hook out towards the drawbridge. It did not engage, so he quickly hauled it in and hurled it out towards the drawbridge again. As he began to pull the rope in a second time, the hook snagged and held. In addition to being the featured player in the drama. Svenson was also the senior member of the group, and he had elected to go across first. Andrews would follow, then McSweyn, Sandman and Maranz. The New Zealander started off on his short but hazardous journey along the wet and slippery rope, hand over hand in the driving, cold rain. Then, just as he was within reach of the drawbridge, a bored guard, who had been sheltering in his sentry box, strolled out to look over the side of the drawbridge. To his astonishment he saw Svenson dangling from the length of rope below him, and quickly raised the alarm.

There was no alternative for the others but to rush back into their quarters, hide the escape gear and rations, and clamber into their bunks. Svenson meanwhile was dragged off for questioning, and would later serve the mandatory ten days' solitary confinement for his escape. Soon after the guards barged into the prisoners' quarters and drove the occupants out of their bunks and into the courtyard before conducting a meticulous search for any concealed escape equipment. It was cold, wet and miserable out in the courtyard, but when they were eventually ordered back into the castle it was with the comforting knowledge that the searchers had not uncovered any of the precious escape paraphernalia.

After ten weeks at Spangenburg the prisoners were transferred to Oflag VIB, Warburg, on 29 September 1941. Not only was their new camp an aesthetic disappointment after the grim magnificence of Spangenburg, but the surrounding land, 40 kilometres north-east of Kassel, was flat and uninteresting farm country. Squatting on a low windy plateau, Oflag VIB was a barbed-wire enclosure measuring 500 by 300 metres which held around 2500 officers and 300 orderlies. Newly constructed wooden huts, each designed to hold around 200 prisoners, had been sited and erected with typically Teutonic precision within the confines of the double wire fences. Guard towers and searchlights looked down on the dusty compounds.

Allan McSweyn's escaping habit was soon in full swing. He participated in two unsuccessful tunnel schemes, but finally escaped Warburg hidden in a bread cart. His freedom only lasted two days before he was spotted by a pair of alert soldiers as he made his way across a paddock wearing a passable camp-made suit, which was actually a modified and dyed RAF NCO's uniform. He was returned to the camp, where he served fourteen days for his escape. Then, belatedly, he joined in a well-planned and highly innovative scheme, which led to one of the most audacious and most spectacular mass escape attempts of the war. It has gone down in POW lore as the Warburg Wire Job.

On the night of 30 August 1942 a total of 40 desperate men with blackened faces stormed the perimeter wires of the camp between huts 21 and 22. Each team of ten men carried hinged ladders which had been manufactured in the camp and disguised as shelves in the music room. The camp lights had been fused moments earlier, while carefully planned and noisy diversions erupted all over the camp.

This escape had been choreographed and rehearsed for months, under the direction of Major Tom Stallard. Four teams of ten men had been chosen for the attempt, but in mid-August the Germans evacuated all army officers over the rank of major – many of whom were involved in the scheme. To keep the four teams up to quota, ten air force officers including McSweyn were recruited to fill the gap. After some minor reshuffling, they were given the responsibility for carrying ladder number four to the perimeter wire and getting as many of their number as they could up, over and away. The men were given as much instruction as possible, but they were ill-prepared by comparison with the other teams. On 28 August the Germans announced plans to evacuate the camp, and Stallard put the escape teams on twelve hours notice. Two days later the camp administrators informed the prisoners' senior officers that the move would take place within 48 hours. The escape committee resolved to go ahead with the escape that night.

At 9.30 p.m., with all 40 men assembled in hut 20, the four teams sprang into action. As the lights were fused and the camp was plunged into darkness, the ladders were pushed out through a window. The designated men grabbed them on either side and dashed through the unaccustomed darkness for their allotted place at the perimeter wire. With bedlam all around them from the sudden loss of lights and the diversions, the teams threw their ladders up against the inner wire. A hinged section of the ladder was thrust upwards and outwards so it bridged the 2-metre gap between the inner and outer fences and the men began to clamber across. Reaching the end of the horizontal section, they grasped the end rung and swung themselves down to the ground. From there on it was a matter of a mad dash into the surrounding countryside.

In all, 28 men scrambled over the wire before the guards managed to bring the mass escape to an end. Although most of the fleeing prisoners were quickly rounded up, three British officers made good their escape through Holland, Belgium and France after making contact with some people from the indomitable 'Comet Line'. Allan McSweyn managed to escape over the 'air force' ladder but he was soon recaptured.

Towards the end of the year McSweyn was transferred to Oflag XIB at Schubin, in northern Poland, where the guards were drawn from the army instead of the Luftwaffe. Here he quickly became involved in yet another tunnel scheme, but once again the German guards frustrated the enterprise before it had a chance to succeed.

With a small team of willing escapers McSweyn then tried to recreate the success of the Warburg Wire Job, but this attempt was less fruitful. Twenty men rushed the perimeter wire on the chosen night but even though others had fused the camp lights, the searchlights were on a different circuit and did not go out. The escape was over before it had truly begun.

Allan McSweyn's next endeavour came when he teamed up with a fellow Australian, Tom Gilderthorpe, in a plan requiring them to cut the camp perimeter wire by night. On three separate occasions they began their attempt, but each time something prevented them from getting out to the wire.

The night we finally made our bid for freedom occurred shortly after a warning had been issued that anyone caught trying to escape would be shot on sight. This threat hanging over our heads did not help to boost our morale as we wormed our way across the trip wire placed ten feet back from the main wires – and beyond which no prisoner could step without being shot at. We could work uninterrupted on cutting the wire for periods of only about two minutes before we had to knock off to lie perfectly still while the sentry passed within a few feet of where we were operating. Obviously, it was not possible to make any quick movements or noise without fear of detection.

Since I could not check accurately on the movements of the sentry patrolling outside the fence, we rigged up a warning system. Tom lay in a vegetable patch, holding a piece of string attached to my right foot – and signalled when the coast was clear for me to resume cutting. However, progress was slow, and it soon became apparent that we would not be able to cut through the full set of wires in the limited time available.

Our minds were finally made up for us when the sentry noticed my presence in the wire. Rather than wait to be arrested, Tom and I decided to risk a wild dash back to our quarters. Separating, we ran as fast as we could – zigzagging to reduce the chance of being shot. The sentry fired only one shot – and, fortunately, this came nowhere near us. When we got back to our barracks, we were able to hide our provisions and escape equipment before the Germans arrived to carry out a search. They found nothing.

The two men had also been participants in yet another tunnel, planning to break from it in the spring of 1943, but the Germans imposed additional anti-escape precautions when the tunnel was almost ready and it was decided to postpone the escape.

Keeping an ear to the ground as always, McSweyn learned that the prisoners would soon be on the move once again – this time to the massive air force camp known as Stalag Luft III in Sagan. McSweyn decided he would stand a better chance of escape from Sagan, but that it was essential he enter Stalag Luft III as an orderly. Officers were not permitted to leave the camps, whereas orderlies and NCOs were regularly required to collect bread, laundry, coal, and German food rations. Casting around for someone who might be prepared to change identities, McSweyn eventually discussed the matter with an orderly from his own barracks – Private John ('Jock') McDiarmid, of the Seaforth Highlanders. The prisoners were roughly the same build, and close enough in appearance. McDiarmid was happy to participate in the ruse but, as both men were reasonably well known to the Germans at Schubin, McSweyn decided to leave any identity change until the day of the move.

As any change would have to be permanent, the two men had to switch identity cards. This was complicated by the fact that the Germans checked identities by comparing fingerprints as well as photographs. Taking a bold gamble, McSweyn joined one of the working parties of orderlies carrying bread from the German compound to the prison camp. On his second work detail he was able to steal three blank German identity cards from the administrative building. Returning to his compound he gained access to a typewriter by breaking into the hospital office – and typed out his particulars and those of McDiarmid on the new cards. The two men then planted firm fingerprints on each other's card.

Gathering suitable photographs would now prove a major hurdle. Despite four attempts McSweyn was unable to steal their photographs from the genuine identity cards, but luck was on his side once again and an opportunity came on the day of the final camp check – but he also received a fright.

On that day a number of orderlies were detailed to help the Germans lay out identity cards for checking. McSweyn dressed himself as an orderly, and in all the confusion he was able to obtain the original cards for both himself and McDiarmid. To his chagrin, he then discovered that the genuine German identity cards had been partly typed and partly hand-written. In addition, certain notations had been made against the originals, which would prevent him substituting the ones he had so carefully prepared. There was little he could do except take the German cards to his hut, where he quickly switched the two photos. On his return he slipped them back in before anyone realised they had gone. His exploits in stealing the cards and typing the information had all been for nothing, and he now had to rely on the altered photographs getting him through the German check.

As it turned out the check was anti-climactic, and a relieved Allan McSweyn left Schubin as Private John McDiarmid.

*

It was now June 1943. When he arrived at Sagan McSweyn managed to survive another identity check. To his surprise it turned out that four others had tried the same ploy, but without success.

Once he'd settled in at Sagan's East compound McSweyn began his orderly duties – much to the carefully concealed amusement of his aircrew friends, who were wise to his game. He also made a point of getting to know many of the guards to reinforce his identity as an orderly. But his plans of escaping while on a working party did not come to fruition, as a watchful guard always accompanied them. He took part in a tunnel scheme from beneath a kitchen floor, but they stored too much of the sand from their shaft in the roof, and it collapsed.

Meanwhile the escaping season was well under way at Sagan, and as McSweyn waited for another opportunity to get out he lent a hand as a 'stooge' on a bold and innovative effort by three English-men – Eric Williams, Michael Codner and Oliver Philpot – to dig a short tunnel under the wire from beneath a wooden vaulting horse. No one really gave the scheme a chance.

As the wooden horse tunnel began to edge out towards the wire, McSweyn was approached by Wing Commander Joe Kayll. One of the three escapers, Michael Codner, had come to him with an alter-nate scheme for leaving Stalag Luft III, apparently in the belief that the vaulting horse scheme was too impudent to work. Codner, a slightly built young man, suggested that he cut through the wire perime-ter fence. Then, dressed as a woman and in the company of another prisoner – ostensibly as a man and his wife – walk off as if they were out for a stroll. Kayll approved the scheme, and asked McSweyn if he would care to take on the role of the husband. He agreed, but shortly after this Codner changed his mind, and decided to stick with the tunnel.

History records that Codner made the right decision. The three men tunnelled free of the camp and caught the train at Sagan station. After splitting up and catching separate ships all three reached safety in neutral Sweden, from where they returned to England. Philpot had taken just four days to reach Sweden, where he greeted Williams and Codner nine days later. It was one of the classic escapes of all wars.

McSweyn next decided to have himself sent to a camp for other rank troops, from where escape would likely be far easier. The first step was to adopt a tactic of planned disobedience; he would volunteer for any task organised by the Germans, then refuse to work. Wing Commander Kayll willingly cooperated in McSweyn's bid by complaining to the German staff that his 'orderly' was intractable, refusing even to work for his own officers. He declared himself most unhappy with the man's attitude and requested he be sent elsewhere. McSweyn's suddenly belligerent attitude had already come to the notice of the German officers, and he was warned that if he continued with his ridiculous behaviour he would be transferred to the less desirable camp at Lamsdorf. This was just what the Australian had been hoping for and he maintained his stubborn defiance. The transfer order was subsequently signed and he was sent in disgrace to Stalag VIIIB, Lamsdorf. Here he was destined to become part of a disconcerting statistic for the German hierachy; there were more successful escapes by airmen from Stalag VIIIB than any other air force camp in Germany, with eleven men reaching freedom. One of these was Allan McSweyn.

At that time NCOs were permitted to volunteer for outside work, whereas privates could be forced to go on any outside work determined by the Germans. The course McSweyn now had to take was abundantly clear. When he reached Lamsdorf early in July 1943 he promoted himself to corporal! This discrepancy was argued by an officious German scribe when McSweyn was entering Lamsdorf, but he persisted, citing slow paperwork. The German could certainly relate to this and he entered the promotion details on his card. Such trivialities mattered little to him.

Lamsdorf (later renamed Stalag 344) was a working camp, and had a floating population of about 30 000 troops, with 6–7000 interned at any one time, but the Australian spent very little time there. As soon as possible he volunteered for a working party and was taken cross-country to Breslau. Here the workers clambered aboard a truck and were driven to a farm where, supervised by an uninterested guard, they were to undertake general duties.

On the fourth day of this relatively enjoyable assignment McSweyn decided it was time to make his break. He waited until the guard and other prisoners had moved off to another paddock after lunch, and simply walked off the property, a pitchfork over his shoulder giving him the appearance of a farm worker. He hoped his absence would not be noticed until the evening check five hours later. McSweyn had earlier decided that his best means of escape lay in trying to reach one of the Baltic ports, so he set off for Danzig, nearly 300 kilometres north, where he hoped to board a ship bound for Sweden. Along the way he met a small group of Polish workers and revealed his identity, asking if they could assist him. The Poles took McSweyn to a place where a little-used bicycle was stored and left him, obviously wanting to be well clear when the airman liberated the forlorn vehicle. He made good time on the bicycle, travelling by day rather than by night, as he felt his chances of being picked up on suspicion were greater in the evenings. On the fourth day he abandoned the bicycle and hopped onto a goods train, leaving it just before it shunted into the marshalling yards at Danzig.

Once here, his principal aim was to locate a French working camp and obtain shelter for the night. Through information gathered from other escapers who had made it into Danzig, but who had been recaptured, he knew of the camp and its location. Eventually he spotted a party of 40 Frenchmen under the control of a bored German guard. When the guard was not looking, McSweyn slipped up to one of the Frenchmen and convinced him of his identity. Once the Frenchman had overcome his suspicions he told McSweyn to return to the camp with his working party that night, and to remain in their midst until further arrangements could be made. He then lent the airman his beret and added that the German security was very lax. This proved to be the case, and that evening McSweyn once again found himself a guest of the Germans.

The camp leader was introduced to the airman and promised he would ask around for a suitable ship. McSweyn did not hold out too much hope for success, but agreed to spend another night at the camp. He marched out with the work party the next morning, slipped away at an appropriate moment and spent the day looking around Danzig, pretending to be occupied on some important task. That evening he was relieved to hear that the camp leader had contacted a Frenchman working on a ship which was scheduled to leave for Sweden at seven o'clock the following evening.

It was arranged for McSweyn to go to the wharves on a work detail, taking the place of a Frenchman who reported in sick. All went as planned. McSweyn entered the prohibited dockside area without any difficulty, and around 3 p.m. he discreetly made his way to the coal bunkers aboard the small ship. He then dropped down through an open hatch and buried himself in the coal, leaving enough space around his face to breathe.

It was a long and cramped wait. Finally, after a rush of activity, the ship pulled away from the wharf area and chugged out into open waters. At this stage the vessel had not been subjected to a search, which surprised McSweyn, but as it headed further out to sea he allowed himself to relax a little and even to congratulate himself. His reverie subsided as the ship's engines stopped and she came to anchor. Before long the ship was subject to a thorough search by police or customs officers. He heard footsteps approaching his bunker, then a harsh voice called out in English, ordering him to come out and give himself up or things would go very badly for him. McSweyn stayed where he was, and the voice came again, louder and more impatient. A few seconds later the hatch covers were flung back and McSweyn heard the disconcerting sound of dogs snuffling and barking right above him. They had his scent, but a meek surrender was out of the question for the Australian. Then a new threat was issued – the use of tear gas. Still he did not move.

However, true to their threats, the Germans did use a tear-gas bomb. Because I was so close to the top of the coal, and since I was in a confined area, I found that it was not long before I was coughing and spluttering. My eyes began to stream, and I had involuntarily to give away my hiding place. Then I had to come up.

The Germans did not handle me particularly gently. When they got me to a type of barracks nearby, I admitted that I was a corporal in the Seaforth Highlanders who had escaped. The Huns were not over-impressed with my story and checked up with my POW camp at Lamsdorf. Fortunately, the check confirmed my story. And, since

I could also substantiate my account by quoting my POW identity number (actually McDiarmid's, of course), the Germans sent me back to Lamsdorf.

Before I left Danzig, I talked to one of the Germans who had helped to capture me. He told me that a Frenchman on the wharves had given me away. The Frenchman had seen me on the dockside and had realised that I was not a fellow countryman. Then, when he had noticed that I was no longer present just before the ship had sailed, he had realised that I had gone on board. So he had told the Germans that he was certain an Englishman was trying to stow away. That was why the Germans had carried out a thorough search – and had caught me so easily.

However, when I was returned to Lamsdorf, the same thought continued to dominate my mind: I was still determined to escape.

In spite of the ease with which he'd reached Danzig, McSweyn decided his best chance of escape might lie in going right across Germany, then down through France, and across the Pyrenees into Spain. The biggest drawback to this or any scheme was that languages were not his strong point. Then he met a New Zealand private by the name of Geoffrey Williamson, who spoke excellent German and French. Williamson's escape record stood at two unsuccessful attempts, and the two men decided to pool their resources and expertise and make a break together.

In working out the details they gained the valuable assistance of two Canadians taken at Dieppe – Sergeant Larry Pals and Sergeant Major 'Mac' McLean. These two men, and a Czech–Canadian NCO, had already organised an escape committee for their section of the camp, accumulating stores of food, clothing, money, identity cards and maps. Asked to help McSweyn and Williamson by the three senior Australian NCOs at Lamsdorf – Army Warrant Officer Ian Sabey, RAAF Warrant Officer 'Mac' Currie and Flight Sergeant Ray Sherman – the three Canadians were pleased to help where they could.

The two escapers examined the prospects of leaving the camp on a working party, but they could not take such essentials as camp-made civilian clothing, food, forged documents and maps. A well-built tunnel, which was all but completed, had been dug under the supervision of the three Canadians, and use of it was generously offered to McSweyn and Williamson. It presented them with a heaven-sent opportunity to leave the camp fully equipped for their hazardous crossing of Germany. Next they enlisted the aid of a German Jew in the camp, who spent six weeks preparing forged documents which identified them as French volunteer workers returning from a munitions factory at Blechhammer. McSweyn would also carry a letter, ostensibly from the camp doctor at Blechhammer, stating he was suffering from acute laryngitis – a ruse he hoped would overcome his lack of French.

On Sunday, 19 September, they were ready to go. Unfortunately the train schedules meant they had to exit the tunnel by daylight. This was a tricky part of the operation, as sentries were posted every 50 metres along the wire. While the two men changed into their workmen's clothes the Canadians took charge of the business of diverting the guards' attention. As McSweyn recalled:

To ensure that the attention of the German guards was distracted, McLean and Pals arranged for a game of baseball to take place immediately in front of the sentry box nearest the mouth of our tunnel. In addition, they organised a football match near the next box along the wire – with some lively scrummages going on to rivet the Germans' attention on the game. Our main danger was the sentry box immediately in front of the point from which we were to break out of the tunnel. A fairly intricate system of signalling was accordingly set up to give us the word when to attempt the break. The danger was complicated by the fact that odd German civilians, some of whom wandered into the camp vicinity on Sunday afternoons, might see us.

Williamson and I waited anxiously underneath the trap at the end of the tunnel. It was not until some quarter of an hour had passed – which seemed to us like an eternity – that, at long last, we received the signal to break. To make certain that the German guard remained completely oblivious to the breathtaking events going on twenty metres behind his back, the baseball game suddenly developed into a bout of fisticuffs between two of the players. The fighting had developed into a violent scrap by the time Williamson and I had managed to push the wooden trap off the tunnel, with a lot of exertion. Then we levered the trap up sufficiently to enable Williamson to crawl out. Immediately, he went into some scrub bushes 30 metres from the camp fence. I came out right behind him. Then I lay flat on my stomach while I gradually dropped the hinged trap back into place. Afterwards I scraped dirt and grass over the top. I patted this camouflage in as quickly as I could so that the tunnel location would remain reasonably concealed, ready for use again at a later date.

This was the most nerve-racking part of the venture. A German could come by at any moment, or a sentry might decide to look around in spite of the distractions. McSweyn knew any guard's immediate reaction would be to open fire.

Everything went as planned, and McSweyn soon joined an anxious Williamson in the bushes. Brushing each other down they decided they would pass cursory inspection. Then, taking a deep breath, they emerged from their cover and strolled nonchalantly down the side of the fence, peering through the barbed wire like any of the normally curious locals. They even paused for a few seconds to watch the fight which still raged in the makeshift baseball diamond. At this a guard wandered over and pointed out that civilians were not permitted to loiter near the camp! Shrugging, the two men moved off. They ambled by the German barrack quarters, then past the main gate of the camp, and finally moved onto the road leading to Lamsdorf station.

Their plan now was to catch a train east to Breslau, where they would pick up the Berlin Express, hoping to reach Berlin by 10 p.m. On arrival at Lamsdorf station Williamson put his German to the test, purchasing two tickets with money supplied by McLean and Pals. Ten minutes later they boarded their train.

At Breslau, Williamson bought two tickets for the Berlin Express. On boarding they mingled with the other passengers, most of whom were German soldiers. At 8 p.m. the train arrived in Berlin, having made a stop at Sagan station, where McSweyn noticed some guards from his former camp waiting on the station. Due to his work as an orderly he was well known to some of these guards, so he kept well away from the windows. The guards boarded several carriages down.

At Berlin they placed themselves in the midst of the crush of disembarking passengers, crossed the road and booked into a small hotel for the night. Knowing the Germans checked all guests' papers at a 9 a.m. inspection, Williamson told the hotelier they had to catch an early south-bound train and asked that breakfast be served in their room at seven. The next morning they left the hotel, travelled across Berlin by underground, then caught a train to Mannheim, on their way to Saarbrücken.

McSweyn and Williamson arrived at Mannheim around 10 p.m., but were unable to obtain accommodation due to the devastating effect of RAF bombardments inflicted on the city. In company with many of the local citizens they spent the night in a crowded air raid shelter beneath the railway station. 'This turned out to be a particularly nasty experience since, for some twenty minutes, we found ourselves on the receiving end of an RAF raid!'

While waiting for their train the next morning, McSweyn and Williamson enjoyed a haircut and shave and travelled around the city by tram. They hoped this would avoid the risk of being questioned by the police, who had thrown a tight cordon around the city to prevent those engaged in forced labour from running off during the confusion associated with bombing raids. Later the two men caught their train to Saarbrücken, where they arrived at 4 p.m. Their next move was to contact a man called Pierre, who was employed on a French working party and was in touch with sympathetic helpers. They located him in a working camp in what had once been a synagogue and established their bona fides as escapers. Pierre arranged for them to be absorbed into the working camp, where they spent the night. The following day they walked around the city as if they were members of the working party on a legitimate assignment.

In all they spent four nights in the synagogue before they were introduced to Georges Monclard (thought by McSweyn to be an alias), a French worker from Marseilles with contacts in Metz and Lunéville. Monclard desperately wanted to get away from the Germans and McSweyn and Williamson decided to go to Metz with him. There, Monclard said, he would make contact with another Frenchman who could get them across the border, which the Germans had relocated to 40 kilometres south of the town.

It was a relatively uneventful trip to Metz, where they arrived just before midday. Monclard instructed them to head straight for Metz Cathedral, where they spent most of the day trying to avoid looking suspicious. At 8 p.m. Monclard arrived and ushered the two men to a cafe, where the owner gave them a welcome meal. Following this he took them to another French working party. They were able to remain in the camp the next day, as there were nearly 300 French-men in the place at any one time, to whom the German guards paid scant attention.

They left the camp around 6 p.m. with Monclard and two guides he had contacted. One was a French adolescent around eighteen years of age, and he had brought along his younger brother, who looked about ten. It was unnerving at first to place themselves in the hands of these two young people, but it soon became apparent that they made a living hopping across the border from Metz into France and back again. They seemed to have no qualms at all about German guards or security, and had readily agreed to take the three escapers over the border.

They caught a train which took them to Moyeuvre-la-Grande, the station immediately before the border, and then walked along the main road towards the frontier. Within a kilometre of the patrolled area, they cut across paddocks at right angles to the border until they came to a point where their guide maintained the crossing could be made with ease.

Despite the youth's assurances, it was far from a simple matter. Armed German sentries patrolled the frontier, and some were aided by Alsatian dogs. Searchlight posts, mounted a little over a kilometre apart, illuminated the area and the border itself comprised two barbed-wire fences about a metre and a half in height and about 50 metres apart.

The men decided to cross straight away, so the guide went first, taking his younger brother with him Williamson followed, then came Monclard, with McSweyn bringing up the rear.

Everything went well until Williamson slipped as he attempted to clamber through the second fence. The wires twanged loudly enough to attract a German sentry, who rushed to the scene of the disturbance and held Williamson up at rifle point. For some unknown reason he did not raise the alarm, perhaps feeling that Williamson was alone, but asked his captive why he was in the forbidden area.

We were obviously in a pretty tough spot, for I realised no matter how good a story Williamson told, he was now quite certain to be arrested. Taking all the factors into consideration, I made up my mind to liquidate the guard. Fortunately, the Hun was so excited as he interrogated Williamson that he was totally unaware of my presence as I crawled silently up behind him. I moved so quietly, in fact, that even Williamson did not know I was in the vicinity. Suddenly I made a wild leap at the guard; I got a good hold around his throat. My fingers closed around his windpipe before he had a chance to yell out. My object was to choke him into insensibility to prevent his raising the alarm.

When Williamson and the others saw what was happening they all rushed to my assistance. Georges took the rifle from the German who had, in any case, dropped it when I had attacked him. Because of the stranglehold I had on him the guard was still unable to utter a word. In the circumstances I had no alternative but to go on increasing the pressure until I felt the guard lose consciousness. As soon as I was absolutely certain that he was unconscious I dropped him to the ground. Then we picked up our packs, clambered through the wire, and raced off at top speed!

They soon reached the small village of Aubouié, where they hid in a shed at the back of the guides' house, following which the two brothers took their leave. Following a discreet discussion with a local, Georges Monclard discovered they could catch a bus out of the village, which they did at first light the next day. However, to McSweyn and Williamson's horror, it headed straight back across the border into Germany.

Helpless to do or say anything, the enraged escapers and the highly embarrassed Monclard could only sit and stew as the bus drove to Briey, a minor rail junction straddling the new border line. When they finally left the bus McSweyn tore strips off the Frenchman, who was most apologetic. He later atoned for his error by contacting the driver of a train about to leave for Lunéville, in French territory, who agreed to taking the three men across with him.

Leading the way down to the marshalling yards, Monclard went up to an engine that was taking on water. His new-found friend invited the trio into his cab, where he covered them with a couple of old greatcoats and some sacks. The driver then shunted up a track alongside the carriages he was waiting to pick up, leant out and opened the door of a second-class compartment. When he got the 'all clear' from a guard on the platform the three men leapt across

320

into the compartment. A few minutes later they were handed tickets by the guard.

By now Monclard's bravado had returned, and he soon began boasting to a French farmer and his wife that he was helping two Allied soldiers to escape back to England. It was an alarming lack of discretion and the two escapers cast withering glares at their companion. Despite their fears of denouncement to the Germans, the trip was uneventful and they soon arrived safely in Lunéville. Through Monclard they made contact with Pierre Banzet, a retired businessman and well-respected citizen of Lunéville, and stayed in his house. Monclard elected to stay with someone else he knew in the village.

Banzet sheltered the two men for three days while making arrangements with another patriot – the Chief of Police – who organised some papers and more money and set things under way to pass them through to Nancy. On the morning of the third day two gendarmes arrived at Banzet's home and politely 'arrested' the two men, placing them in handcuffs. McSweyn and Williamson thanked Banzet for his help and his pariotism, and then allowed themselves to be escorted to the local police station. Here they were reunited with Monclard and were provided with some temporary papers and extra money. Their next stop was the railway station, where Monclard, the gendarmes and their two 'prisoners' boarded the train.

On arrival at Nancy the gendarmes directed their charges to a department store where they had photos taken. These were then affixed to their new identity cards, which were now totally genuine. Their next stop was a cafe, where the owner would accommodate them until contact was made with the next lot of helpers in the escape line.

Time passed slowly, with McSweyn and Williamson becoming increasingly concerned at Monclard's open bragging, which reached the ears of far too many citizens. When told to keep a lid on his boastfulness he was painfully dismissive; he would not hear that any of his loyal countrymen could give them away. Fortunately their stay at the cafe went without incident, although the promised contact did not come about.

After a day and a half had passed McSweyn grew impatient. Not knowing how long they could trust the cafe owner, he asked Monclard if he would return to Lunéville and get in touch with the Chief Gendarme once again. The Frenchman was pleased to do so. On his return he was accompanied by the same two gendarmes and another Frenchman by the name of Pierre Lenoir. A sergeant with the French Spahi Regiment in North Africa, Lenoir had come to France on leave and had decided to try for England and the Free French Forces.

With the return of the gendarmes things finally began to happen. The Chief of Police sent word that a mix-up had occurred, but help was at hand. A couple of anxious hours passed before a young woman by the name of Odille arrived and told the men that their future travel was being organised. They would go by train to Lyon, where they would stay with a local businessman and his wife who were relations of Lenoir. Their small group would be broken up for the journey to avoid suspicion. McSweyn was teamed with Lenoir, and Williamson with Monclard, thereby ensuring that each pair had a French speaker.

Five hours later they arrived at Lyon and proceeded to the house owned by Lenoir's relatives.

On their way there the small party had a bad fright when a German patrol cordoned off the street just metres ahead of them and began apprehending citizens. As they watched from behind the barrier the men were thankful they had not moved too quickly from the station, as they would have been swept up in this security blitz. Three or four citizens were arrested, and one was shot in the back as he made a desperate lunge for freedom. The escapers later discovered a German had been murdered the day before and reprisals were taking place all over Lyon, under the direct orders of the notorious Kommandant of Lyon, Klaus Barbie, who was ultimately responsible for the deaths of untold numbers of Frenchmen.

Badly shaken, the party arrived at the house, where they were warmly welcomed by Lenoir's relatives, who proved to be magnificent hosts. That evening a sumptuous meal was produced for their guests. McSweyn was a newcomer to delicacies such as frog's legs and garlic snails, but found them quite delicious.

At 8 p.m. the house was visited by a 19-year-old Frenchman named Maurice de Milleville, who spoke excellent English and told McSweyn: 'You are safe now. We will get you back to England!' It was then that the reality of the escape hit home for the Australian, and it was some time before he could subdue the involuntary tremors and elation which swept through him. There was bad news for Lenoir and Monclard – de Milleville's organisation would only take responsibility for the two airmen. After some fond handshakes and embraces the two escapers left for Ruffec, in the Franco–Spanish border area, with de Milleville and a young woman named Ginette.

Ruffec was the headquarters for an important escape line set up by de Milleville and his mother, the Comtesse, to pass escapers and evaders through to England via Spain. They were placed in the Hotel de France under the care of the owner, François, and later met the remarkable Comtesse, known as 'Marie Lindell', 'Marie-Claire', or simply 'Madame Marie'.

She was a small, dynamic woman with an indomitable spirit: a lover of all things British and a hater of Germans, she was one of the most remarkable persons one could ever hope to meet. Dressed in an International Red Cross uniform with British, French and Russian decorations across her breast, she was very anti-German; in fact she wasn't all that much pro-French, but very pro-English, and didn't make any attempt to conceal her identity, or the fact she was working as hard as she could to upset the Germans whenever it was possible. She was a magnificent woman – imperious in nature (which didn't always endear her to people in France or England), but I could just never speak too highly of the magnificent job she was doing. Her small group of helpers included the Regeon family, who owned a small garage and who were made up of father, mother and daughter (Yvette and Therese), the city engineer Monsieur Cottu, a fellow named Gaston, Armand Debreuil from a local resistance group, and the local Chief of Police, Lieutenant Paul Peyraud.

It is worthwhile digressing for a moment to take a closer look at the incredible life and courage of the colourful 'Marie-Claire'.

She was born Ghita Mary Lindell in Sutton, Surrey, in 1895. Impeccably English in manner and deportment, she spent much of her youth in France, and as the Comtesse de Milleville enjoyed an esteemed position in Parisian society. During the First World War she volunteered as a nurse in England, and later crossed into France, where she joined the Red Cross. She served in the field throughout the war and was decorated for her gallantry. In 1919 she set up home in Paris with her family, but remained fiercely proud of her English background. In 1940 she once again joined the Red Cross, wearing her English medals with pride over those from France and Russia. She soon became involved in clandestine activities, assisting British escapers along their way to Marseilles.

'Marie-Claire' was finally caught and sent to Fresnes prison in Paris. Following her release nine months later she travelled to England through Spain and offered her services to MI9 in July 1942. She then underwent an extensive course in coding, wireless operation, and the training of agents in laying out flare paths and signals for pilots of Lysander aircraft, who made daring, secret landings in France to aid and supply the work of local resistance groups. She returned to France aboard a Lysander and with the help of Maurice set up her escape organisation under the very noses of the Gestapo. Among her many magnificent accomplishments, she was responsible for returning the two surviving members of the famous 'Cockleshell Heroes' commando raid safely to England.***

The Comtesse told her guests that the best way home was to cross the Pyrenees into Spain, then proceed to a British Consulate, or, failing this, press on to Gibraltar. Lieutenant Peyraud, the Chief of Police, saw to it that their papers were right (McSweyn was identified as a deaf mute named Roger Binault), and they were soon eager to move on.

*

*** Six weeks after McSweyn's group had passed through the Comtesse's hands she was arrested by the Gestapo in Switzerland. On the way back to Paris for interrogation she dived from the train in a bold escape bid, but was shot in the back of the head and a cheek by one of the guards. Her life was saved, but she was sent to Ravensbruck concentration camp on 3 September 1944, from where she was released by liberating forces on 24 April 1945. She died on 8 January 1987. One of the bravest and yet least acknowledged escape-route organisers of smaller lines, her *No Drums, No Trumpets* is a fascinating book about a remarkable woman.

Despite McSweyn's eagerness to get on with the six-hour crossing of the Pyrenees, his presence was something of a godsend to the Comtesse. The French resistance people had little practical knowledge of the type of terrain a pilot needed to make even a minimally comfortable landing and take-off, but here was a trained pilot who could assist in determining suitable local sites for Lysander operations. She contacted MI9 in London and advised them of his presence; in turn they requested his help prior to making the journey into Spain.

Accompanied by Peyraud, McSweyn went out into the countryside several times on night excursions, and soon the resistance had a map of suitable and relatively safe landing sites and drop sites. The Comtesse was grateful to McSweyn for his help and suggested to London that he and Williamson be picked up by a Lysander on one of its missions. For all its gratitude, London said this was out of the question.

While they waited at Ruffec, McSweyn and Williamson were joined by two Polish flight sergeants, Bakalarski and Raginis, who had been serving with the RAF. They too had escaped by changing identities back at Lamsdorf and slipping away from a prisoner work detail. It was decided that the four men would cross the Pyrenees from Foix, not far from the border, but an unforeseen problem occurred on their first trip, necessitating a return to Ruffec. A second attempt was also aborted at Foix when they heard of a German blitz on the frontier. To McSweyn's dismay, when a new route was organised shortly afterwards, he had to stay behind. A great danger of interrogation existed on this route, and he was the only member of the party who could not speak fluent French. He was distraught, but understood.

When he farewelled his good friend Geoff Williamson and the two Poles his emotions ranged from regret to envy. He was not to know that this change in plans almost certainly saved his life. The party had started out quite confidently after taking in another RAF sergeant escaper at Pamiers. But as they pressed on the conditions deteriorated rapidly, and within 36 hours Williamson was dead – the victim of the fierce blizzard.

Williamson had grown weaker by the hour, fighting his way through the knee-deep snow in atrocious conditions. Bakalarski was ill as well, with intense pain in his legs. Raginis and their Basque guide decided to keep going; the Pole would press on into Spain while the guide promised to locate some help and come back for the others. He never returned. Bakalarski and the RAF sergeant supported the New Zealander between them as best they could and moved on, but five hours later Williamson died. Eventually, the two men reached civilisation and safety and were returned to England, where they were reunited with an overjoyed Raginis.

Meanwhile, back at Ruffec, Allan McSweyn continued with his covert operations. Two days after Williamson's departure he was joined by four more airmen on the run. They were Captain R.B. ('Buck') Palm, of the South African Air Force; Michael Cooper, an RAF flying officer from Kenya; and two Canadians from the same crew – Flying Officer Harry Smith and Sergeant Len Martin. These were the men with whom he was to make his final desperate journey to freedom.

After farewelling the Comtesse de Milleville they began their journey with a certain degree of comfort, sitting in the back of a truck, but as the vehicle negotiated a winding mountain road the back axle snapped. The group left their truck and pressed on to Tardets, from where they would begin their trek across the mountains.

In talking with the Comtesse, McSweyn had heard stories of escapers being given rough treatment in Spanish prison camps, so he carried with him letters addressed to the British consuls at San Sebastian and Barcelona and to the British Ambassador in Madrid. These letters advised the British authorities that the escapers had crossed the frontier and would be in a certain area. Once he'd added the name of the place in which they were most likely to be imprisoned, McSweyn simply had to post the already stamped and addressed envelopes at an opportune time. The letters, he felt sure, would help to hasten their release by the British authorities.

Around 1 a.m., and led by two Basque guides, they set off by moonlight on what they hoped would be the last phase of their journey. After walking steadily for an hour a light rain began to fall, which soon developed into a steady drizzle, soaking them through. Harry Smith was already feeling the strain of the difficult trek, and by four o'clock was suffering severe chest pains and found it impossible to continue without some rest. They agreed to stop for a while, concerned that Smith might even suffer a heart attack with the exertion. Meanwhile the guides revealed that they would soon have to cross a main road patrolled by Germans, and then over a bridge which was normally guarded.

Leaving Smith to rest for a while in an old cattle barn, the other men reconnoitred the area, hoping to find a way to avoid the patrols. The road did not present too much of a problem, but as they approached the bridge in the darkness they spotted an ominous dark shape, complete with rifle, standing guard. They noticed an occasional small movement in the head of the figure, drew the reluctant conclusion that the bridge was under guard, and withdrew as quietly as they had arrived.

Crossing the mountain stream without using the bridge involved a long detour which would disrupt the guides' plans, so they decided to wait until daylight to see if there was some other option. Morning brought with it something of a shock when they discovered that what they had imagined to be a German guard was in fact an old post leaning against the railings. The 'rifle' was another piece of wood and the movement they had all seen was a bag flapping around at the top of the post.

By the time they'd enjoyed a snack at a small inn on the other side of the bridge, Smith had improved to the point where he felt capable of carrying on. They were soon trudging up a steep incline, but the weather closed in and worsened. The incessant drizzle became sleet, which developed into a snow storm, and this finally ushered in a blizzard. As the snow on the mountainside grew deeper, it became increasingly difficult to walk. Eventually conditions were so bad it was almost impossible to maintain any decent footholds.

At one time the group had to cross a razorback ridge connecting two peaks. The width of the track was less than a metre, with a sheer drop of 100 metres on either side. With a relentless wind tearing at their clothes, the men had to cross this ridge on their hands and knees, but they all completed the tricky crossing.

That evening, exhausted, they came to a dilapidated mountain shack, where they decided to spend the night in an attempt to regain some warmth and vigour. This proved fruitless – they were so cold and wet that rest proved impossible. Discussions had already taken place on the possibility of retracing their steps and trying another time, but they felt they could endure the conditions just a little longer. They had been told it was just a six-hour crossing in fine weather, but the trip ahead of them would eventually take three days and two nights. After their brief stopover they kept heading south-west, knowing that at least they were moving in the right direction.

Halfway through the day their guides rebelled and wanted to turn back. They'd had enough. However, the escapers were now more determined than ever to press on and told the guides they must continue towards Spain, although it was obvious the Basques were feeling the strain as well. They finally agreed, but as the trek contin-ued their protestations grew increasingly vehement. McSweyn and the others argued that the men had been paid well – 15 000 francs each to take them across – and they must fulfil their obligations. Muttering darkly the guides headed off once again.

Mike Cooper was now giving the others cause for grave concern. Staggering uncontrollably, he finally grabbed McSweyn on the arm and gasped that he needed to sit down and rest, but McSweyn urged him on. To remain immobile in the terrible conditions was to die.

An hour later he turned for his periodic check on Cooper, only to find the man had disappeared. He alerted Buck Palm and the two of them trudged back again, treading in their own footsteps. They found Cooper 300 metres away, lying in the snow in a low state. The two men hauled their companion upright, pummelling and slapping his body to restore his consciousness and circulation. When he'd recov-ered enough to keep going they turned and retraced their steps.

Before long Harry Smith began to complain of complete exhaus-tion, while the older guide was showing signs of cracking up. His feet were so badly frostbitten he could barely walk. Soon the man was in such pain that he found it impossible to continue, and collapsed into the snow. McSweyn and Palm sat him up and desperately massaged his hands and feet to restore his circulation, but he quickly slipped into unconsciousness. The remainder of the party now faced an awesome decision. If they remained with the Basque guide in the open, the rest of them would soon die. If they left the man where he was for any length of time, he would never regain consciousness. Taking all factors into consideration, they decided they had to go on.

As they tried to make the guide comfortable, the men were astonished to see another traveller heading through the snow. He was a Spaniard, who kindly gave each of them a drink of light wine he was carrying in a skin water bag. He also tried to force some wine down the throat of the unconscious man. Five minutes later, unable to help further, the Spaniard continued on his way.

Having covered the Basque with a groundsheet, they left him and moved on. Two kilometres later, McSweyn was dismayed to find that Mike Cooper had disappeared once again. Rather than leave him to the same fate as the guide he gritted his teeth and turned back, finding Cooper twenty minutes later. As McSweyn worked hard to restore life to the frozen and almost unconscious airman, Len Martin came back to tell him that a small hut had been spotted, down by a creek bank two kilometres away. They decided it would be best if Martin rejoined the others and brought back help for Cooper.

Invigorated by this life-saving news, McSweyn decided to return to their Basque guide and somehow get him into the shelter of the hut. Leaving Cooper, who had partially recovered, he hurried back through the snow as fast as he could. Eventually he saw the man ahead, covered by a thin blanket of snow, but it was too late – the man had frozen to death. McSweyn tramped back to the huddled figure of Mike Cooper, where he was soon joined by Len Martin and Buck Palm. The three men were able to half-drag and half-carry Cooper down the hill and on to the banks of the creek, where they met up with the others.

The door of the empty hut soon gave way under some hefty shoulder blows. It was well stocked with dry firewood and they were soon able to dry their clothes in the warmth of a crackling fire. Fatigue quickly took over, and in the midst of this comfort they fell into a deep sleep of exhaustion. The following day, much refreshed, the men followed the remaining guide as he led them down the river, hoping they would soon come across a Spanish village.

Arriving at the junction of two streams the guide was adamant they follow the one which branched off. McSweyn and the others were confused, maintaining that the direction of this new stream was wrong. Obviously lost, fatigued and confused, as evidenced by his failure to fully grasp the earlier loss of his countryman, the guide was so insistent they reluctantly fell in behind him. Ten minutes later McSweyn checked their bearings with the compass and decided to turn back and follow the original stream. The others followed suit. The guide, barely hiding his annoyance, tagged along.

Their persistence paid off when they came across a main road which led them to a small frontier outpost. Since they were all in a bad state they gladly surrendered themselves to the startled policemen, who managed to put a small meal together and later accompanied the ragged party to the police station in the nearby village of Utaroz.

The surviving Basque guide was obviously well known and liked by the guards, and he quickly relaxed in their company. McSweyn asked the man to post his precious letters, stating that he should do this before they were officially placed into custody. Eventually they were taken before the Chief of Police in Utaroz, who was unsympathetic to their situation and uncooperative. He did, however, organise some food, although it was given in exchange for a couple of the watches and pens the men possessed. The food was appalling but filling, and over the next two days the men's supply of watches, pens and rings dwindled as they bartered for more of the unsavoury but nourishing food.

After two days they were removed from the gaol and placed under close watch in a local hotel, where all four men and a guard stayed in a single room. The following day, to their immense relief, they were collected by a representative from the British Embassy in Pamplona. It seemed their letters had reached the right hands.

Not long after they were taken to Gibraltar, arriving there in December 1943. Here the four escapers made their farewells before being sent on their separate journeys back to England. To McSweyn's delight he found he was to be flown across the Channel in a Dakota aircraft.

When our Dakota came in to land at Bristol airfield a strong cross-wind was blowing. The pilot, it seemed to me, was not making a particularly good job of his landing. My judgement was, in fact, borne out a moment later. Immediately after touching down our aircraft swung right off the runway, skidded across the grass and bowled over a parked Avro Anson. Eventually the Dakota came to a rather ignominious stop, with one wing badly damaged and the undercarriage messed up. All of us eighteen passengers heaved a sigh of relief at having got down safely. However, though I had made a somewhat shaky arrival, my escape was now, thank goodness, all over. I was a free man at last!

McSweyn's arrival in London and his exhilaration with his new-found freedom were soon tempered by the sad news that his New Zealand friend Geoffrey Williamson had died in his attempt to cross the

Pyrenees. At his MI9 debriefing McSweyn told the full story of his escape attempts, and was on the point of leaving their offices when he happened to overhear another debriefing taking place in an adjoining room, with a trio of men from Stalag Luft III. This turned out to be Eric Williams, Michael Codner and Oliver Philpot, who had continued digging their tunnel beneath the wooden vaulting horse long after McSweyn had left Sagan. Incredibly the Germans had never woken up to this audacious scheme, and the three men had turned their wooden horse escape into a triumph of daring and ingenuity by making a successful 'home run' back to England.

When McSweyn had recuperated fully he undertook a refresher flying course at Cranwell and was posted to 105 Transport OTU at Bramcote, near Nuneaton in the Midlands, training operationally expired crews for transport or civil aviation duties. As a returned escaper, operational flying was prohibited to him, as was any publicity concerning his escape – mostly because of his assumed identity. Jock McDiarmid was still in the camp at Sagan, ostensibly as a pilot officer, and the authorities felt it best that this duplicity continue. McSweyn gave his full attention to the new posting, where he soon became Flight Commander and sometime Commanding Officer.

Prior to being shot down McSweyn had become engaged to a cypher officer named Barbara, whom he'd met on a golf course while undergoing training at Lossiemouth. In fact he had borrowed £9 from her in order to buy their engagement ring. On 6 March 1944 the two were married in Winchester. By gently tugging on a few important strings, McSweyn managed to have his bride transferred to Bramcote.

Allan McSweyn's Air Force Cross, for his post-escape work flying and instructing, was duly gazetted. On 10 July 1945 he was presented to King George VI at Buckingham Palace to receive this medal, as well as the Military Cross for his escape. This unusual combination of the two medals was remarked on by the King, who warmly congratulated the young bomber pilot. Allan McSweyn returned to Australia with his wife on the ship *Rangitana*, arriving on New Year's Day, 1946.

Eager to stay in the aviation business, McSweyn joined Lester Brain's fledgling Trans Australian Airlines and was instrumental in opening offices in Sydney and Brisbane for their first operations. He served as TAA's Queensland manager before leaving ten years later. After spending four years in business for himself, he joined Amatil as a director and general manager of an engineering subsidiary before retiring to Sorrento on Queensland's Gold Coast. Interviewed by the author in 1993, Allan McSweyn recalled that fire in his belly as he set off on his long and determined journey home, and the defiance and never-say-die determination of a young airman hell-bent on escape. More than anything, he wanted to acknowledge the incredible courage, patriotism and compassion of those who helped him along that lonely, perilous path to freedom.

> They were the unsung heroes; I salute them as most laid their lives on the line for complete strangers because of their love for, and loyalty to, their country.

A few months after our interview, on 24 April 1994, Allan McSweyn, MC, AFC, passed away in hospital following a long illness. For this truly bold Australian escaper, the immortal words of poet Richard Lovelace must surely apply:

> Stone walls do not a prison make,
> Nor iron bars a cage.

ACKNOWLEDGEMENTS

I STILL TREASURE THE MEMORY of the truly amazing contacts I made all those years ago when I started researching and writing this book, and while I made sure I thanked each person individually at the time, I now offer them – sadly, in almost every case posthumously – a collective and heartfelt thanks for sharing and trusting me with their stories.

I would also like to thank the following individuals for material used in this book, many of whom are no longer with us since the book was first published.

Chapter 1 Escape fever: Hugh Clarke and Sid Marshall.
Chapter 2 From the clutches of the Kaiser: Henry Lamert Thomas, Neil and Margaret Gibbs.
Chapter 3 Freedom or death: Bill and Gwen Jinkins, Ben Amor, Ron McPherson, Ron Gabriel, Rhyll Rivett, Ian Macrae.
Chapter 4 Tunnelling out of Gruppignano: Bob and Gloria Hooper, Jack Stewart, Bruce Gardiner, Mason Clark,

ACKNOWLEDGEMENTS

Garven ('Snowy') Drew, Eric Canning, Richard ('Dick')
Head, Bill Kelly, Andrew ('Bluey') Rymer, Noel Ross.
Chapter 5 In the footsteps of the dead: Nelson and Colleen
Short, Keith Botterill, Owen Campbell.
Chapter 6 Airmen on the run: David Radke, Jack Garland,
Bob Gemmell-Smith.
Chapter 7 Defiant odyssey: Allan McSweyn.

Material drawn from published sources is suitably and gratefully
acknowledged throughout the book.

I would also like to express my thanks to Dr Joan Beaumont
for allowing me access to her voluminous research on Gull Force
(2/21st Battalion, AIF), and to the late historian Don Wall for his
kind permission to reproduce quotes from his magnificent book,
Sandakan: The Last March. Similarly, other quoted oral extracts
are reproduced with permission from Hank Nelson's *Prisoners of
War: Australians Under Nippon*, which in turn is based on material
recorded for an ABC radio series by Tim Bowden. The late Colin
Simpson's 'Six from Borneo' radio documentary provided further
subject quotes, and the reproduction of his evocative poem on
the Sandakan death marches is gratefully acknowledged.

A former prisoner of war in Germany and longtime friend, the
late Mike Moran, once expressed to me how he felt in looking back
over those seemingly endless years of incarceration:

The French have a phrase, *la nostalgie d'hier* [the nostalgia of
yesterday], and as one grows older one's understanding of that
sentiment becomes more and more clear. The memories and
experiences of our yesterdays are the basis on which many of us live

our todays. The companionship, the shared loyalties, the standards which we hold so dear, the men who were our particular chums – these are all part of the nostalgia as, indeed, is the awareness that as young men we were privileged. Life did not pass us by as it might have done had we belonged to another generation. The nettle was there to grasp; it had been placed within our reach. But its stings, for most of us, had no lasting ability to hurt. Rather, with the passing of the years they became an enrichment to our lives.

In acknowledging with gratitude those who have helped to make this book a reality, and particularly this revised and updated edition, my sincere thanks go to the amazing people at Simon & Schuster (Australia) in Sydney. They have done an outstanding job and in saying that, I must single out the tireless assistance of former associate publisher (nonfiction) Brandon VanOver, my brilliant editors Michelle Swainson and Katie Stackhouse and the masterfully meticulous proofreader Mark Evans, as well as Luke Causby for his outstanding cover design. I am indebted to them and the entire team at Simon & Schuster.

INDEX

INDEX

INDEX

ABOUT THE AUTHOR

COLIN BURGESS WAS BORN IN suburban Sydney, Australia, in 1947. In 2002, after 32 years' service with Qantas Airways in a variety of roles, Colin took an early retirement in order to concentrate on his writing career.

His first published book was *The Diggers of Colditz* in 1985, co-authored with Colditz veteran Jack Champ. This was followed by *Destination: Buchenwald*, the harrowing story of 168 Australian and Allied airmen illegally held in Buchenwald concentration camp. Since then, he has had numerous non-fiction books published on a wide variety of subjects. In recent years he has not only turned his attention to writing books on the history of human space exploration, but was appointed series editor for the Outward Odyssey series of books on that subject, published by the University of Nebraska Press in the United States.

His most recent completed undertaking was a set of six books relating the stories of each of the six manned Mercury flights in the early 1960s. To date, he has written or co-authored nearly 40 books.